AFRICA
—— VIA ——
ANTARCTICA

SIXTY SUNSETS IN THE
SOUTHERN HEMISPHERE

Enjoy the adventure!

BY LAURA VAE GATZ

ABOUT THIS BOOK

When Laura Vae Gatz, avid adventurer and photographer, discovered that the company she worked for offered a sabbatical program, she knew exactly what she wanted to do: take a two-month trip around the world, one of her life-long dreams. After procuring her boss's blessing, Laura started planning, figuring out how to put her daily life on auto-pilot for sixty days, and pack for it all in two rollaboard suitcases.

Laura set out to explore places she'd read about in National Geographic magazine and seen on television - legendary, remote and wild places. She sailed past Cape Horn, south through the Drake Passage and beyond the Antarctic Circle, kayaking around blue glowing icebergs, sitting surrounded by rock-stealing Adelie penguins. She explored the windswept volcanic fields of Rapa Nui (Easter Island), communing with the giant stone Moai at sunrise. She traversed the north and south Islands of New Zealand learning of the native Maori, glimpsing the mysterious glow worms in a dark forest grotto. She trekked across islands in Botswana, tracking bull elephants, a pride of over a dozen lions, and encountered a large pack of endangered African Painted Dogs.

Fueled by a passion for exploration, Laura Vae Gatz travels around the southern hempishere, seizing life one day at a time, recording her daily encounters with locals both domesticated and wild, and relaying the fantastic stories of the characters she meets.

LAURA VAE GATZ

First edition, 2011

Published by:
Colorado Peeks, 2601 Nova Dr., Garland, TX 75044
www.lauragatz.com

ISBN: 978-0-9831664-5-0
Library of Congress Control Number: 2011902189
Non-fiction
1. Travel - Photography.
2. Arts & Entertainment - Photography - Nature & Wildlife.
3. Arts & Entertainment - Photography - Photo Essays.

Editors: Donald F. Gatz, Joanne E. Gatz, and Elizabeth Grimm
Typesetting, Cover Design and Photographs: Laura Vae Gatz

eBooks available online for Kindle, Nook, iPad, etc.,
on Amazon, Barnes & Noble and iBookstore

For Lisa,
my "Seester," who would have loved to take this trip, but
has already departed on the ultimate adventure.

And for my parents, Don and Joanne
who have always been amazing examples of faith and love,
and who tirelessly support me in all my endeavours.

SABBATICAL STOPS

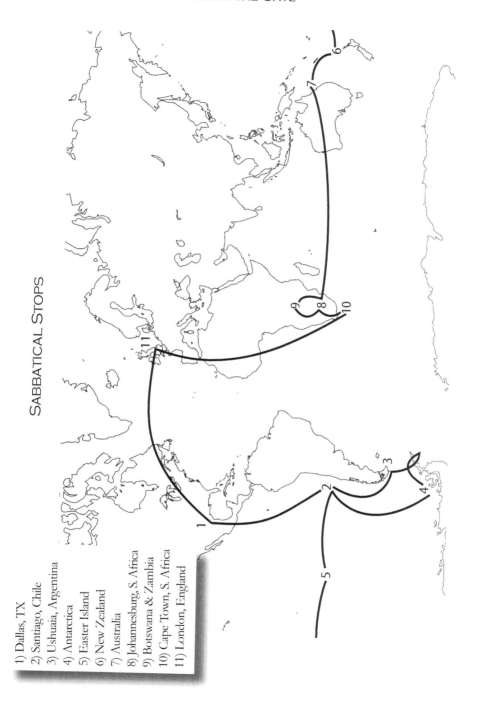

1) Dallas, TX
2) Santiago, Chile
3) Ushuaia, Argentina
4) Antarctica
5) Easter Island
6) New Zealand
7) Australia
8) Johannesburg, S. Africa
9) Botswana & Zambia
10) Cape Town, S. Africa
11) London, England

TABLE OF CONTENTS

About this Book..3

Preface..11

Planning..13

Travel Day!...37

Land Ho!..57

Paulet Island 67

Deception Island 81

Cuverville & Neko Harbor 87

Port Lockroy, Lemaire Channel, Booth Island 91

Inside the Antarctic Circle 97

Headed Back North 101

Ocean Motion 105

'Round Cape Horn 107

Kicked off the Ship 111

Easter Island aka Rapa Nui, Isla de Pascua 125

Church on Easter Island 137

Dinner at Edmundo's 143

Excursion with Edmundo 151

Last Day on the Land of the Moai 163

Kiwi-Land!... 179

Tour Time.. 185

Holy Hikoi! 189

On to Rotorua.. 197

On to Queenstown 209

Trek to Milford Sound... 213

Dart River Jet boat 225

Pinot Noir Country 231

Big Blue Glacier.. 237

Sick... 243

On To Christchurch... 247

Bahhh! 253

Walk Around Christchurch.. 255

On to OZ... 261

Koalas, Kookaburras and Kangaroos, Oh My! 265

Great Barrier Reef - TRULY GREAT! 271
Skyping Beth's 4th Grade Class 277
Sydney – City of Sails 279
Mother in Bollywood.. 285
Jo'burg 297
Flight to Maun 309
Deception Valley Lodge... 325
Bushman Walk 331
Leopards & Lions oh my!... 343
Delta Camp 349
Impala, It's not just a car 359
Meno Akwena 369
Santawani: Three Wishes Granted 385
My What Big Teeth You Have! 397
Stuck in the Mud 403
Up In The Air 417
Back in Jo'burg 429
Lots and Lots of Luggage.. 433
Driving on the Left, Again 435
The Long Way Home... 453
Appendix A: Resources.. 459
Appendix B: Packing List 463
Appendix C: New Zealand Slang 469
Appendix D: Animals and birds I saw at each Camp in Africa 473
Appendix E: Health Tips 477
Appendix F: Laura's Travel Principles 481
Appendix G: Recommended Books 483
Author Bio... 485
Other books by Laura V Gatz... 487

LAURA VAE GATZ

I.

PREFACE

TUESDAY, FEBRUARY 2, 2010

"Land Ho!" The shout erupted from my fellow passenger on the *National Geographic Explorer*. I followed his gaze and extended arm, pointing at a faint outline of land barely discernable, just off the port bow. Moments later an announcement from the bridge was heard throughout the ship, confirming the sighting, and reminding us we'd been sailing, out of sight of land, for over 30 hours. The energy onboard suddenly became palpable. Already excited passengers clutched their cameras a little tighter, and the bow became full of activity, each fellow traveler, a little bundle of excitement and anticipation.

Suddenly, as if welcoming us to Antarctica, a beautiful black and white Orca breached off the starboard side, and cameras that had been poised at the ready suddenly sprang to life; mechanical clicks of excited photographers accompanied a chorus of oohs and ahhs from everyone on deck. The captain slowed the ship and slightly changed course, to match the direction of the whale, giving everyone as much time as possible to marvel at this first Orca sighting.

Eventually the excitement died down to a low level buzz, the whale slipped off silently into the dark, iceberg-littered seas, and folks breathed happy excited sighs of a grand morning in the Antarctic. Some passengers went inside to warm up, while others decided it was time for breakfast and a hot cup of coffee. I stayed on deck until it was almost deserted, soaking up the atmosphere. As we silently passed a small iceberg, textured from wind and water, I took a few moments to reflect on how I came to be here.

I'd always dreamed of taking a trip around the world. Six months ago the company I work for moved all the IT departments to another division, which meant a change in benefits. One of those new benefits was the ability to take a sabbatical. So, I seized the opportunity and started to make arrangements, starting with getting the appropriate official approvals.

PLANNING

TUESDAY, SEPTEMBER 15, 2009

Wahooo! Last week I got the go-ahead to start planning my trip around the world! After getting the thumbs–up, I did a little happy dance. There was skipping involved, I believe, and my heart took flight. That's one of those feelings you don't experience every day, but you know it when it happens; it's like someone you love is giving your heart a big bear hug. You almost want to burst with joy, sing from the rooftops, hug everyone you come across whether they're a stranger or not.

There's a lot of planning to do before I leave, but I think it's all part of the fun. Right now I'm trying to figure out what I'm going to do with my two free months. Wow - two whole months! What should I do?? In the last few years I've spent many moments dreaming about where I would go if I ever got a few months off from work.

That evening I lay in bed with my eyes towards the ceiling, seeing far away lands: icebergs, crashing seas and billowing sails, giraffes on the savanna, and pyramids standing tall behind the Sphinx. How could I decide where to go? There were more countries and locations calling to me than I would have time to visit. Even with the gift of eight weeks, I could select only a handful of places.

So I thought about my dream list - that list of places I've always dreamed of visiting. The first on my list was Easter Island. As I daydreamed about Easter Island, Antarctica was tapping me on the shoulder reminding me not to forget about it. I whispered back, "Yes, but you're so expensive!" The voice in my head, which sounded like my mother, said, "You'll never know if you don't ask." Too right!

National Geographic and Lindblad Expeditions have hooked up to take groups of people on "expeditions" instead of "tours." They assemble knowledgeable researchers, biologists, oceanographers, and other naturalists, who travel on their ships to enhance their expeditions. Their clientele tend to be passionate about nature and wildlife, not just shopping or checking countries off a list. Lindblad visits some of the most fascinating places on the planet. When Dad and I were in the Galapagos we saw one of their ships. Having been impressed with what I'd seen there - the new-looking zodiacs, the videographer who followed the group, and the crisp lines of their ship - I found Lindblad's web site was full of short videos on various trips, interviews with expedition leaders, and trip notes from trips currently in progress. I was hooked. One trip literally gave me goose bumps – an Antarctic expedition.

I called Lindblad Expeditions, feeling my heart aflutter in my chest. I asked about the last Antarctic trip of the season, sailing from Ushuaia, Argentina, on February 5th. "Is there another woman traveling alone who I could share a room with?" I asked hopefully. There was! That would cut my cost in half, and as if fated to be, there was another two thousand dollars off the price, making it an amount I might actually consider. "Wow," I thought to myself, "This could happen. I could actually go to the Antarctic in less than 6 months!" Woo hoo!

Click. Two pieces of the puzzle fell into place. I'd fly to Santiago, take my trip to Antarctica and return, and then fly on to Easter Island. I had figured out the first and second leg of my trip.

When I told my parents about the trip, Mom's voice perked up and she said softly, "Maybe I could come with you, at least for part of your trip." What a great idea! So I asked her, "If you could visit anywhere in the world, where would you want to go?" Mom has always wanted to visit New Zealand. Maybe that could be the next destination. As luck would have it, there is a direct flight from Santiago to Auckland, New Zealand.

Then fortuitously my dad's brother asked if Dad could come stay in their home, to be near their 96-year old mother, while they were away for three weeks. Where are they going? New Zealand! So I emailed my aunt to ask what company they were traveling with, knowing that any trip my aunt and uncle were taking would be a well vetted option. OAT – Overseas Adventure Travel was the answer. Further research with Trip Advisor and the OAT website revealed it as the perfect fit for Mom and me.

OAT specializes in "mature active adults," and offers a bit more adventure than you normally find on a cruise ship. Their group sizes are very small – no more than 16 people. Additionally, because it is a land tour you are able to experience more of the culture and land than on a cruise. That's another specialty of theirs – really getting into the culture. Their guides are locals. Not having to be back on board a ship every evening is a plus. The downside to a land tour is that you're moving many nights from one hotel to another.

This particular departure date requires a post trip to Australia, including the Great Barrier Reef. That is on my dream list as well. And we'll have a day or two in Sydney, touring the Opera House and seeing some of the neighborhoods around town.

Click. Three weeks in both the north and south islands of New Zealand, with a side trip at the end to the Great Barrier Reef and Sydney. Three sections done! And three dream locations scheduled.

From Australia it was going to be just as easy to keep going around the world, and if I did that I would be able to purchase a "OneWorld" ticket, through the One World Alliance, which is priced based on the number of continents you visit.

Africa is the last piece of the puzzle and another of my dreams - my sister, Lisa's, too. We often talked about making a five to ten year calendar of the trips we wanted to take, scheduling them several years out, so we had a "master plan" of exciting trips we were planning. Unfortunately we never got around to making that calendar. She got sick early in 2006, and died of lymphoma before the end of the year. I miss my best friend and traveling partner in so many ways. Whenever I start planning a trip my thoughts inevitably turn to her, wondering if it's a trip she would have been interested in. I fancy that she can experience the trips I take, through my eyes. Yeah, I know that's probably just a fantasy, but it's a nice thought. That happy thought distracts me from the tears that inevitably come. If I'm lying down, they leak out of the outer corners of my eyes, and drip down the sides of my face, and straight into my ears, which is mightily uncomfortable. Squishy ears are usually enough to rouse me out of my sadness and set me back to planning.

I want a safari experience, but I don't want to have to take out a second mortgage on my house to do it. Now that I've done a little research, I've found that Botswana is quite the safari Mecca. Who knew? Luxury safari choices seem to be endless. Never could I have imagined the number of opulent lodgings available in the bush. Many look like they're straight out of a movie – complete with canvas tents, four–poster beds draped with mosquito nets, teak chairs surrounding white linen tablecloth covered tables set with hurricane lamps, china and silverware. All with the African bush or a river delta for a backdrop.

I knew nothing about planning a safari. It's not like planning a trip to Europe. The Internet came in handy once again. Although I don't remember what I searched for, I do remember finding the web site for the company I would eventually go with: Expert Botswana. Their site was the only one I'd found whose main page explained that there are a few main things to consider when planning a safari. How much can you spend? What time of the year are you going? How much time do you have? What do you want to see?

What a logical approach to a web site! Eureka! I liked these guys. The way they explained basics to "Joe Traveler" was so easy. Those four questions were all ones I could answer. The site also answered basic questions such as "How does a safari work?" I imagine that, like most people, my idea of a safari was developed from movies like *Out of Africa*. Driving through the African plains in a jeep, setting up camp each night and dining under the stars on linen table cloths, real silverware and candelabras. Yes, it is a romantic version of reality. A notion I'm happy to live with and have be a part of my world until proven otherwise. This type of safari is called a "mobile safari," and it still exists, but most safaris nowadays have base camps which you return to in the middle of the day and overnight.

Occasionally I have to take a break from my travel research, around the time my eyelids start to droop and my head starts spinning. Then it's list–making time. I've always wondered how people plan for a long trip. It seems to be a secret. All the numerous books I've read about sabbaticals, gap years and extended vacations mention the basic preparations necessary to leave your house and bills for months on end, but never in any detail. How frustrating! How am I supposed to figure out how to do it if there's no book that tells me? Maybe I'll write my own book on it!

SUNDAY, NOVEMBER 1, 2009

My grandparents had a cottage in Wisconsin on the Chain of Lakes, near Waupaca. They had a small row boat with a small motor mounted on it. There's a photograph of me at age two, carrying the cushions that used to double as life preservers. I seem to be behind everyone, struggling to catch up, but I'm so small and weighed down by too much stuff. What is funny to me about this picture is that I seem to be a little overwhelmed with what I have to carry. As a single traveler, this "overwhelming" feeling is often on my mind. How does one pack for a two–month trip? Not only that, but how is it possible to stay within all my airline baggage restrictions and pack for the Antarctic AND Africa? It's quite the conundrum.

So this weekend is a packing dry-run, like a dress rehearsal. After gathering most of the substantial items on my packing list I place the two suitcases I plan to bring with me on my bed, along with my "sucky bags."

Sucky bags are a beautiful invention. They are clothing–size, thick plastic zip lock bags with one-way air vents that let the extra air out but not back in. I buy many of mine at REI outdoor gear and clothing store where their name for them is "clothing compression bags." Having used these bags for many years I've gotten very good at folding my clothes in just the right proportions to fit perfectly so that when rolled they compact efficiently, and are the right width to fit nicely into the suitcase. Amazing how sucking air out of your belongings helps the packing process along.

After rolling all the clothes I plan to bring with me for the entire trip, I find that they all fit into one suitcase – along with my bulky Antarctic rubber mucklucks (knee–high boots). A very happy surprise!

As my packing list grows longer and more complete I remember back through the years when I dreamed of taking off for a year. A gap year. A true sabbatical. Sailing around the world. And every time I tried to make real plans or think through the details, I would get stuck and mired down in the details. How exactly could I be gone for that long? What about the mortgage, paying bills, insurance on my car? My stuff. Should I pack everything up and store it? Sell it? How do people leave for an entire year?

As an avid traveler, always planning my next trip, one of my favorite types of books to read are the ones where a couple quits their jobs, sells everything and travels around the world, or someone who simply takes an extended vacation of more than a month. I eagerly scour those books for details on how preparations were made. Often I come up kind of short. There just aren't a whole lot of details to tell you how to do it. I started thinking it was kind of a secret elite club that only those travelers belonged to – that you couldn't belong until you took a trip like that. The rule for "the club" is how you prepare to go away for an extended time must be a closely guarded secret that must not be divulged to the average Joe. Their adage being, "If they're serious enough to want to go, they'll figure it out on their own!"

Actually, I think it's a rite of passage; figuring out all the details to vacate your life for a period of time. If it was easy it wouldn't be as rewarding. But each person's details are different, so if I provide a bit of an outline it wouldn't be cheating too much, right?

There are several phases, and each phase leads to the next. Every few years I get slightly discontent with life and I start dreaming again. Last time this happened was right after my sister died. Knowing I couldn't take a big trip real soon afterwards, that a little time would have to pass first, I decided to do a little planning nonetheless. That's my first suggestion.

If you've ever imagined a dream trip, **it's never too early to start planning.** Much of what you discover won't change over the years. You can decide where you want to go. What time of year is best? Is there a route that makes sense? Which airlines fly to each destination and what are some of the central hubs for flights around the world? Trip planning got me through some of the rough times in my life when I really wanted to just chuck it all and hop the next sailboat headed across the closest ocean. It gave me a hope that the dream might actually happen. Planning, for me, is all part of the fun of traveling.

When I found that I could actually take two months off, my mind drifted back to the last planning session I'd had a few years earlier and I dug up those notes. Although I didn't have the whole trip planned, I'd gotten as far as Australia in my planning.

With a rough idea of where I wanted to go, I needed to pick a time of year; something that worked well for my employer, gave them and me enough time to plan for my absence, and gave me enough time to plan my trip. In September I talked with my boss, who already knew that someday I wanted to take a big trip and most likely take time off from work to do it. My plan was to be gone in February and March, returning to work the beginning of April in time to work two months before the end of the fiscal year – which is always a busy time for us. That gave me 5 months to plan.

In order to make planning easier, I found one-month calendars of February and March online for free, downloaded them and printed them out 11x17, making several copies. At home I marked off possible travel dates, figuring in flight times and the International Date Line along the way. As pieces of my trip clicked into place, I would add them to these calendars.

MONDAY, NOVEMBER 23, 2009

I'm at the airport, on my way to Florida for Thanksgiving, with some of the luggage I'll be taking with me on my trip. One thing I've discovered already is that there is NO WAY I'm taking this backpack. It has about fifteen pounds in it now and is dreadfully uncomfortable. Fully loaded, it's twenty-six. I'm going to have to find another backpack. Preferably one that has a few inflatable helium balloons on the side...to make it lighter on my back.

When deciding on the daypack you are going to take with you, there are several factors to think about. What will you need to carry with you? How much does it all weigh? Does your equipment need to be cushioned or protected from moisture? For a backback feature, perhaps a built-in "camelback" (water bladder) would be important. Maybe you want a daypack that is a combination of a daypack and a camera bag.

In my research, I packed up a bag I already have with all the things I'll take with me during a typical travel day. Then I drove to my local outdoor gear store (like REI) with my stuff and found the store subject matter expert. I showed them my bag and named some features that are important to me in a bag -- things like weight distribution, the need to stay as cool as possible, the need to carry my bag on the plane, the need to keep the items inside dry.

The staff at REI were so helpful. They keep different weight sandbags in the backpack area to help customers try out a pack with some weight in it, making the experience of wearing the pack more realistic. I found a few backpacks that were close to the size I was looking for, sat down on the floor with them, and, one pack at a time, stored away the items I'd brought with me, looking for just the right inner pocket or zippered pouch to put everything. Then I tried on each pack, wore it around the store for a while, allowed the staff to adjust it correctly for my body, and ended up finding the perfect pack for this trip!

Finding the right bag is similar to looking for a car or a camera — you have a set of requirements, features you want your purchase to have. And it's a matter of looking until you find what you want. For me, each trip seems to require a different bag. Maybe it's just that I like buying bags, but I suspect there's more to it than that. Each trip has different physical requirements, different climates, and requires different gear.

With a daypack you're also looking for features. Look at this exercise as a troubleshooting mission and part of the fun of planning a trip. You have a set of requirements and you need to know what is going to fit your needs. And remember, it's all part of the fun of preparation. I enjoy the preparation and search for the perfect bag as much as I enjoy the trip sometimes.

Once you have your bag, don't just stick it in a drawer until your departure. Get it out and use it. It's like a pair of shoes -- you want to have broken them in, gotten used to the feel, and feel comfortable in them, before you go. Load it up. Put the items in your bag that will be in it when you're traveling. Figure out where everything goes. That way when you're ready to set off on your trip you'll already be ahead of the game. You'll know which pocket holds your iPhone and where you are going to keep your keys. Being organized on the road can reduce frustration a considerable amount. It's so frustrating to be traveling, KNOW you brought something with you, and not be able to find it. Happens all the time to me. However, sometimes, I know exactly where I've put it because I bring a bag I've used before, and know which pocket that item "lives" in. Although I may not always put things away when I'm at home, when I'm traveling I'm fastidious about putting things back where they belong.

If you're buying other new things for your trip, don't use them on your trip for the first time. Get them out. Take them for the proverbial spin around the block. Wear clothes and wash them. See how they do in different climates. That stretchy cotton weave may end up soaking up a lot of moisture and being hotter than you thought it would be. Wear hats. Break in shoes. Carry your new backpack around the house or to work fully loaded. Practice using your travel wallet.

Speaking of being organized, I'm doing some homework ahead of time so that I'm prepared for some of the strict luggage weight restrictions I'll encounter in Africa. I'm working on clarifying some of the weight restrictions for my luggage in Botswana. The kind of safari I'll be on involves flying from one camp to another on "light aircraft." These aircraft are very small and carry anywhere from two to four passengers. Luggage is stored in the back of the compartment behind the third and fourth seats, or under where the pilot sits – just on the bottom side of the plane, in a compartment that is ten inches high. What I need to clarify is the exact weight limit and what that includes. Also I need to understand what can be carried on. Is there room under the seats to store a small bag? When checking luggage, do I drop the bag off plane–side or does it disappear down a rabbit hole to be whisked away to the plane without me? These small details dictate how I will pack. The last thing I want to face is making a decision between leaving several camera lenses behind in a town I'll never return to or having to pay to have my equipment flown in on the next flight. I have six "light airplane" flights to make it through, so my luggage weight better be within the limits!

One option I've discovered is that if you know ahead of time that your luggage is going to be over the weight restrictions, you can pay for another seat on the plane, which gets you an additional person's worth of weight. It, in essence, doubles your luggage allowance. The question now is, "What would that cost me?"

I'd say about 80% of my luggage weight is in camera gear and electronics. Being a serious photographer and writer I'll be carrying two digital SLR cameras, 5 lenses, a pocket point and shoot, an underwater housing, 50Gb of memory cards, 100Gb of USB drives, multiple camera batteries for each camera body, battery chargers, filters, monopod, laptop, iPhone, solar charger and assorted cables. It's a veritable cornucopia of electronics and a thief's dream. Unfortunately, for what I have planned it's necessary.

Despite all the information on the Internet, I've had a hard time finding many of the details I need. It might be time to call in an expert – Richard Wilt, who has been on these planes and knows firsthand what's what. I'll email him and see what he says. Richard is an avid birder and a friend of my parents. After Richard retired, he and his wife took a year to travel in 2000 with the goal of seeing 2000 different bird species. They did it, with time to spare. One of the countries they visited was Botswana, so they have flown on planes similar to those I'll be flying.

Upon arrival at work this morning I discovered that my glasses are not adjusted right and my right ear hurts. While this might seem like a small thing, if I had to deal with that pain for two months I would not be a happy camper. I'm thinking I really need a second pair of glasses that are the same prescription. Not just a backup pair, but one that I could actually wear for most of the trip if necessary.

Back at the airport before Thanksgiving, I find that I miss being able to use the first class lounge. I'm so spoiled! There's different air out here. It's full of tension and anxiety. The lounge is quiet and relaxed – full of people who know their next seats will be comfortable and accompanied by warm hot face towels and porcelain bowls of salty nuts. The huddled masses are eating squished peanut butter and jelly sandwiches on Wonder bread while sitting cross–legged on the floor. Not really. But that's what the difference feels like.

Onboard my flight I've given into my Mother's suggestion of wearing a mask to protect me from all the germs wandering around the cabin. I've had over 40 years of discovering, over and over, that she's usually right, as much as it sometimes pains me to admit it. But with the H1N1 scare and the proliferation of various colds and other flu at the moment, I think it's a pretty darn good idea to employ whatever germ evasion techniques I can.

It's an interesting experience to be on a plane, in the United States, with a mask on. I get a lot of looks, but people don't say anything to me. It's a warm, humid environment inside the mask, so it's more comfortable for breathing, and actually healthier than the bone–dry airplane air. For those of us with eyeglasses there is a downside – they tend to fog up. But being fairly sedentary on the plane minimizes that issue. It's not like I'm on a hike working up a sweat or breathing heavily. (See appendix E for additional health tips.)

I remember flying to St. Thomas by myself. The day had started off fine. On the flight into Miami I started to feel cold. By the time I deplaned I was feeling strangely drained. Unable to figure out what was wrong with me I found a quiet corner to curl up in for a nap until my plane took off. I boarded my last flight and as we descended into St. Thomas I started to get hot. Oblivious to the fact that I was getting sick, I thought that the Caribbean air they'd let into the cabin was just really humid and I was adjusting to the change in climate. As soon as I'd checked into my hotel room I pulled out my handy dandy thermometer (I WAS a Girl Scout! Our motto was "Always Be Prepared!) to discover I had a fever! Oh no! I'm sick! Aha! On the entire trip down it never dawned on me that I could be getting sick. What did I do next? Pull out my cell phone to call my Mommy, who was not home! Waaaa. I want my Mommy! Luckily I had a 24–hour bug and by that time the next day the fever had broken and I was feeling almost back to normal.

That brings me back to the Girl Scout Motto. It's a good one to follow when traveling. To a degree. When applied to travel it doesn't mean "Be prepared to have a blue pair of pumps to match your blue handbag and slacks." It doesn't mean, "Be prepared with 10 pairs of earrings so that you have a pair that matches every outfit." It means more along the lines of "consider where you'll be traveling to and only pack the items you won't be able to get during your trip." In Asia or in Muslim countries it can be hard or impossible to find tampons. Take extra prescription medication in case you are delayed coming home. Take a first aid kit. A snakebite kit if you're going to be in a remote area with snakes. Going to be in an undeveloped country? Pack toilet paper. Duct tape does wonders in a variety of situations (all having nothing to do with toilets!). No need for a whole roll, just roll it around a broken pencil, winding it around like a roll of toilet paper without a core.

So the magic number of pounds I can take with me on safari is (drum–roll please!)...44! On top of that I can take a small bag – like a small purse or a bag that would hold my wallet and a small camera. I called Expert Botswana, and they filled me in on the whole "light airplane" scoop.

When flying from Johannesburg, South Africa to Maun, Botswana I'll be on a jet, where the normal luggage rules apply. But once in Maun the traditional airport rules go by the wayside. Apparently you collect your bags from the jet flight and then walk out to the small aircraft where you are introduced to the pilot. He will take all your luggage and store it in the wings, and then you get on the plane. That's about it. So, that means that I'll be able to keep my luggage in sight until it is put on the plane. I'll be able to pack my rolling duffle with camera equipment if necessary. I should also bring another small bag such as a fanny pack.

When I tell my friends I am taking a two month sabbatical, the second question I get after "Where are you going?" is "How are you going to pack for that?" Often my response is "Carefully!"

First I checked all the luggage restrictions on the various airlines I am flying. The long–haul flights, like from Dallas to Santiago, Chile, and from Santiago to Auckland, New Zealand have the most lenient restrictions. Those aircraft are very large and are made to accommodate both a lot of checked luggage and good size carry on bags. The flights I needed to check most closely are the shorter flights on smaller aircraft. For instance, my charter flight with Lindblad Expeditions from Santiago to Ushuaia, Argentina. And the regional flights around New Zealand. And the most restricted flights of all on my trip – the light aircraft that will fly me from camp to camp on my safari in Botswana.

There are a number of factors to consider when determining luggage weight limits: airline, class of seat you're in (economy, business, etc.), and frequent flier status. Often frequent fliers with special status on an airline will be able to take additional pounds of luggage.

Luggage falls into two categories typically: checked and carry on. Each category has its own set of rules determined by the criteria above. My habit is to carry on all my luggage. This encourages me to travel light, and I am assured of having my luggage upon arrival at my destination. With this trip I will be unable to do that during parts of my travel. In Antarctica there are special gear requirements that mean I need to bring more items than I'm used to; things like waterproof pants and knee–high rubber boots. Once I'm done with these special items I'm going to send them home to my parents so that I don't have to pay an extra charge for flying with one bag more than allowed.

In college I spent spring semester, junior year, studying abroad in Germany. At the end of the semester my sister, Lisa, flew over to travel with me through Germany, Austria, Italy and Greece for almost a month. All we took with us were what we could fit into backpacks. It was amazing how little we needed to have with us in order to be comfortable. A few changes of clothes, underwear and socks, and some toiletries. After living in a world where we surround ourselves with creature comforts and any other item that can be found a short drive from home, it was enlightening to realize that there is a great divide between things I need and things I want. Food, shelter and clothing are things I need. A portable backgammon game, my favorite shower gel and and iPhone are things I want. Well, I might argue about that last one as a necessity, but you get my point. Not all items I want to pack are things I really need.

And this is where it can get dicey. Do I need an antibiotic with me? I might. What if I'm in the bush without a drug store within one-hundred miles and I get an infection? Do I need a miniature stain stick? Well, it might be pretty convenient due to my limited wardrobe but it's probably not a necessity. I have to weigh the benefits with the additional weight, figure in how close to civilization I'll be, and compromise on some items. My packing list will be in the back of this book as a reference. Keep in mind this list is what I thought I needed for the locations I was traveling to, for the amount of time I was going to be gone, and because I am a writer and photographer. Your packing list may be different.

Being a product of my mother I plan a lot for "just in case." This was a tenet that served me well in the hotel business when I was fresh out of college. I'd moved to Santa Barbara to attend Brooks Institute of Photography. During that time I needed to earn some money and found a job at the local Sheraton Hotel across the street from the beach. The first few weeks I was there I remember encountering a guest whose reservation was nowhere to be found. My colleague told me to give the guest "a Justin Case" room. I said, "what's that?" thinking that Justin might be counting on having his room reservation available when he arrived. They repeated "Just In Case," slowly, and I got it. Ah ha! How smart! Plan ahead so that when you're faced with a difficult situation you have a back up plan. That's how I view preparation and packing for a trip.

At work I am a Project Manager. I make sure things get done in a timely manner and I follow up with folks to make sure they meet their deadlines. These skills come in handy when arranging a long trip. Additionally, my mother raised me to be a list maker. For some reason, conditioning probably, lists motivate me. If a task is on a list, chances are I'll get it done. If something doesn't make it to a list, chances are I won't remember to do it.

I've found organization is key to being ready when the date comes to leave on your trip. For this trip I've been making lists from day one. As soon as one thing came off my list, 2 or 3 things replaced it. Once you know where you're going and have reservations, you've only just begun. Here's a sampling of some of the items that have been on my list:

- Research and purchase travel insurance.

- Measure myself for winter parka for Antarctic trip.

- Figure out how much digital memory I need to be able to back up my photographs during the trip.

- Find a lightweight rolling duffle bag.

- Go on seatguru.com to find out which seats I want on each airplane.

- Create an itinerary that has all my travel details in one location.

- Decide on which two pairs of shoes I'm taking.

- Set up visit to Passport Health so I can make sure I have all my immunizations and arrange for anti–malaria medication.

- Log onto the Australian web site
  to request my travel visa.

- Make sure that from the date I return
  home I still have 6 months or more
  left before my passport expires.

- Scan my passport and email it to
  my parents and myself.

- Call my credit card companies a few
  weeks before I leave to let them know
  where I may be making charges.

- Forward my mail to my parents.

- Set up automatic money transfers into my checking
  account to compensate for my lack of paycheck
  so I am able to pay my bills while I'm gone.

- Make sure my cat sitter is lined up.

- Stock up on cat food and litter.

That's just a fraction of my list, but it gives an idea of the organization that is required for a trip of this length. I love it. But then again, crossing things off lists makes me happy (if that's the case, I should be ecstatic!).

SATURDAY, JANUARY 16, 2010

"Why am I going to Antarctica again?" That's the thought that hit me last week when temperatures in the teens hit Dallas. Not only was it cold, but it was also windy and damp; the trifecta of chill! Then a few days later on NPR's "Wait, Wait Don't Tell Me" radio show I hear a guy from Antarctica call in, live, to the show. He said it was a balmy 40 degrees where he was — at a research station down there. Wait, now that's not fair. It can't be warmer there than here! Hmm, maybe the warmth will last. Well, I don't want it to be too warm. If it's too warm all the penguin poo will defrost. That wouldn't be good.

Twelve days to go. The days have started flying by. I have 4 days left to prepare. The rest of the days are consumed by work. I'll be ready. This is all part of the fun, the preparation! The items that drift to the front of your mind, making their way onto lists, lists that lengthen, change, morph, and shorten again. Accomplishments in small things. One last hair cut, one last tank of gas. Packing those zip lock bags. Purchasing a few more media cards for my camera. All the tasks I've been meaning to do finally have to get done.

Time to order Chilean Pesos. Great. Possibly the worst time in the last 12 months. Actually, it IS the worst time in the last 12 months. The dollar has tanked. It saw a brief spark of life over Christmas, and then sank back down into the murky depths. But, I am out of time, that is, if I want to be able to take the pesos with me. C'est la vie. Just part of the cost of travel. Like I've always said, there's never a perfect time to travel. My hairstylist reminded me this morning that it's just a trade off. Fewer people are traveling, so there are some great travel deals right now. A little less money on the front end, and a little more on the back. It's good to look on the bright side.

One more full week of work plus an additional three days until I leave. It will be a week full of tasks to finish, too. My temporary replacement should be starting Monday or Tuesday, which means I'll be talking all week. Probably more than I talk in a month normally. Too bad it's not possible to do a Vulcan mind meld. That would be quite a lot easier. Well, it will be a fun challenge. It will be like an hourglass, these last 8 days of work, time inevitably ticking away. Hopefully by the time all the pieces of sand in the hourglass have succumbed to gravity, I'll have all the loose ends tied up; tied up enough to not come unraveled in my absence.

My final Antarctic documents have come. Baggage tags, nametag, a cool baseball cap. Why is it that such small things make me so happy? I'm pretty happy with the baseball cap. It's the kind that comes down a good ways on your head, you know, not chintzy.

SUNDAY, JANUARY 24, 2010

My little tan cat is gazing at me with his big, round, innocent eyes, trying to convince me to feed him snacks. How can I leave this sweet little face? Max was my sister's cat. He is so loving, but also quite a little mischief–maker. When my sister died three years ago I brought him home and he's been living with me and Furgus, my other cat, ever since. However, about a year ago a he got a whiff of something that had been my sister's and he got upset – leaving a nice steaming present for me. And the problem has been getting worse. The theory is that Max has anxiety triggered by smells and the fear of being left. Of course, being a traveler I'm not helping his issues any.

I wonder if my leaving will destroy all the hard work we've gone through in the last month. Max has been visiting with the kitty psychologist. Yeah, I know, it makes me laugh too. Until last month I had no idea kitty psychologists existed. So, over the last month, despite the fact that I know it sounds crazy, Max has been going through a program to train him to "do his business" where he's supposed to, and to lessen his anxiety. We'll see how my being gone for two months affects him. Only time will tell. As I heard on the radio this morning, "We'll know when we find out."

Lying in bed this morning, enjoying the difference in temperature between the cool room temperature and the warmth underneath the featherbed, I realized the nights left in my own bed are almost over. That thought made me want to stay in bed longer. Odd to think that I'll be traipsing around the southern hemisphere for two months. That seems like such a long time. But when I recount the different legs of my trip to friends or co–workers, the sum of weeks doesn't seem to be as long as two months. Perhaps it's the same phenomenon experienced when opening up credit card bills. The total says you've spent $2000 this month, but the individual line items are all small. $50 here, $80 there, another one for $120, and another for $45. You think to yourself, surely that doesn't add up to $2000, but it does.

Saturday morning I was up by 8:30, and started cleaning right away. No breaks until a phone call at 12:30. Four hours of solid cleaning was very productive. Amazing how motivating a time–specific deadline can be. How dirty can two cats make a house in two months? Sounds like a math problem. "Two cats are contained within a house for two months, each one sheds 1000 hairs in one week, eats 8 ounces of food a day, and drinks 6 ounces of water a day. If one cat uses the poopy box 4 times a day, what is the greatest distance a piece of cat litter can travel from its point of origin within 24 hours?"

My iPhone continues to increase in its usefulness. Currently I'm using several apps to organize my trip. One is called Packing, by Quinn Genzel. As items are packed, they can be checked off. Another app is called TripCase into which I've loaded all my flights, hotels and car rentals. TripCase connects to the Internet and tracks flight delays, gates, terminals, and alternate flights. There's a place to enter additional notes so I can remember luggage restrictions, meals served, etc. OneWorld (coincidentally this app has the same name as my around the world airplane ticket!) assists with translations from one language to another. Antarctica cached information on local wildlife from Wikipedia.

During my travels other apps start to become useful. MyDiary allows me to make notes about my trip at any time of the day. In combination with writing, there's also a sound recording app that I've used to capture sounds such as the cicadas in the Cambodian jungle on the path to a temple, or traffic sounds in old town Hanoi. Sometimes I'll use it to record a conversation. A favorite that I've captured is a verbal showdown between a Vietnamese cop and a boat driver discussing whether or not the boat driver took my camera. Although I don't understand one word, it's very evident what is being said, and none of it is friendly!

One very simple app I use is Notes. It simply allows me to list out things to be done. In the three or so months I've been planning this trip that list has never been this short. There are only one or two more things on it. Can't believe I'm almost ready to go. My bags are packed. I've weeded through them several times taking out things not really needed, duplicate items, extra paper; I'm also taking items out of my backpack that don't really need to be in there, and sticking them in my luggage.

THURSDAY, JANUARY 28, 2010

My workday is done for two months. Yeah, I know, y'all will still be here when I return, along with all the work. But, for now I leave all my work acronyms behind: POS, NFC and EMS. I have new acronyms to think about...tomorrow I fly DFW to SCL on AA. 3B is waiting for me...

I wonder what stories wait for me tomorrow. You can bet I'll be back to tell you. I'll have several hours at the airport to transition from this life into my temporary travel life...I need a travel name, a travel–alias. Too bad my name isn't Sue – I could be "Sabbatical Sue." Maybe I'll make a new word and become "Sabbaticalaura," like a little travel–superhero. I better stop writing now and go to bed. Wonder if I'll sleep? Tomorrow I travel!

I.

ANTARCTICA

TRAVEL DAY!
FRIDAY, JANUARY 29, 2010

It all started to feel real this morning. Nothing like "travel day" to get me out of bed bright and early. That's always a real motivator. How come I don't feel like that on a daily basis? In the first two hours I was awake this morning I checked off half the items on my to do list. There was the early morning run to the post office to send the last of my Netflix back and make a FedEx drop to Mom and Dad. Then I dropped off my paper recycling, and I was back home. Unload the dishwasher, wash the other dishes, scoop poop, refill cats' water, pack miscellaneous last minute items in what tiny voids are left in my suitcases. Put Max (my anxious cat) in the bathroom so I can haul the luggage downstairs without him seeing.

Time is ticking away. I think I have everything done. My fridge is empty, extra food has been disposed of, the thermostat is set, lights on timers, mail forwarded, keys I don't need are put away.

It's quiet in the house. Max is sleeping next to me, content, but aware that something is going on. The cats' water fountain makes nice watery sounds and the clock above the doorway to the kitchen ticks, ticks, ticks. It's been raining and the traffic on the road behind my house makes a nice wet swishing noise.

Hard to believe that in twenty-four hours I'll be roaming around Santiago, Chile. Maybe I should plan something to do. Nah, I think I'll take it as it comes. I'll get settled into my B&B and then ask my host for a few suggestions. I hear there are great markets selling local fruits, vegetables and crafts. The Cementerio General sounds very interesting (I've always like cemeteries – yeah, it's a little odd, but I find it interesting to wander through them). I've got Santiago's underground system on my iPhone and my B&B is just a few blocks from a station. Who knows, maybe I'll just wander around on foot and see what kind of local food I encounter.

But first...two and a half hours until I leave the house. Get ready kitties....

The drive to the airport was perilous, at best. I don't know what it is about Texas drivers, but any sort of weather other than sunny and dry seems to freak them out. Add a little water to the roads and you'd think it was ice or oil. The traffic report sounded like army troops reporting in with heavy casualties.

My friend, Trisha, who was going to take me to the airport, is out of town on business. So she left me her car to drive to the airport. I'm leaving it there for her to pick up. She'll be flying in around the same time my plane departs. I've texted her phone with the location.

The one thing she asked me to do, though, I didn't do. I'm pleading innocence on this one though. Well, innocence or ignorance, I'm not sure which. She'll choose the latter I think...She asked that I leave the parking ticket in the car. Well, I didn't get a parking ticket. Hmmm. Ooops. Thinking I'd get a parking ticket when entering the parking garage, I went through the toll tag lane. After parking I realized there was no ticket to leave in the car. Sorry, Trish!

The Admiral's lounge in Terminal D at DFW (Dallas/Fort Worth International Airport) is ok. It's nice, quiet, and has high ceilings. Plenty of space to sit, and adequate power plugs for electronics. They even provide free wi–fi and computers for use. As far as food goes there's not a lot of selection. However, there are some really slick lounge chairs against a far wall – 6 of them, with footstools. I can get soda water with a lime for free, but other drinks cost money. Upon arrival you're given two free drink tickets. I usually try to find someone to give mine to.

Ok, this will make Mom cringe, but it's all part of the story. I'm comfortably settled into one of the slick lounge chairs, soda water with lime by my side, luggage tucked in nicely next to the wall, laptop on my lap. Nice view of the room. Sleeping, cowboy–booted, baseball cap–wearing man snoozing in the chair next to mine. All is good. Then the consumptive comes and sits on the other side of the greenery from me. I hear her say into her iPhone "I'm starting to get over my cold." Run away, run away! Don the oxygen masks! Spray her down with antibacterial! *Sigh*. My perfect little spot, ruined by invading germs. I look in her direction; scarf casually draped across the lower half of my face, and stare daggers into the back of her head. How dare she come sit by me...go sit by some other poor schmucks who don't mind getting sick. I try my powers of mind control "Go away. Go sit somewhere else. Don't you want to go to the gate now??" She finally goes away after about 10 minutes, hacking up one last fur ball as she departs. A parting gift, perhaps? Germs settle and all is right once again in my little corner of the world.

The flight from Dallas to Santiago, Chile is 9 1/2 hours. Not bad. Well, not bad if you're in business class or better, which I will be. When deciding to take this trip, I decided that if I was going to fly around the world, I was not going to be doing it from coach. No way. I'd make sure I had enough money saved to upgrade to Business Class. So, I have dinner and breakfast with real linen to look forward to. Think I'll take in a movie during dinner, and then turn in, sleep about 6 hours and we'll be there. La, la, la. I must decide what to do with my Friday. Oh, the tough decisions that come with travel! (picture me in a dramatic pose, back of my hand across my forehead, head tossed back) Tee hee. I'm off!

FRIDAY, JANUARY 29, 2010

I'm on my plane, a Boeing 767, from Dallas to Santiago, Chile, which is 3 hours ahead of Dallas.

It's funny how iPhone users are about staying close to their phones...it's almost like affection for an inanimate object. I often say it's "my everything." By that I mean that it's my GPS, journal, phone book, camera (well, one of them), Bible, collection of games, subway map, Internet, computer, email, portable communication hub. When I travel I don't like to be parted from it in any way. I feel best when I can actually feel it. In fact, most of the time I travel in my "travel pants," lightweight, quick drying pants with lots of pockets. One pocket is my iPhone pocket, about mid–thigh. I pat that pocket frequently, almost like a talisman. "Got my iPhone? Ok, good." It kind of reminds me how my cat Max is, with me. When he is in the room with me he likes to always have at least a paw on me, reaching out to make sure I'm still there.

iPhone owners spot each other and give a "knowing" smile and nod, thinking, "Oh yes, you have one too. You KNOW, don't you? Yes, you're one of the cool ones, I see." A man hanging out in one of the slick lounge chairs in the Admiral's lounge found a place to recharge his iPhone, and he said to the 3–4 other iPhone users within earshot that he felt particularly odd about having it out of arm's reach. It was the furthest he'd been from it in a long time and that made him uncomfortable. We each contributed our affirmations that we understood and felt the same way. In the last 2 years that I've had my phone I can't think of anything else that more quickly forms a bond between travelers.

This 767 seems to be quite a bit different (read: smaller) than the 777s that I've gotten used to for long haul flights. The seats are narrower, the bathrooms smaller and fewer, the in seat televisions kind of jury–rigged as an afterthought, into the back of the seat. In fact these screens aren't built in, they are small, modified, self–contained computers with touch screens. Not very responsive touch screens, I might add.

All of a sudden it's daylight outside. Passengers are starting to stir and the bathrooms stay busy. Folks are chugging their overnight bottle of water, feeling dehydrated after a night of breathing bone dry cabin air. Kind of feels like someone stuck the inside of my mouth into one of those dehydrating machines you stick fruits into to turn plums into prunes.

The sunrise was brief but colorfully intense. A narrow band of dark saturated orange at the horizon, separated from the sky by a deep purple band of clouds. As the sky lightened the contrasting colors of orange, purple and blue were simply beautiful. God's hands at work.

The mist has risen now and all is light blue – clouds and sky.

Small, fast moving, wispy clouds sail past us. Their cousins below, a carpet of patterned cotton, keeping the land we fly over hidden from view. Ok, that's enough waxing on about the clouds. I think breakfast is imminent. Then we have just a few more hours in the air.

The Andes were, well, I'm not sure I possess words to describe how beautiful they looked from the air, an hour or two after sunrise. Clothed in morning fog the waves of mountains reached to the horizon. Simply stunning. I was reminded of those posters we bought as kids, that hung in Spencer's or WalMart. You know, the ones next to the cute kitties in a basket – the thin horizontal photograph of mountains and more mountains in the distance, each one fading a little lighter blue–grey.

My airport pick up went smoothly. After checking into my B&B, which turns out to be the owner's house, because his actual B&B building is under construction, I took a shower, paid up for both nights I'll stay and the two taxi rides, and wandered down the block to Liguria, a restaurant that had been recommended. I figured out how to order a bottle of water with gas (soda water), and a straw. However I just took a chance with the food and pointed to something on the menu that I could see had pesto in it. Noquis al Pomodoro y Pesto. They bring out the hugest bowl full of gnocchi that I've ever seen. Uh oh. What are gnocchi made out of? Wheat? Potato? Neither is good, but potato won't kill my stomach. So as luck would have it, it's carb city for lunch today.

Sitting outside on the sidewalk, under an umbrella, shielded from the sun, the sounds around me were simply the din of other eaters until a saxophone player walked up 5 minutes ago. I have to say his playlist ability really stinks. He's gone from the Jewish wedding dance to the theme from Titanic and on to "Happy Birthday."

Ricardo is the owner of the B&B where I am staying. Naturally he speaks Spanish. My Spanish is next to non–existent. I have a few words, and can get around, and I can understand more than I can speak, but sometimes it's just not possible to communicate with me in Spanish. After walking around his home I asked him if they had Ikea here. He looked at me quizzically and walked over to the computer to translate the word. We went to Google instead and I typed "Ikea" in. Then his face lit up and he exclaimed "E–kea!" That's how they pronounce it here. Rick said he used to live in Germany and while he was there he had a lot of Ikea furniture. "Sprechen Sie Deutsch?" I said. And he said "Ja." Finally we had a language we could communicate in a little more effectively. Although I am far from fluent in the language, and many of the words I've learned have rattled around in my head so long, they've molded themselves onto other words to make entirely new words that don't really exist. Since we discovered this new communication option, we've been communicating in a mixture of English, German and Spanish.

"Gerglish?" Oh, it hurts my brain, but it's good mental exercise.

On the plane, while traveling here, I was thinking to myself, "Oh, why did I decide to take German in high school?" I totally should have learned Spanish. You'd think that logic would have helped to make that decision back then, but I don't think that was part of the equation. If you look at the parts of the world where Spanish is spoken vs. German, and if your goal was being able to communicate outside of your country, Spanish is the clear choice.

Last summer while in Europe it was so enjoyable to be able to walk into any German town and open my mouth almost without thinking, and communicate my need. How nice it would be to do that here. I was so busy at work and preparing for other aspects of the trip that I never got around to preparing common phrases I might need here.

Working for Kinko's for so many years our catch phrase has been "just in time printing," and now I suppose it's "just in time shipping," since I now work for FedEx. Sitting at Liguria for lunch this afternoon it was "just in time Spanish." Just the phrase or words I needed at the moment I needed them. Perfect.

SATURDAY, JANUARY 30, 2010

This morning I woke up and devised a plan to find my toothbrush in my luggage without having to search through all its tightly packed contents. Success! Found the toothbrush in the second little bag I looked through. Toothbrush, toothpaste, and hairbrush in hand, I traipsed down to the bathroom, which I'm sharing with Ricardo, because the other couple staying here wanted an "in suite" bathroom. Ok, here we go. Toothpaste on toothbrush. Get it a little wet. Start brushing. Just like any other day right? While contemplating that the new batteries I recently put in my electric toothbrush really made a huge change in speed from the old ones, (gee, they must have been on their last legs) I freeze. Uh oh! This isn't any other day. I'm an idiot! I used water from the tap! I spit. Then run back to my room quickly to grab my water bottle and hightail it back to the bathroom, mouth full of toothpaste. Rinse spit, rinse spit. Envisioning little bacteria already worming their way into my bloodstream intent on wreaking havoc with my intestines. Rinse spit, gargle spit. Hmph. Man, I'm just not fully engaged in "travel mode yet." I'm somewhere in–between.

In between? What's that, you might ask. I have a theory (yes, hold onto your seats, here it comes!). Travel is a different reality than our normal world. To get there involves a change in your mind. Getting to that reality takes anywhere from 2–3 days, sometimes longer depending on how long you've been ensconced in your normal reality. There are several examples from movies and television that spring to mind that illustrate the point. They are similar, if somewhat more science–fictiony. In "The Twilight Zone," think of the episode where department store mannequins get to come to life for a time period. Or in the movie Avatar, when they transition their conscience from their real body to another body. Or possibly even the disorientation associated with time travel. While none of these examples is perfect, they all have an element of what it is like to travel – especially for any extended period of time (say, for more than a weekend) outside of your own country. Different things become important. Instead of commuting, getting to work on time, and meeting deadlines, the important things become making sure you have all the items you started off with, can I drink the water here, and have I captured the images that make this place special? Some items are logistical, some creative. Some are electrical.

Crap! At some point in the near future the travel smarts that I know I've amassed, really need to kick in. My parting gift to Ricardo was popping one of his fuses. Luckily it was a circuit-breaker and only needed to be reset. But I think my cute little travel power strip is toast. Literally. Toast with a nice coating of ozone. Crap. You can always tell something is dead when it starts smoking.

Now I'm at the Grand Hyatt. Grand is right. There are people just standing around waiting to help you. Room 1401 is mine. A cute mini–suite. Contemporary, with large black and white photographs of local scenes on the walls. Two steps down bring you into the "living room" with floor to ceiling (well, almost) windows looking out on the periphery of town and foot hills. A large flat screen TV, wired sound system, and a selection of power plugs to choose from, including the U.S. standard. I will NOT be blowing up my laptop. First of all, I'm smarter than that, although I am starting to doubt that as a fact.

In a few minutes I'll be stepping out to find the shopping center down the road that will have a USB to RJ45 (internet) connector. Don't know what I was thinking not bringing one. Suppose I thought that the prevalence of wi–fi would be much higher. Rick did try to put wi–fi in his place, but it won't work because of the construction of the building. Apparently buildings made of metal don't let the signal through.

It was quite the busy day today: my little shopping trip, a little swim around the outdoor pool, which has a wonderful waterfall wall, and then a late lunch because I am pretending I am a Hobbit, having had first and second breakfasts today. Hey, who can pass up a really kick-ass buffet? Yes, Mom, I was good. I only had one small pastry and one piece of bacon, which was balanced with watermelon and a fabulous glass of fresh squeezed orange juice, hence the need to do a little swimming! Then at 2:30 there's a short city tour and a reception at six. That's our first get together as a group. Afterwards is dinner. Luggage must be set outside the door by 10:00 p.m.

At first I was only going to check one piece. But after thinking about it, I think I'll check both large pieces. This is a charter flight. All luggage is tagged and kept together. There is a very small chance that it will get lost.

Speaking of lost luggage, as I was waiting to let the Lindblad representatives know I'd arrived and pick up my packet of information, the people in front of me were having just that issue. On the flight from Miami to Santiago their luggage got lost. What had happened is that during their check in at the airport, the luggage tag that was affixed to their luggage was another person's tag. That tag has the other people's last name on it. I try to be so careful when checking in to make sure that the tag put on my luggage has the correct 3 letter code of my final destination, however, I've never thought about making sure that the name on the luggage "receipt" has the correct name on it. It's just one more thing to think about... and be careful of.

What a great, busy day. Part of it was spent looking for a cable that I didn't really need. Once again, I forgot what I had brought with me. That's part of the down side of packing too far ahead of time. If I'd stopped to think about it before reacting and heading out to try to buy the cable I needed, I would have realized that there's no way I would have left home without it. This cable is a USB to Ethernet converter. I have a MacBook Air, which does not have an Ethernet connection; it relies on wi–fi to connect to the internet. Silly me, thinking we'd have wi–fi a few more places. So, before we head off into the wild cold places, I thought perhaps I should go buy the right cable. The mall is just down the road. After a nice walk in the shade, I walk around the mall looking for the store the door man recommended, which, incidentally has moved out of the mall. However, I spy an Apple store. Bingo! The salesclerk helps me find the cable, and I look at it carefully. It's a USB to RJ12 (phone connection). No bueno. Guess what? They're out of the one I need. After looking in 3–4 other stores I'm referred down the block to the large store that's like a Walmart. Also, no dice. Head home, look through my luggage, holding my breath each time I open the next pocket, bag, or crevice I think the cable might be in. Finally – *voila!* Success. See, no way I'd leave home without it! Hate it when I start second guessing myself.

After my hot walk to the mall, it is time to go swimming. As I look for my bathing suit, not immediately finding it, I wonder if it's sitting in a drawer at home. Nope, I know it's packed. And it is. The pool is very cool. Kind of Mickey Mouse ears and head shaped with a wall of waterfalls and inter–tubes to float around in.

The Lindblad reception and dinner are over. There are great people on this trip! My mind keeps transporting them from reception garb in tropical Santiago, and placing them in Blue hooded parkas on the snow and ice. Kind of makes me smile. I just love not knowing exactly what is ahead. I'm so excited that I feel like a little kid waiting for Christmas. Once we fly into Ushuaia tomorrow we head straight for Tiero del Fuego National Park to have lunch on a catamaran. Tonight we met a few of the staff photographers who will be aboard ship. They're going to become my new best friends. Especially the one from National Geographic (tee hee). Can't say I've ever met someone who worked for National Geographic.

Did I say I was excited? I have an "excitement" headache. I'll never be able to sleep tonight.

At the same time our dinner was taking place, a wedding was taking place on the edge of the pool. Looked like an Orthodox wedding. The priest was a figure to behold. A huge house of a man, with serious black beard to match, draped in an intricate gilded tapestry-looking thing. It was wider and more substantial than our Lutheran "stole." This man chanted the liturgy and the vows in a lovely resonating baritone. I could hear it all the way down in our ballroom full of one-hundred and forty-four excited travelers. I just had to go watch for a while. The "main stage" area was like a "huppa" without a top – just three sides of a structure, just a few upright and horizontal bars, wrapped with material, and clear glass vases hung with wire, each filled with one red rose. Beautiful and simple. It framed the area so nicely.

SUNDAY, JANUARY 31, 2010

During our orientation at the Hilton, we hear, "We're going to Antarctica, it's kind of cold down there." The ship's hotel manager, during our initial welcome and "how–everything–on–the–ship–works" talk, went on to say that during an emergency, we should return to our cabins and put on warm clothing, and they don't mean a long sleeved shirt and flip flops. They mean real layers, a warm hat, our special boots and parka.

Today started off early. I got up at 4:00 a.m., mostly because I gave up on sleeping. Just too excited to sleep. I got a little sleep, but probably not more than three to four hours tops. Turned on the TV and found "Friends" in English. Bonus! And it was an episode I'd never seen. That never happens. I didn't know there were any episodes I hadn't seen.

The process of going through the Santiago airport as a group, for our charter flight, wasn't bad. It took about an hour all told, but it was warm in the terminal, and by the end sweat was rolling down the middle of my back. The flight from Santiago to Ushuaia was about 3 1/2 hours. My seat was 8L – the window seat on the coast side. Clouds covered the land most of the time, but sometimes there were breaks in the clouds and small areas of land showed through. Mountains, and glaciers! I've never seen so many glaciers in my life. In fact, I don't think that cumulatively in my entire life I've seen as many glaciers as I saw today. Must have seen at least 20.

When we landed in Ushuaia, Argentina, and walked into the terminal we ran into the last Lindblad group that had just returned from their trip to Antarctica. They were on the other side of the immigration barrier, which was a glass wall. So they pantomimed that the Drake Passage was very wavy. I gave one a "thumbs up", and the returning passenger shook her head to indicate that a wavy Drake Passage was not a good thing. Another one indicated that flat was very good. I shook my head back "No," as I love the sea and adventure on it. I wonder what it will be like when we're in their position. What will I have seen by then? What amazing experiences wait for us over the next ten days?

Airport arrival formalities were simple and quick. Customs was perfunctory and seemed unofficial. Immigration consisted of an officer asking me if I had anything that I shouldn't have. I said no and he let me through without looking in my bag. Once through the official "welcome," we got onto buses to take a little tour. Our destination was Lapataia Bay where catamarans were waiting to take us along the Beagle Channel for lunch. To get to the bay we took the Pan–American highway. We drove to the end of it. This highway goes all the way up to Alaska. Maybe someday I'll visit the most northern point as well!

The land here reminds me a lot of Colorado. Tall, rocky mountains, bright orange lichens on boulders, short, scrubby ground cover, thick forests, wind blown trees similar to the ones up on Trail Ridge Road outside of Estes Park, Colorado.

We boarded the National Geographic Explorer around 5:30p.m. on Sunday. There was very little to do for check in – just leave a credit card and get a photo taken for my ID card. The ID cards also turn on the lights in the room and the AC/heat. So, it's important to have them. I think a lot of people wanted to go to their rooms to get unpacked right away, and skipped the check in process, but then realized that if they wanted light in the bathroom, they were going to have to check in.

The ocean has been very calm. Although I know I shouldn't wish for rough weather, it's too calm for me. There's a part of me that really wants to be tested – to be scared and live through it so that I know what I'm made of. These gentle rolling seas remind me exactly of sailing around the Caribbean. The gentle sway, the long rolling swells. It makes for ideal sleeping conditions. I slept so well last night! Since Windjammer went under a few years ago I've really missed being on the water. The almost elliptical roll of the ship, like we're going in slow vertical circles, is very relaxing. Makes it harder to think about what needs to get done. Harder to stay focused. Yes, I'm on vacation, but it's a working vacation. Logging the trip in photographs and words takes some dedication. If I get behind I'll never catch up. So that's why I'm in my room trying to concentrate, so that I can catch up on my writing and photograph downloading. Then I want to start absorbing all the amazing experience and knowledge of the staff on this ship. The staff has been with Lindblad for so many years. Some started coming down to Antarctica in the 1970's!

In the middle of the night I woke up, took stock of the rolling of the ship and had to restrain myself from exclaiming aloud, "That's it??" That's the extent of what the Drake Passage is going to bring? How sad. Oh, I know I should be glad. Perhaps on the return trip we'll have "The Drake Shake" instead of "The Drake Lake."

Our wake up call this morning startled both my roommate and me. A soft male voice said, "Good morning." Bev and I looked at each other, wondering who had snuck into our room without our hearing it. And then we realized it was an announcement. Bud, one of the crewmembers, was giving us a wake up call. His voice in the morning is smooth and soft like cream. It's a nice, but slightly odd way to wake up. I almost felt as if God was speaking to me — the disembodied voice hovering over me like an apparition.

Our bird talk this morning was given by Stephan. He discussed many of the pelagic birds that are found in this area and farther south — albatross, petrel, and shearwaters. There are generally regarded to be between thirteen and twenty-four species of albatross. Most are pelagic, which means that these birds live on the water and go to land only to breed. Many are endangered species.

Wandering albatrosses are one of the bird species that have been following the ship. Albatrosses are the only birds that have divided nostrils. If you find a bird skeleton on the beach you can tell if it is an albatross or some other kind of bird because on albatros each nostril is divided into two openings - one is for getting rid of excess salt and the other one is for incoming air. When an albatross has taken in too much salt for its body to handle, the excess runs out through the nostrils. Very often, if you look closely at an albatross in flight, you'll see a drop of water at the very end of its beak.

Pelagic birds have a gland above the ridge of their eye that acts like reverse osmosis. It's the only way they can get fresh water. Otherwise they would need to find a lake to get fresh water. That certainly wouldn't work very well for birds that stay on the open ocean most of their lives. I think God creates some pretty cool features in a lot of animals.

Over and over again, in the last two days we have heard about the destructive results from introducing non–native animals into the wild down here. First it was beaver from Canada being brought down to Ushuaia to create a fur trade. The problem was that Ushuaia is not as cold as Canada, so as the beavers multiplied, their coats became thinner and not as luxurious. As a result, the beavers were never hunted and their population exploded. They started to create their own habitat, gnawing down trees and making dams. As the area flooded, trees died and the flow of the rivers were changed.

On Marion Island in the Southern Indian Ocean, cats were introduced in the late 1940s to kill the mice that ships brought. However, the cats found it easier to kill the petrels and albatrosses because they're so clumsy and slow on land. Not only did the cats not fix the problem, but they also kept multiplying. A "cat virus" was introduced and that reduced the population a lot, but as usual some of the population was immune and the population simply re–expanded. At the lecture where we learned this I joked to the woman next to me that they should have just introduced dogs next! By the 1990's, after organized nighttime hunting parties killed a number of remaining cats, traps were used to catch the remaining population. It's now believed that the feral cats have been completely eradicated from the island.

While in the observation lounge today, I saw some penguins porpoising out of the water, about five or six of them. So beautiful and graceful, and fast! They're truly at home in the water. Like slick little bullets. Immediately I thought of my binoculars, but they weren't around my neck. I haven't gotten in the habit of walking around with them yet, but now I have an incentive to do so.

LAURA VAE GATZ

LAND HO!
TUESDAY, FEBRUARY 1, 2010

Today we will see land. We've made very good time – about thirty-six hours from the time we left port in Ushuaia. I believe we left at 7:00 p.m. on Sunday, and land should be sighted about 7:00 a.m. this morning, Tuesday.

It's 4:07 a.m. Yes, I should be sleeping, I know. We have a big day ahead of us. The crew has moved breakfast up by an hour and a half so we can take full advantage of the day. The big surprise yesterday was that we are going to try to make landfall (in the zodiacs) at Elephant Island, the infamous location where the Shackleton crew made landfall for the last time, and sent the Captain out in one of the lifeboats to find help (which he succeeded in doing). Depending on the waves, we may or may not be able to disembark.

It's starting to get light outside. The fog has cleared a little and visibility is now probably at least a mile, although, without any distance reference in the open ocean, it is hard to tell. We may see mammal activity this morning – large mammals –, which means whales. If there are any early morning sightings from the bridge, they've promised to announce it.

Breakfast at 7 a.m., mandatory IAATO (International Association of Antarctica Tour Operators) and zodiac (inflatable boat) procedure meeting at 8:30, then it's back to our rooms to get dressed for our first excursion. The IAATO briefing covers the procedures and guidelines that ensure safe and environmentally friendly visits. Only one hundred people can be ashore at any one time. We can only approach wildlife within fifteen feet. However, the penguins don't understand these rules, so if we're planted and they wander up closer, then it's fine. We also were instructed on how to not disturb the environment. Don't leave anything behind, don't remove anything, and don't walk on small plants or lichens found on rocks.

Our first trip out sounds like it will be mostly a zodiac cruise. This will be a good first dress rehearsal for spending time on land. All of us will be trying out our new gear – new boots, clothing layers, waterproof pants and our spanking new National Geographic blue parka.

As for me, I'll be using my new backpack and Think Tank camera pouch for the first time in the field. Sure, I carried the backpack around through the airports in order to get here, but didn't use it practically. Now it only has in it what I'll need for the day. All the extraneous items have been taken out.

Seas have consistently been eight to ten feet. On the bridge yesterday I noted the sea temperature log, taken once an hour, which tracks the sea temperature down to a 10th of a Celsius degree. It had steadily been rising all day until about 3:00 p.m. when it started to fall, much more quickly, as we passed out of the Drake Passage into the Southern Ocean.

Sleeping onboard has been most pleasant. The gentle rocking of the ship is like being rocked to sleep as a baby. There are those that would disagree with me. Those with inner ear issues. Those that don't like being on the water. But, to me, it takes me back to sailing with Windjammer and all those fond memories of sailing around the Caribbean, on old wooden sailboats, with my sister.

Of course the cabins here are much larger and more luxurious. There's actually room for both my roommate and me to walk around at the same time. The bathroom has a separate shower that is behind a glass partition, and it's not actually possible to stretch out your arms and touch all opposite walls at the same time, like it was aboard the Windjammer ships. There's a flat screen television for tracking our progress, GPS location, and to sneak a peak to see what is going on outside in front of the ship. That way I have an idea of what is going on in front of us before I get all dressed. Maybe there is a spectacular sunrise or iceberg that deserves recording!

Sitting here in bed, under the fluffy white comforter, pillows supporting my back, I find my stomach is rumbling. Did I eat too much or not enough last night? I have been trying to be good. Bread is offered at every turn. Desserts are simple and delicious. Staying hydrated can also be a challenge if I don't make a conscious effort to keep water with me as I wander around the ship.

I can hear the waves crashing around the hull. Walls creak and pop. And when I'm lying down, the cotton of my pillow makes a low squeak against the fitted sheet in rhythm to the rocking. This ship has excellent stabilizers. I can hear them working when the ship rolls. Well, it's either that or the hull of the ship smacking back down on the surface of the water and I really don't think that we're moving enough to do that. Every 20 or 30 seconds there is a deep clunk in the bowels of the ship, as if a heavy weight just ran into a bulkhead. I picture large, sofa size lead weights on tracks sliding from port to starboard to counteract the rolling of the ship. Perhaps there's a way to get a tour. I've been wearing earplugs, yet it's hard to not be aware of the sounds, especially when my mind is racing with all the new information and knowledge I'm trying to absorb into my brain.

Chris Rainier's camera workshop yesterday afternoon was fantastic. Chris is the National Geographic Photographer on board as part of the staff. It was like a class at Brooks Institute of Photography, condensed down into one hour. Although I already knew most of what he was saying, and I mentally ticked off each of the techniques he mentioned, his practical knowledge and good photography habits have already added valuable techniques to my shooting. Lying in bed this morning I was reviewing them in my head, eager to practice them on the zodiac this morning, or possibly earlier if we spy whales in the vicinity.

For instance, I had no idea I could keep my ISO ("speed" of my camera, like film speed) at 500 as a baseline. I'd been following old principles learned in the film days, trying to keep my ISO as close to 100 as possible given the light conditions. Michael, the other staff photographer on board gave me some practical insight into protecting yourself from camera vibrations and wind shear. It's pretty windy, even gusty on the back of the ship. Many of us were out there yesterday photographing and watching the birds with binoculars. I had donned my 100–400mm lens with 5 inch lens hood. Michael came out with his large lens and monopod attached to his camera body. Walking up to him, I asked if the vibration of the ship made it difficult to photograph with a monopod or if there was a shutter speed that could compensate for the shake. He said that with a wooden deck most of the vibration is absorbed. He uses his feet to gauge vibration. If you pay attention it's possible to feel the vibration in your feet. Also, the monopod foot can be placed on the top of your foot to further absorb vibration.

My definition of "bracketing" was also expanded yesterday.

Bracketing can refer to more than exposure compensation. You can "bracket" composition, taking both vertical and horizontal compositions, as well as zooming in and out on a subject. Change your perspective. Work a subject. Take a photo with and without a polarizer. Adjust your white balance (this can be done in the camera if you have time, but can also be done on the back end, on your computer). Why not take ALL your options and combine them in different ways?

Polarizers can be used in cloudy situations as well as sunny ones, especially if you're on the water. They'll take a bit of the glare off. They also work well on clouds and snow.

Chris said that Canon has had the contract for imaging with the U.S. government for a long time. So they have lots and lots of R&D (research and development) dollars at their disposal. Their focusing technology is superior to Nikon's. When he was in Serajevo, he saw war correspondents with Canons, sticking only the camera out of hiding to get the shot, relying on the autofocus to do its job. He thought, "Heck, why do I want to stick my neck out and take a chance at getting shot when I can get a Canon and do it like they do?" Then he started shooting with Canon. His point was that with Canon you didn't have to look at what you were shooting – you could point your camera in the right direction and press the shutter down, leaving the lens to autofocus for you without having to put your head in the line of fire.

Being on board this vessel with her staff and all their knowledge can be a little intimidating. We heard that many staff members have been with Lindblad for at least seventeen years and some as many as thirty. Some have traveled down to Antarctica every year for thiry years, three times a season or more. At first you think to yourself, "Whoa, that's something else; I can't go to talk to them!" Then you realize that they're here for you. You're all on the ship together for a week, and you want to soak up as much of their knowledge as they'll share. Shyness falls away and you find yourself walking up to the author of "The Antarctic Primer" or the National Geographic photographer. No time like the present!

All the other guests are just as interesting. It's fascinating to talk to each person. Everyone is full of stories: what brought them here, why they're interested in the Antarctic, how long they've been wanting to come, or stories from their other travels. And a common thread amongst us is that we're all excited about where we're going and what we're going to see. The excitement is almost palpable.

At first I was a little surprised at the diversity of the passengers. There are a lot of older folks (meaning older than me). I suppose that's not surprising, they're usually the ones with the time and money to travel. However, I have a hard time imagining some of them getting into a zodiac or making a water landing. But they all have a sense of adventure, and they're here! Some want to complete their complement of continents, some love penguins or whales; others are simply fascinated with the idea of an uninhabited continent (yes, there are people who live in Antarctica, even year–round, but there are no real towns). It's a land ruled by the elements and animals. Is there anyplace more remote, frozen, and otherworldly on this planet? Actually, there may well be, but my point is that Antarctica is special. It takes effort to get here. It's not a place that you happen upon. Being here stems from a specific intention in each one of us. Each person has his or her personal reasons for being here. And that makes all these folks who were strangers just a few days ago fellow adventurers, fellow dreamers. It gives us a bond – a singular purpose. We're all here to Experience.

This morning I experienced stretching on the ship. Doing it on a ship takes it to a whole new level. The movement of the ship accentuates the stretch, in waves. As the ship rolls up your body is pressed to the floor, and as it sinks, the stretch relaxes a little. And because the ship is moving in a lot of different directions it adds complexity to the stretch. If you're stretching standing up, working core–stabilizing muscles, then balance becomes an additional challenge.

Because there is no way to get to the exercise room without going outside, I settle for stretching in the lounge, but not before attempting to access the room. We are currently at 60.35's 55.47'w and it's 6 a.m. I have on thin, long underwear and an oversized man's shirt that I sleep in. "I don't think I should be going outside," is a thought I have as I try to unlock the wrought iron door that opened onto a cold, wet, windswept deck. Only one other person is out there, practicing with her camera. She's probably practicing some of the tips learned yesterday. Of course it's important to avoid falling over...

Icebergs and Whales!! Saw my first iceberg today. The little ones are called bergy bits. It sounds like a good name for a breakfast cereal. You could take little rice bits, dye them blue and call them "Bergy Bits" or "Blue Bergies." Then have black and white marshmallow penguins. Apparently the name depends on the size. Bergy bits stand between one and four meters above the water. On the smaller side there are growlers, which stand less than one meter out of the water. Brash ice consists of tiny bits of ice, all floating in close proximity, usually shards from other forms of icebergs. Then there are tabular icebergs. Those are huge, and flat on top. They can be several square kilometers in area, and several stories high. The blue color they emit is so amazing. Aqua. Almost glowing. Weathered icebergs can have holes and arches and spectacular shapes. Pancake ice is formed when small bits of ice are packed together, turning the outer edges up.

Ice and icebergs appear blue when the ice is very old, and most of the air has been forced out of the ice from great pressure. Air reflects light, and would make the ice appear white. When there are no more reflective properties within the ice, the ice will appear blue. Why? It's the same principle that occurs when diving in the ocean. The farther down you go, the fewer colors you see. Blue becomes the dominant color. This happens because blue is the wavelength of light that is filtered out last.

We prepared for going out in the zodiacs this morning. Everyone signed up for a group, splitting us into six groups of twenty-four. There are one hundred and forty-four passengers on board. Our group number remains our number for the rest of the trip. Each zodiac holds up to twelve people.

The waves have been surging about five to ten feet today. We were to be completely ready to get on the zodiac before crossing the threshold to the area where we step down several stairs to an open doorway a few feet above the water line of the ship. When I was next to step into the launch, the waves broke over the doorway and temporarily flooded the platform of wire mesh I was standing on with about a foot of freezing sea water. It was kind of cool to still be on the ship, but be standing in so much water. I took a step up onto the platform, preparing to step onto the zodiac. The zodiac dipped down at least five feet, in synchronicity with the waves. As the two crew–members maneuvered the boat into position left to right, they indicated when I should step in. Grabbing their hands with a sailor's grip (wrist to wrist), I stepped on board, took one stride across the boat, and quickly sat down on the far side. Whew! Although I've done this many, many times with Windjammer, there's something a little more at stake when the water is almost at the freezing point. Ten of us got on and then we took off.

Well, we took off until the motor died. Hmmm. When it died we weren't too far from the ship, but it still made me wonder what would happen. Everyone on the zodiac was silent. After less than a minute our zodiac driver coaxed the motor back to life and we headed towards a lounging Leopard Seal lying around relaxing on a medium size chunk of floating ice.

PAULET ISLAND
WEDNESDAY, FEBRUARY 3, 2010

Today we arrived at Paulet Island. Leaving Elephant Island, of the South Shetland Islands, we traveled into the Weddell Sea to get to here. I smelled it before I saw it. The smells from the penguin colony permeated the ship, all the way into our cabin. Once outside, the full smell was apparent. Fishy, but not too unpleasant. I'd thought it would be more intolerable.

It snowed all day, sometimes more than others; big fluffy flakes. From the ship they almost seemed to be floating upwards as if the sea were precipitating.

Up early this morning. Around 4:00 a.m. I woke up and wrote a bit, then wandered up to the bridge fully clothed for the weather, camera in hand, and shot photos of the magnificent icebergs we passed. Occasionally penguins were hanging out on the ice, running around or tobogganing down slopes.

Around breakfast time the announcement came about which groups would be going ashore first. 1–2–3–4 going ashore, 5–6 going on a zodiac cruise. My roommate, Bev, and I ran off to our room after breakfast to don our Antarctic gear. One day behind us, this was the real deal – going ashore for a few hours. One last bathroom break, and then we started to get dressed. The first time we'll actually be going ashore. We're both extremely excited and slightly flustered. Feeling as if we're in a bit of a hurry, we don't get the order of the clothes quite correct the first time, and spend almost as much time undressing as getting dressed. First, knee-high socks, long johns, second pair of socks, fleece pants, and then the waterproof pants. Then thermal top, thin sweater, fleece and parka. Next, life vest, backpack. And last, belly pack and camera pouch. As Bev said the first time she saw me in this getup, "Oh my, you look like you just gained 40 pounds!"

Observing each other getting dressed was like watching the three stooges; well, two out of the three, anyway. You wouldn't think that putting on a life vest would be very difficult, but these life vests are a little different from most I've seen. There's a firm horseshoe shape that goes around your neck and down your front. Then from the curve of the horseshoe is a strap that goes down the middle of your back from neck to waist, terminating in a belt that is fastened in front. I tell you, it took all week to figure out how to get into the life vest quickly. Every day I would hold it up in front of me and just shake my head. "How did I do this yesterday?" I wasn't the only one having trouble. While waiting to board the zodiacs I saw several folks holding their life vest in front of themselves and just shaking their heads.

We toddled out of the room and down the corridor to the stairwell that would take us to the Mud Room. I felt like I was all geared up for scuba diving or possibly walking on the moon, with lots of layers and gear hanging off most sides of my body.

In the mud room expectant passengers were making last minute adjustments to their clothing, making sure coats were zipped, hoods up, camera equipment covered and stowed. Glove liners and over—mittens on, hands free. Ooops, where's my key card? I've got to check out before going ashore. Gloves off, parka pulled up, pants pocket unzipped. There it is. Scan the barcode at the computer station. Bleep. Ok, now I'm official.

Then the call came to start loading the zodiacs. Before stepping through the threshold into the loading dock area, you must be completely ready to go, no fussing with equipment and your hands must be free. As you cross into the exit area there is a bin with foam rubber soaked in disinfectant, which must be stepped in to ensure you're not taking anything onto or back from the island. A zodiac pulls up, the swells much calmer than the day before. I step onto the platform, then onto the boat, and sit down. We're off!

It's a short ride from the ship to the island. Less than a football field in distance. The zodiac pulls up on a black basalt rock shoreline, the dark rocks tumbled round by waves. The island is covered with a fresh layer of snow, already dirtied and trampled by thousands of penguin feet and guano. Groups of Adelie penguins line the shore, honking a reception.

The correct way to disembark is to sit down on the side towards the bow, and swing your legs over in the direction of the stern. Dropping my feet into about 10 inches of water, I grasp the offered hands and arms for support, and slide off the edge. Climbing up onto shore I stop at the large baskets that are ready to receive our life vests, then select a walking stick.

Oh! So exciting! Penguins everywhere! Where to go, what to do first? Remembering that I must stay at least fifteen feet away from all wildlife, I find it takes a while to make progress. The penguins are busy – diving into the ocean, hunting, and hopping back onto land. They make their way back to their nests. Other penguins seem to be indecisive about what they're doing. "Should I go in? I don't know; it looks awfully cold. That's a big drop down to the water. Bob doesn't seem to want to go in either. Maybe I should go back to my nest. I know Susie is sure to be rock stealing again."

Adelie penguins are rock stealers. It's what their nests are made out of. In order to attract a mate you've got to have a big nest. Rocks are currency to the penguins. The larger the nest, the more assured they can be of their eggs staying high and dry when snow and ice start to melt in the summer. If the eggs don't stay dry, they won't stay warm, and then there won't be any baby penguins to hatch.

Watching the penguins' behavior was so amusing. I'm going to name a few penguins for my illustration here, just for fun and ease of understanding. Bugsy and Sid both have their own nests. Sid goes off in search of that perfect rock. While Sid is gone, Bugsy waddles over to Sid's nest and steals a rock. Now Bugsy is up one rock and Sid has broken even. I wonder if they know they're not actually scoring additional rocks when this happens? Do they notice one is gone? Or do they think that by adding rocks that their nest must be growing? I guess we'll never know what they're thinking.

However, during one of our "Day's Recap" sessions Stephen was giving a short talk about the Adelie penguin behavior. He said that the females pull a fast one on the males. Apparently the female behavior that indicates she's interested in the male is the lowering of her head, while the male sits on the nest. The male will acknowledge by stepping out of the nest. This is when the female makes her move and steals a rock. She'll do this over and over again, and the male never wises up. Apparently, his hormones override any suspicion.

The penguin chicks are about the same size as their parents now. It's early February and they're starting to molt. I'm reminded of junior high; everyone tries to act grown up, but looks dorky and a bit geeky. Each chick has a different molting pattern. One looks like a punk rocker with a Mohawk; another is just patchy all over. Another has down stuck to his beak. Yum, a beak full of feathers! Most of them could use a bath. They have what I'd call "guano butt." I'm amazed at how dirty some of these guys are; even the adults. I'm amused to observe the difference a dip in the ocean makes in these guys' appearance. Dirty going in, clean coming out. The ocean is one big penguin washing machine.

I walk as far along the shore as I can, pausing along the way to let penguins cross my path. It's slow going, but amusing. Finding a rock, I sit for a while watching the penguins on parade. Listen to the low buzzing honk coming from the shoreline when the penguins think they might actually go in. The sound reaches a crescendo and then dies down. No one has gone into the water. It surges again, a few taking small tentative steps closer to the edge. Then one takes the plunge. His friends hesitate for an instant then follow in his wake. Many more go, then strangely, one hesitates, and the process begins all over again.

After a bit I wander up the hill, crossing several rivers of guano and melt water. The round black rocks are slippery, covered with a mixture of guano, ice, and slushy snow. In spots my feet sink down into, well, I don't know what it is. It's certainly not mud. Perhaps an accumulation of guano? It looks like mincemeat pie covered with a light crust of powdered sugar.

Making my way to the top, I pass another grouping of nests. This one contains a crèche. A crèche is a gathering of chicks, late in their first season, standing together. As each chick sees its mother, it breaks off from the group and chases her down. It's funny to see this fat, mottled downy mass chasing after the sleeker black and white version of itself. This must be the time when parents start to encourage their little ones to start hunting on their own. February is close to the time that the chicks will need to leave the island and start hunting on their own – not relying on parents for their food anymore.

One little chick was running after Mom, and when Mom stopped, it maneuvered its beak as close to Mom's beak as possible. Mom kept turning her head, beak in the air, attempting to avoid her persistent chick's begging.

Farther up the path was a ridge, from which could be seen a large, mostly frozen lake, penguin nests overlooking it from the far edge. Those penguins have a really long hike from the beach; at least 45 minutes to an hour commute each way.

Off in the distance I see penguins doing just that, coming down from the slopes and returning from hunting; a little penguin highway, some walking, others tobogganing on their stomachs down slopes then standing to walk again. After walking across a fairly open snowy expanse, I settled on a rock to watch. Fascinating.

After approximately 2 hours, I'd apparently stayed on the island past my "allotted" time. This is not a big deal; they give you as much time as you want, but if you want to do another activity, there are set times to depart from the ship. Once back on board I asked the shuttle loaders if I'd missed my opportunity for a zodiac cruise. The first answer I got was "yes," so I went in search of a different answer. Today both sides of the ship were being used for loading and unloading of passengers. So I headed to the other side. There I got the answer I was looking for. One shuttle loader asked the zodiac driver if he could take me out to join one of the cruises. He first took me along the shore where we watched the penguins queuing up to jump of a squatty cliff, into the water. Eventually a zodiac with a few people on it pulled up and I transferred from one boat to the other.

The current was swift just off shore today. The little icebergs and bergy bits floated past at a good rate. I asked the driver if he ever gets into situations where the ice closes in and it's not possible to get out again. The answer was "Oh, yes."

Because the water is crystal clear, it's possible to look over the edge of the craft and see the bottom. Close to shore the bottom is a field of round black rocks of varying shapes and sizes.

After everyone was back on board, around noon, we sailed through Fritchoff Sound where we saw a legion of porpoising penguins. There must have been 500 at least. Then we sailed into the Antarctic Sound where the most amazing tabular icebergs sat regal and imposing, waiting for us.

Michael, the photographer, had given me a heads up that I'd want to be ready to take photographs because this part was going to be impressive. And it was. And, oh, so much more than that! The videographer was out on the bow with us, taking footage. She said this is one of her favorite bits of ice; and that she loves to see people's reactions and hear their comments.

These icebergs are attached to the bottom and are not floating around. Their walls are vertical and therefore safe to sail close to. These tabular icebergs originate from the Larsen Ice shelf, farther south in the Weddell Sea, which is a permanent ice shelf; ice that is thousands of years old. Then the wind comes along, and a piece shears off and drifts north with the current. Around the Antarctic Sound the easterly winds catch them and some are blown into this area. Most of these bergs draft about 700 feet. The entrance to the Sound is deeper than that, but eventually they run into the shoals and get grounded. This is the area in which we sailed around.

As I mentioned, these bergs start off with straight sides. Over time the water erodes areas around the water line, and bits around the top can crack and fall off. As this happens over time, the part in the water can end up wider than the top. However, the parts close enough to the surface to interfere with the draft of the ship (15 feet) can clearly be seen as light aqua through the clear water, and that makes it fairly safe to sail close to these icebergs.

The tabular iceberg area we sailed in was spectacular. Tall bergs rising straight out of the water, towering above us, varying shades of blue and aqua. Averaging about 150 feet tall or more, they stood, each unique. Some had overhanging snow, like snow flowing slowly off an angled roof, curling around the top edge like frosting on a cake. Other bergs sat close together creating long narrow passageways; cold blue hallways of the Antarctic. In some places ice pillars had formed within the iceberg walls, reminiscent of a frozen Petra. Ice caves with deep blue interiors, crusted with icy stalactites. Rich blue cracks extending down from the peak. A hundred different animal and human face shapes spring to life from the cold walls. My imagination lets loose as I attempt to capture these amazing sights.

Silly me. I left my gloves in the room. Once I ran back to the room to get them, grabbing my hat, thinking the gloves were stuffed inside. Once out on the bow I was unable to tear myself away even for the 2 minutes it would take to run downstairs and back to get them. Towards the end I came inside, to the chart room, to beg a pair of gloves from a friend who was done going outside. My savior! Occasionally my mind flashed back to the scene in "Titanic" where our main two characters are on the deck when the ship sails impossibly close to the wall of the iceberg they've just hit.

When we left the "tabbies" (Antarctic slang for tabular icebergs) behind, we left the Antarctic Sound and sailed into the Bransfield Strait to reach Deception Island.

LAURA VAE GATZ

Deception Island
Thursday, February 4, 2010

W e've got wind blowing at fifty-five knots here at Deception Island. Neptune's Bellows is the entrance to the flooded caldera, named Port Foster. Deception Island is an old volcano. We cross into the bay, which although calmer, still has winds gusting at fifty knots now. The first groups have gone ashore. Several hearty souls signed up for, and took the hike up to Neptune's Window. I've enjoyed watching their progress and antics from the warm bridge. Some have lost their gloves in the water along the shore; some apparently have been blown off course. We've seen at least one backpack go in the drink. Some hikers have turned back early. Along the other end of the shore are several old buildings from whaling times; two wooden boats, permanently frozen in the ground; large rusty round tanks used to hold the whale oil rendered from blubber; several old buildings, starting to crumble.

I'm reluctant to go ashore and yet I know I must. Soon I'll be putting on all the clothes I've brought with me. And yes, I'm very thankful for the loan of Dad's fleece facemask with the pointy nose-piece; it will be a godsend today.

What a blustery morning! The short trip to the shore took all of twenty seconds; then we were disembarking. Feet swung over the side from the stern end, into the water, which on this island, is lined with black sand. A fresh snowfall covers the land and mountain peaks. Low clouds and snow obscure the view in the distance. Photographs of this bay are printed in one of the books I've read. Interesting to see it in person, when, at the time, it all seemed very remote. Well, it is. It's just that we are now here, in this remote area. Unbelievable.

Bev and I head up the beach several yards to look at the boats. There are the remains of two there, apparently used to haul and store drinking water. We take turns snapping photos of ourselves, bracing in the wind to keep from blowing away; trying to keep our eyes open against the sting of hard blown snowflakes.

After Chris's lecture this afternoon, where he showed us some of his amazing black and white images from around the world, Bev and I were sitting and talking with both Chris and his brother Peter. Bev had just asked Chris to recount the quote he'd mentioned at the beginning of his talk. The quote was from a Buddhist monk who had just come out of a cave where he'd been in seclusion for a year. As the monk was walking away, Chris asked him what he'd learned, and he said, "Everything will appear as it should." We thought that was profound, and became our phrase of the week, repeating it to each other in our cabin and throughout the day, when we were uncertain about what would happen next, "Everything will appear as it should."

As we were talking, we all were looking at this amazing iceberg in the distance. One of us mentioned how cool it would be if we could go over there. I volunteered to go talk with the captain. Bev came with me for reinforcement. The short story is that he said yes, and changed the ship's course. The surprise is, well, there are several; it wasn't only one iceberg, it was three. Two with ice caves and one extremely tall thin one. And there were humpback whales on the way, and chinstrap penguins hanging out on the low blue part of the tall iceberg. The captain took the ship's nose right up to the base of the berg, where we hung out for several minutes. The iceberg even "calved" while we were there (icebergs don't calve, only glaciers calve, but that's the action that occurred). It was amazing. The captain even announced the viewing opportunity. Lots of folks were out on deck shooting photographs.

This was a great learning opportunity for me. Although I had two camera bodies with me, I did not have any extra memory cards; what a shock it was when my LCD screen blinked "CF FULL" indicating that I was out of luck. Crap. Now I was down to one memory card and two bodies. Then I realized that one of my bodies was still set on "fluorescent" for color balance. Double crap. Guess I'll be deleting a number of shots. Oh well, that's why I shoot a lot.

Photo Tip: when there is a little time before you know you're going to be shooting, get your cameras ready. Check all the settings and make sure they're all correct. Speed, battery charge, ISO, color balance, room left on the memory card.

This trip is interesting in so many ways. Too many to count, but some include the numerous stories that everyone on board has to tell. I'm fascinated by people's stories of how they came to be here, or what they do "in real life."

Shipboard friendships sprout up quickly. Before you know it, you've met almost everyone and have formed relationships based on random things. Bob shoots the same camera that I do, Susie grew up in the same town my sister worked in, we both love whales, we've visited the same places. Whatever the reason, we're all here for a little adventure, to see this remote place, and we're all bound together by the excitement that is this trip.

None (well, very few) of us are distracted by our everyday lives. Bills, chores and work are temporarily forgotten. World news marches on without us. Television seasons start and it's of no consequence. We're all completely engrossed in our days. We're here and now, present in our surroundings, soaking up the experiences like dry sponges. Tonight we cruised around in a quiet, still bay, surrounded by tall black pointy peaks and a semicircular wall of glaciers. We watched whales play, seals lounge, and icebergs crackle and calve while the sun started to set behind the clouds. What a beautiful, peaceful evening.

CUVERVILLE & NEKO HARBOR
FRIDAY, FEBRUARY 5, 2010

Cuverville is one of the largest Gentoo Penguin colonies on the Antarctic Peninsula. Ashore we shed our life vests, select a walking stick, and walk across the rocky beach, trying to avoid crossing paths with penguins. Remember to stay at least fifteen feet away! This is harder than it might seem. Sometimes the penguins hold so still they aren't immediately apparent. Multiple times I've been walking along and all of a sudden realize I've invaded a penguin's space, the result of which might be several squawks, a blank stare, or they might simply waddle away.

More passengers were arriving at the research station around the time we were waiting to go back to the ship. As they walked up the stairs towards the station I held out my arms and in a bad imitation of a Russian, I said magnanimously in a booming voice, "Welcome to Antarctica! It's been such a long time since we've seen anyone!" I got a few chuckles, but I thought I was funnier than anyone else thought I was.

Our zodiac cruise began right from the research station. Off we went, in search of wildlife, finding three different species of seals – Leopard, Weddell and Crabeater. The Weddell seal has a very tiny little head. The Leopard seal has a very funny face if they're looking straight at you. Like a bald kid, with no eyelashes, who has just eaten a chocolate chip cookie very messily.

After we got back, the ship departed for a very scenic passage on the way to Neko Harbor. However, the katabatic winds beat us there and we had to choose an alternative destination. The winds were just brutal. Katabatic winds originate in the mountains and sweep down out of them with a vengeance, stirring up snow and decreasing the windchill temperature by several degrees!

So instead, we went to Paradise Bay where the ship dropped anchor and we split into two groups – one to go ashore on the Antarctic mainland, at the Argentinean research station called Base Brown – and one to go on zodiac cruises.

Ashore, Bev and I took turns taking each other's photographs in front of the research station sign and in front of the penguins. This colony of Gentoos had some chicks that were much younger than we had seen, still sheltering under their parent's legs, to keep warm. Some appeared so fragile they almost seemed like a noodle, too limp to stand up under their own power. A pair of them was flopped down on the warm rock face, apparently recharging their batteries and cooling off by panting. Since penguins are birds, they can't sweat, and must cool off in other ways. One way is by panting, much like the family dog.

Other passengers climbed up a steep, snow covered hill, and took in the view from the top. Apparently the way down was a little different method than the way up. We saw little blue shapes descending on their posteriors, some more quickly than others. From our vantage point it looked very steep and a little scary. Somehow Bev and I missed the information about the "snow slide" and didn't know the hike up the hill was an optional activity.

LAURA VAE GATZ

PORT LOCKROY, LEMAIRE CHANNEL, BOOTH ISLAND
SATURDAY, FEBRUARY 6, 2010

Originally Port Lockroy was called Port LaCroix. It was a whaling station in the 1920's. Today, Port Lockroy is a restored historic British Antarctic base. In the 1930's it was used for British expeditions. The building that we visited was built in 1944. The earth's atmosphere, animals and plant life were topics of study. It remained a science base until 1962, afterwards being left to the elements. It was falling into disrepair and the British government had gotten a few complaints from visitors to the area once the roof started falling in. In order to remove the eyesore and maintain some dignity, they restored it in 1996, and it has been running as a living museum and post office ever since. Penguins moved onto the station in the 1980's and the building was declared a historic monument in 1995. It is designated as Historic Site #61 under the Antarctic Treaty. Items used in the early 1900's are displayed much in the same way they would have appeared when in use: food rations, clothing, and research equipment.

The current staff members run the gift shop and have to live with the Gentoo penguins that inhabit the base area. Rachel, Eleanor (postmistress), and Claire are this year's residents. The proceeds from the gift shop go into maintaining the building and other historic buildings in Antarctica. I do believe our shipmates made a tidy little donation to preservation today. I think the average bill in there was over $125 USD.

Painted on the inside of the gift shop door is a portrait of a woman who looks like Marilyn Monroe, painted by the original "overwinterers". It was never finished; she only has one arm, and the one arm she does have doesn't have a hand. Although it must have been meant to remind the men of the beautiful women back home, I think the painting is a little creepy.

The baby penguins are everywhere around the station. They especially like the boot brush, for cleaning boots, which is at the base of the ramp leading up to the front entrance. They walk right up to the door, peeking in, wondering if they should go in to get a cup of tea. The Snowy Sheathbills have also made themselves at home here, hatching chicks under the front door grate. The grate allows for snow to fall through it from the front walk. These chicks are easily visible from above, and are seemingly happy, protected from traffic.

The researchers told us that part of the Gentoo population of this island is a control study. They are studying the effects of tourism on penguins – comparing where people interact with penguins versus where they don't. I'd be curious to know what they find. One of the researchers from the National Geographic Explorer said that they often find that the group with human interaction tends to fare better because humans have a tendency to scare off Skuas that would otherwise prey on the penguin chicks.

A new building was in the process of being constructed. This is to be the new lodging for the residents. I think they'll be quite happy with it considering that currently they stay in the old base that is not well insulated, has no running water, and through which come all the tourists. There's one main room they live, sleep, and eat in. Each person has a bunk in one of the four corners of the room. They must find it hard to have strangers looking at where they live all the time. It must be hard to allow yourself to truly feel at home in a place that is always on view. Once we've all gone back to the ship, the researchers are invited onboard to take showers, do laundry and join us for dinner. This is a tradition with the ships that pass through here. I'll just bet they look forward to each ship coming through!

Port Lockroy is a quiet, safe anchorage and is where we spend the night, at anchor. All the better for sound and deep sleeping.

After leaving Port Lockroy we sailed through the Lemaire Channel, a fairly narrow waterway leading between towering walls of snow covered cliffs, beautiful and imposing. Here is where we met the most ships we've seen all trip. One miniscule sailboat that I imagined was lost – it was so small that I couldn't imagine sailing it around down here in any sort of storm. It couldn't have been over twenty feet. An old Russian research vessel sailed past us, and a passenger ship that was roughly the same size as our ship. So far I think I've seen a total of five ships in the waters down here.

Just before dinner tonight we got a fantastic surprise. Instead of turning the ship around to start heading north, we're going to continue south past the Antarctic Circle, which lies at 66'33S. Not all of the Antarctic trips make it this far south. I think we are able to have this experience because we made such excellent time in the Drake Passage (Drake Lake!) and because the weather has been, is, and is expected to be very good. Speaking with the first officer this morning on the bridge, he said this is the best weather he's seen down here all season: excellent visibility, calm seas, and sunny. Usually it's fog and driving snow. We have been truly blessed with fantastic weather our entire trip, except for the day on Deception Island. However, I find it important to have a bit of contrast, just to be able to understand, in even a small way, the driving forces that are the weather down here. I'll never forget those sixty mile-an-hour winds and the scoured black and white landscape.

Today Bev and I received a dinner invitation from Chris and Peter Rainier, to eat in the chart room. Apparently everyone gets to eat up there once during the trip. There are 12 nights and 144 passengers, so the math works out perfectly because each dinner party is a group of 12. What a lovely time we had. Our evening started with champagne and a few toasts; then appetizers and main course. And a special Argentinean dessert, called Don Pedro; Ice cream with toasted almonds and whisky. Our dinner conversations were lovely: just the right group of folks gathered to guarantee an interesting conversation.

The night continued after dinner, in the lounge, where Tom, one of the staff members, was sharing some of his life's stories with our group. He's written a book, which he was selling and signing. I was reminded of my little book signing sessions up in Michigan this summer. I find it an interesting experience when people are interested in having me sign their book. A spotlight I'm not 100% comfortable with, yet one that brings a warm feeling of satisfaction, knowing that I've created something other people are willing to pay for.

INSIDE THE ANTARCTIC CIRCLE
SUNDAY, FEBRUARY 7, 2010

Last night was a late night for me, but that didn't keep me in bed for the sunrise this morning. I hadn't gotten back to my room until about 1am. Fabulous and engaging post dinner conversation kept us in the lounge well past O'dark–thirty. Well, actually, I suppose last night was only O'dusk–thirty. At midnight we'd seen the last of the sunset slip by, and by 12:30 a.m. it was dark. By 1:36 I was on the bridge looking at the lightening sky. Discovering that sunrise wasn't officially until 4:39(ish) this morning, I head back down to my cabin to get at least a little snooze before donning my Antarctic gear for an early morning photo session with our first scenic sunrise. Keeping my iPhone under my pillow, so as to not wake my roommate, the tower bells "ding–dong" in my ear at 4:30. I sit up, shake off my lovely dream, catch a glimpse of intense orange and blue in the sky and rocket out of bed to shimmy into my pants, grab a memory card, shoes, hat, gloves and parka. No more outside shooting for me without gloves. I think I've learned my lesson.

Slipping on my coat, zipping it up and pulling my hat on as I stumble out of the side chart room door, lifting my legs to clear the foot and a half water barrier, I stumble out on deck with an "oof," startling two of my fellow shipmates who were serenely taking in the sunrise. "Good morning." I sleepily greet them. "Beautiful!" I exclaim and start to take photos, checking my camera settings for the correct speed, color balance and ISO. Wow! Stunning. Back through the door now; inside and up the stairs to the bridge where I greet the new watch and slip out the bridge's side door for additional shots. Only a few souls are up this early today; most of them must be sleeping away last night's complimentary Guinness, heads buried deep within their pillows.

Being here, at the southern end of the globe, beyond the end of the world, has been a journey, not just in terms of miles or distance traveled; it has been a journey of the mind and senses. When the whole world is peeled away from you like shed skin, you're left with your naked self, the core of who you are. That can take a little getting used to if you've never experienced yourself without these layers. Most of us become so comfortable in the world that we forget that it's not actually "us." All the media hype, television shows, competition on the roads and at work – those are all just society and "wrappings."

What I find on a ship is that your immediate surroundings become your world. You're isolated from all that you've been told is "you." All your belongings, chores, and obligations drop away temporarily, and you can, in essence, step out of your role – all the expectations people have of you, who they think you are or should be to them – and experience your wants and passions. Dropping the bands that hold you down, hold you to a place, you're free to explore your dreams and what's next in life.

No media intrusion, no television adds, no access to Internet or email. All the things we come to use and rely on in our everyday lives are suddenly not available. At first it's a break. It's nice. And throughout the entire journey I enjoyed not knowing what was going on in the world. I like the media blackout. It's one of the things I look forward to during my trips. But once in a while I found myself wanting to look up some information and had no way to do it. How frustrating. I had to find the information another way – perhaps by talking to people? Unheard of! So I started to ask people if they knew the answer and eventually I would find out. This time I was looking for the amount of memory available on a DVD, something I didn't know off the top of my head.

But back to the present. What an amazing morning; two firsts for me. One, I'm inside of the Antarctic Circle. We are at 67.31"S and 67.52"W. Two, I saw an Emperor Penguin!! One lonely guy on a little iceberg. The captain announced the sighting and it was like someone had just announced, "abandon ship!" Doors were flying open and slamming shut, sounds of feet on the stairs stomping upstairs, people in motion running and donning parkas, trying to balance hat, gloves and a camera. People barely awake following their instinct to "get the shot!" To "see the Emperor!"

Then a stillness falls over the ship as we barely motor forward. Ever so slowly. The ship appears to be sneaking up on this penguin, because the penguin, by virtue of where it is standing, is behind an ice ridge taller than it. So as we approach, this ridge hides us from view. I can feel the excitement in the air. Literally 140 passengers poise, ready, almost holding their breath. And then, as we inch closer, finally a head can be seen, then the chest, and then the whole penguin. He (or she) just watches us approach and hardly moves. Little turns of the head, an extension of the neck, and then, as we circumnavigate the little berg, it starts to walk and slips on the ice, falling down. This penguin species is much larger than the Adelie, Chinstrap and Gentoo — at least two to three times the height. So when it falls, it's a big fall - one large penguin tipping over.

For the morning's activity I jump ship and trade group activities, choosing to go ashore rather than stay with my group that is going on a zodiac cruise. I don't know if you can call it karma, but you can certainly call it the wrong call. Although I very much enjoyed my time ashore I apparently missed the best humpback whale sighting many of the old salts on board had ever seen. It circled and played around all the zodiacs for about 45 minutes. It sounds fantastic. I'll be going on the afternoon zodiac tour just to see if the humpback is still in the area. If he was curious this morning, maybe he'll be curious this afternoon (turns out he wasn't).

HEADED BACK NORTH
MONDAY, FEBRUARY 8, 2010

I think the sign, on the back of the captain's chair on the bridge, sums it all up. "I Brake For Whales." And he does too! Not only will he brake for whales, but he'll break for seals and penguins. He brings the ship in slowly, sneaking up on the wildlife so that we don't scare them off. Once in position we just hang there for several minutes, watching and observing, and of course, taking photographs. Then, just when you think it can't get any better, the Captain takes the ship in a slow arc around whatever it is we're viewing, giving all angles a chance to be seen and accommodating passengers on all sides of the ship.

Ohh, the mountains down here are absolutely spectacular. I never tire of looking at them. The warm colors in the early morning (I'm talking 5:00–6:00 a.m.), the clouds that wrap themselves around the peaks, the glaciers and varying blue colors hidden within the nooks and crannies. The subtle shading on snow fields that look like marshmallow fluff. And the jagged black basalt peaks and vertical walls. Then, to throw the entire landscape into perspective, an iceberg will drift across your field of vision as the ship continues on her way.

The icebergs are another wonder all together. Floating, their behemoth bulk rises up out of the ocean. Sheer walls eroded at the waterline by repetitive wave action, sometimes tilted on their axis from erosion happening under the water. Occasionally we'll see one roll over, sending out a small wave surge. Ones that have flipped have a wonderful pockmarked appearance, something akin to a golf ball.

Our zodiac cruise today was all about the icebergs. Big ones, little ones, ones with "pools," ones with clear ice blue crevasses, smooth or textured. A few had little separate bits standing almost alone, a little ways away from the main berg. Little spires, connected somewhere under water.

Where the ice spreads out under the water, the water's color intensify from deep blue to the Caribbean aqua. This color combined with the blue–white of the iceberg, and deep blue of surrounding water with the blue sky and cloud patterns can make for spectacular and dramatic photographs.

Today was our last chance ashore and in the zodiacs. We went ashore at Useful Island. It had a slightly different geology than the other islands we've been on. This one had large smooth rounded slabs of rock. Many had cracks, and most were slippery and guano covered. I successfully avoided injury when I slipped, not more than 10 paces from the tender. My boot must have been wet on the bottom, and that combination with the smooth surface caused me to slip. It happened in slow motion and I was able to go down gracefully – hand, knee, hand, and knee. I didn't bruise anything or damage any equipment. Yeah me!

Useful Island has many colonies of nesting Cormorants (Shags), Gentoo and Chinstrap penguins, and fur seals. The fur seals were particularly frisky today. They're territorial and wickedly fast on the ground. And they bite, kind of like a dog bite, apparently. I'm content to give them a wide berth and not find out the validity of that claim. Walking around, it is hard to keep all the animals in sight. You think you know where everything is and all of a sudden you hear a deep bellow and see, out of the corner of your eye, a large dark mass quickly moving your way. Time to back off.

Yesterday the Skuas were spirited. They had nests on the island and we could see their chicks, on a slight rise, in the rocky field we were crossing to get to the far side of the beach area. Our guides had us turn around to avoid being dive–bombed. I've heard that an agitated Skua will attack your head and can fly off with your hat.

I hiked up the hill on Useful Island and made it about ¾ of the way. I kept looking up thinking that the top must be close, but the further I went the more there was to climb. I made it as far as the first mixed Gentoo–Chinstrap colony, and was happy to sit there enjoying their antics. Adults were displaying what is called "ecstatic behavior," which involves pointing their beaks to the sky, fully extending their neck, flapping their flippers back and forth, and emitting a loud sound; an undulating gravelly squawk.

I took some video of this behavior. Over and over again it made me laugh. What an amazing time. Beautiful, majestic views of the surrounding snow covered mountains, penguins running around, chicks losing their balance and falling on the rocks, then trying to figure out how to right themselves.

I'd found a flat rock to sit on. Hiking up the rocky hill had made me warm and a little rest would cool me off. Stripping off my camera gear, parka, hat and gloves, I sat down to relax and take in the view. Amazing. Snow covered mountains peak out from a thick frosting of glacier ice. There are peaks everywhere. The further south we travel, the snowier the mountains become, it's as if a giant kid came along and dumped an entire bag of powdered sugar onto the mountains.

OCEAN MOTION
TUESDAY, FEBRUARY 9, 2010

The Drake Passage was not as much a lake this time. It wasn't crazy either. What we had the most of, was wind: wind and chop. Because of the wind, although the swells were fairly small, the boat had a lot of roll, up and down, which stresses the hull. Walls creak. The metal hull bangs as the waves impact from the starboard side, reshaping the outside of the ship with temporary dents. Packing becomes a floor activity. There's no use packing on the bed, things just slide off, and I lose my balance, falling onto Bev's bed. Going to the bathroom becomes an adventure. I start off in one direction, only to be forced off balance and end up facing the wrong way. Maybe crawling would be easier.

'ROUND CAPE HORN
WEDNESDAY, FEBRUARY 10, 2010

How exciting to see the Horn! It's been one of my dreams for so long. I stand out on the upper deck with my eyes closed, enjoying the feel of the boat under my feet, rising and falling with the waves. Rocking from side to side, keeping my balance by hanging onto the railing, sea–spray in my face. Visualizing the globe and where I am on it brings a smile to my face. Reaching back, I think of all the times I've talked with friends saying that I've wanted to sail around the Horn. Of course, in my dreams, it's always been a square–rigged schooner, but hey, any ship in a storm!

Everyone is busy around the ship, walking with purpose. Picking up passports from reception, packing, finding lost items, and getting email addresses from new friends. Remembering things they need to do, washing penguin guano off boots, weeding out extraneous items they don't feel like taking home. You should see the mudroom – the designated place to take your cast–offs – it's already full of boots, jackets, instant hand warmers and fleeces.

It seems I have developed a new fashion statement with my jeans. Cuff–height salt stains. They're crispy and white, very haute couture, fashionable in the sailing circles. I believe they're going to get washed on Easter Island.

We just had our last day's recap. All the crew got dressed up in suit jackets and ties. They clean up so nicely! I almost didn't recognize a few of them. Mike, the photographer looked dapper in a dark blue suit and white shirt, the dive master in a grey pinstripe suit with black and white wingtip shoes. Steve had on a penguin tie. The captain was stunning in his dark blue uniform with his gold stripes adorning his shoulders.

An air of melancholy seeped into the room as the crew addressed us one by one. It has been an amazing journey; one that I don't want to end. There's a warm feeling that encompasses me here on this ship, this ship that has become my home, my little floating home on the cold, cold ocean; my home that allows me to venture far south, to see these things that defy description. To have experiences that will be impossible to convey to anyone who has not experienced Antarctica. Those who have been here will understand, at least those who have been able to get out on land.

One of the staff who spoke read to us a "journal" that had supposedly been passed on to him from another ship's crew, which had been left behind by a passenger, apparently an older, married woman. Day 1. Got on board the ship. Had an invitation to dinner from the captain to sit at his table. What a nice man. Day 2. Had another invitation to have dinner with the captain, in his private room. He's quite dashing. Day 3. Another invitation from the captain. After dinner the captain asked if I would spend the night. I said, "No,

I am a married lady and I cannot be unfaithful to my husband. Day 4. The captain asked me to spend the night again. Again I said no. He replied that if I didn't sleep with him he was going to have to sink the ship. Day 5. Today I saved 1, 671 passengers. Twice (Well it went along those lines). Everyone roared. The next few days, jokes were flying around the ship regarding if anyone had saved any passengers recently.

As the captain spoke and mentioned that we have to "get the boot" tomorrow, I looked around the room at these people who had become my friends -- most of whom I'll never see again. Some I will. Some will be a mystery — I may see them again. A little tear gathered in my eye and I wiped it away with my finger. Then more gathered and I had to employ the use of my scarf to keep up with the flow. Geeesh, I tell you, I'm sentimental to the end.

LAURA VAE GATZ

KICKED OFF THE SHIP
FEBRUARY 11, 2010

The last sunset before our feet hit solid ground in Argentina was beautiful, with rays radiating out from dramatic clouds, silver and gold light. Dark clouds backed by blinding white light. The sparkling Beagle Channel.

So, I'm running around the ship after dinner, and I run into the shop girl who asks if I'm going into town. "No," I say. "Oh, why not? She asks. "Is there something to do?" I query. "Yes, there's a little Irish Pub and we're all going to be there. You should come." So, I do. Bev has already gone to bed, so I let her sleep. On my way off the ship I run into Rod, one of the old salts on board, on his way back. He'd been to town to buy gifts and liquor. It's all tax and customs free here. He says he'll walk with me if he can get his purchases stowed first. I say sure and wait for him. I would never have found the bar if he hadn't led me there. It's warm, comfortable, and playing 80's music. After hanging out for a while, listening to the music, talking to crew and passengers, I head out and walk up and down the streets. It's after 10 p.m. and the streets are full of families. People eat late here. Kids are still up and the restaurants are a–buzz. The smell of roasting meat makes my mouth water.

But I don't want to leave. One of the crew said jokingly, "there are lots of good hiding places on the ship, but don't tell anyone I told you so." Apparently the lifeboats are good spots – they have food and water provisions!

One last wakeup call this morning with Bud sneaking into our rooms on the sound system. This morning at 6:15 he was a little more loud and lively than he normally is. We're used to hearing a gentle "good morning," like a smooth cup of joe. This morning was a cappuccino, and I was up, sitting on the edge of my bed. 15 minutes to get dressed and have our luggage in the hallway.

One last breakfast, one last trip to the room. Check it one more time. Has anything been left behind? Nope. Attach my butt pack and camera pouch, hoist the backpack onto my shoulders and head out. The crew is outside by the buses ready to say one final farewell. Hugs and handshakes all around. Thank-yous and wishes for future voyages together. Smiles and a bit of sadness ring the normally sparkling eyes. We're loath to leave; the crew knows they have another group in only a handful of hours. Time to "rip off the Band–Aid." This is a term my sister, Lisa, and I came up with during our Windjammer sailings. At the end of the week we never were ready to leave, but eventually we had to. We called leaving the ship "ripping off the Band-Aid," because it hurt, but when you decided to do it, doing it quickly was the best tactic. Time to move on to the next part of my trip. Bye bye! Thanks for the memories!

Our first bus ride was short, just down the street and up the hill to the Maritime Museum of Ushuaia. I went in to get a stamp for my passport and then went out to wander on my own. I enjoyed being out on my own in the fresh air. It's nice to be able to be alone and not have to stay with the group or within sight of a guide. I wandered down to the shore for some photographs, remembering that some weather had been blowing in from down the channel, creating a nice gradation of grays on the receding hills. The rain started back up. I covered my camera case and put my raincoat on over my photography vest.

I hung out at the railing along the shore, taking in the scene, appreciating where I was, and the down time, and then wandered slowly down the walk, as if pulled back to the ship by a magnetic force. I didn't get very close but did walk towards it. I tend to fall in love with ships. After a week they're my friends, taking me new places, revealing their secrets and strengths. Learning their inner passageways, I get to know them like a new home. Favorite hangout spots develop. The corner in the lounge, the little wind shielded balcony just off the bridge, the mudroom during preparation for excursions.

As we loaded onto buses for the last time and sped back down the gravel Pan American highway, I am amazed at the lush green of the grass. Until we returned to Ushuaia I'd not realized the lack of green in the Antarctic. In fact, the color palette is fairly limited there – white, blue and grey, and some black. Sunsets and sunrises are another story if there's a hole in the clouds. The lush green of the grass on the side of the roads and in the forests here is a sight for my green–starved senses. It looks so incredibly lush and fertile; like an oasis.

One of the nice things about traveling with an outfit like Lindblad is that they take care of you. From the ship to Santiago I won't see my luggage. It's so nice to not have to lug it around. My photo backpack and waist packs are enough weight to carry.

At the airport, we see the incoming group. They're going on a three–week trip to South Georgia Islands and the Falkland Islands. They look excited, much as we must have two weeks ago. This time the roles are reversed – same piece of glass, except this time we are the ones just coming back from an adventure, and theirs is yet to happen.

At our final daily recap the captain mentioned that we would be seeing this new group, just like we saw the returning group as we arrived. He asked us to please not do "this." Meaning don't take your hands and make large waves with them, indicating a rough crossing. So, of course, that's exactly what we did. We thought we were so funny. One of our guys even held up a packet of seasick medication. He thought he was pretty funny too. I think we were funny. We were all just yucking it up and laughing.

They're a bright group. It's very windy today, and they shot back with hand signals indicating that we were in for a rough flight back to Santiago. Good for them.

One lady wanted to know about the penguins. It took me a long time to figure out what she was asking. The thick glass wall doesn't allow for any sound to come across. So all communication is done with pantomimes. Anyway, it was an entertaining 15–20 minutes. Something to keep us busy until we could board the plane.

I can't wait to see what the rest of the trip brings. I think this next week is going to be interesting. It's less planned than the last two weeks. Well, actually, our Antarctic itinerary wasn't really planned until we knew what the weather was going to be. The National Geographic Explorer had to submit an itinerary last June. When the guys got here they took a look at it and said "that's crap" and decided that they'd determine their own itinerary depending on the winds and weather. And it turned out beautifully. Takes me back to Chris's phrase "Everything will appear as it must." Everything will happen as God ordains. Mom will join me in New Zealand, inshalla (God willing). Because we all know if God's not willing, it's just not going to happen.

When I get to Easter Island (also known as Rapa Nui), I think I'll take a few days to get oriented around the island — figure out how to get around and figure out which places I want to plan to be at for sunrise and sunset. Line up a horse back ride or two, see if Edmundo is going to be available, and then let the winds and Moai take me where they will. It will be a good time for reflection, for drawing parallels between Antarctica and Rapa Nui, two of the most remote places on the planet. Antarctica as a whole is the most remote, but Rapa Nui is the farthest from any land.

I'll be on my own again; that always takes a little adjustment. Not a long time, but I do tend to get comfortable wherever I am. The people I'm with become my temporary traveling family. It's sad to see them go. Most of them I won't see again, just a special few. I'll have to fend for myself, find meals, and remember to eat. That last one shouldn't be hard. I'll even be able to stock up on a little food for the week and carry some with me. That will be a nice change of pace. Now, if only I can get a good Internet connection and upload this blog! That would be fantastic.

LAURA VAE GATZ

II.

EASTER ISLAND

GOIN' TO RAPA NUI
FRIDAY, FEBRUARY 12, 2010

Sitting on the "right" side of the plane yesterday going from Ushuaia to Santiago was a wonderful experience. Bev and I headed toward the back of the plane, past the wing, so that it wouldn't be in my shots. I ended up sitting in row 19 on this particular 767. I would sit a few more rows back if I could do it over again, but the view from there was still great. We had patches of clouds, but it was mostly clear with nice dramatic clouds.

Now, I don't know for sure but I think I see the "famous" pointy Patagonian mountains from the plane, the ones I see in photographs. It is so exciting to see them that I poke my friend in the seat in front of me and say "Look, the famous pointy mountains." Yes, I'm sure they have a name but I just don't know what it is.

Thrilling to see them. They're right on the edge of a large lake.

There are a lot of lakes in Patagonia. So much fun to see them from the air. Some are definitely from glacier melt water, and others from rainfall or at least not incoming streams. Their colors are different. The glacial ones are milky blue and the others are a deep aqua blue. So many glaciers. So easy to see their gouging results on the mountains. So much is more readily apparent from the sky.

Talk about perspective. That's the way it is with life. If you can get a different perspective so much becomes clear. If you're on the ground looking at a range of mountains, it may not be easy to see the effect glaciers have had on them. Get up in the sky and the troughs pop out. The same, I think, is true for our own lives. Stay in the same old comfortable rut, the same routine, and it's hard to see your life, where you're going or even what your goals are. Get out of the house, out of the routine, and up in the sky, and some things start to take on a distinct shape. Passions become apparent, goals clearer. Of course leaving the daily obligations behind doesn't hurt.

All that clutter that occupies our mind interferes with our "journey." Of course it's all necessary. We have to pay bills, clean the house, take care of the pets, and oh yeah, go to work, but nonetheless it doesn't allow us time to see our dreams.

It's not that this kind of travel isn't work. It is. It's just work I thoroughly enjoy and don't mind doing until I can barely keep my eyes open. It's a passion. And that makes all the difference. Although I did lighten up on myself towards the end of the Antarctic trip (and got a little distracted from writing) I only allowed myself two naps — one for fifteen minutes and one for an hour. When I wasn't on shore, on deck, or in a zodiac, I was writing, downloading, editing photos, charging batteries or cleaning equipment; very little time for sleep, especially when the skies don't get dark until midnight and sunrise is at 4:40 a.m!

These weeks are such a gift. The pie in the sky dream had been to take a year off; however 8 weeks is almost three times longer than I've ever traveled continuously. It's a goodly time to be gone, to shed my everyday skin for my travel skin, travel mind and travel eye, and short enough that my cats won't completely commit mutiny when I return. Although I suspect there will still be some hard feelings there. Cats are oh so good at letting you know they're miffed at you. Like a fellow traveler said — she only saw the cat's behinds for two months after they brought a new dog into the house.

I find it so hard to believe that the first leg of my journey is over; three more legs to go, each so different. From the land of snow, icebergs, blue hues, penguins and those amazing giants of the deep; to Easter Island's land of mystery, towering stone carvings and isolation to New Zealand with its sheep, mountains, rivers and grand vistas; to Australia's Great Barrier Reef and on to Africa with its contrasts between the large cities and the bush, full of wild animals just waiting to be discovered. I am very much looking forward to having time to discover parallels and differences between each place.

The clouds over the ocean were beautiful on the way to Easter Island. We flew through patches of clouds on the way here – sometimes little round patches that remind me of pancake ice, then towards the end, big fluffy clouds right at eye level. Then we broke through the clouds and Rapa Nui lay below. Green and lush, contrasting nicely with the blue blue blue of the sky. I looked for the famous large stone statues, called moai, trying to pick them out of the landscape below. I didn't see any.

The Easter Island airport is nice and small. I like small airports, they're easy and quick to navigate, and usually fairly relaxed about security and customs. This airport doesn't have jet ways; everyone walks outside, across the tarmac to climb up roll–up stairs, onto the planes. There is one small room to collect baggage. There's no carousel, only a 15–foot metal shelf onto which the luggage is placed. There's not enough room for all the luggage at once, so in order to keep the system flowing, passengers have to watch for their bag and take it as soon as it's available.

The arrival "hall" doubles as the area where the ticket counters are. Most folks waiting for arrivals are outside. I walk slowly, looking for a sign with either my name on it or with "Te'Ora" on it. I don't see one. I look around. There's nowhere else to go. As I lean on a pillar, one local woman sees I look lost and asks where I'm staying. After I say Te'Ora, she says that Sharon is running a little late and she'll be there in a few minutes. I smile, and say thank you. What a great, friendly, little community! Sharon pulls up a few minutes later, with lovely fresh flower leis in her hand. She greets me and puts one over my head. It smells great, and the petals feel cool and smooth against my warm, damp skin. We're waiting for one other couple and then we'll be on our way. A couple walks up. Sam and Mark. Sam's the girl. They're from Britain and both quit their jobs to travel around the world for 9 months. They have a few months left, I believe, and just arrived from spending a few months in South America.

We walk over to Sharon's vehicle and drive slowly through town. Town consists of one main street, with a few side streets, and an area by the water. About 3300 people live in town, Hanga Roa, and it's the only town on the island. 90% of the people on the island live in town. Sharon points out key intersections to aide us in way-finding throughout the week, restaurants she recommends and ones she doesn't. She's created a great hand drawn map that she gives each of us a copy of. On it are the good restaurants, post office, Te'Ora, the car rental and Internet café, the mini–marts and market, craft market and church. It's one of the most helpful maps I've seen from a B&B. I can tell she's put a lot of thought into it. The tour through the town is very helpful too. Although it's a lot of information in a short time, during that time in which you always feel slightly discombobulated and out of sorts, having just flown in from "another world," it's well worth it. It's really hot though. I have sweat threatening to drip into my eyes and it's making a major river channel down the center of my back. I believe we all sigh collectively when the car starts moving again heading for our next point of interest. It must be just about one mile from the airport to Te'Ora. The main roads are paved with uniform sized bricks, and the side roads are unpaved.

Te'Ora is on the southwest side of the island, just across the road from the ocean. It gets lovely breezes that keep both the patio and rooms cool. There are three rooms for rent, two on the ground floor and one above the room where Sharon lives. Two of the three rooms have a small kitchenette for cooking meals, and a refrigerator. The smallest room shares a communal kitchen with Sharon, and we're all invited to use it as well. Just outside my door is a patio with a table large enough for six, kept shady by a large umbrella. Around the entire building is a wooden fence, which makes the area feel private and closed off from the road. As you enter the gate from the road, tropical plants line the walk on either side of stepping–stones that lead past a miniature moai that stands 9 feet tall. Usually Michigan is there to meet you. Michigan is Sharon's dog. He's very friendly and will go for walks around the island with you as long as you don't plan to walk for too long. He has free range of the island and Sharon says he takes care of himself and not to worry if he wanders off.

My room is very comfortable. Two of the walls are made from local volcanic rock, giving the room a great rustic texture. A large window looks out onto the patio and is my main source for a breeze through the room. There are power plugs in convenient locations. My bathroom is just around the corner from the kitchen and has a small window to the back of the building. The shower is also a tub. In the front room are two sliding glass doors, one faces the patio and the other the communal kitchen. When I'm home I have them both open to invite the breeze in. There's also a round table to eat at, and two comfy wicker chairs with cushions. This will be a great place to call home for a week.

LAURA VAE GATZ

EASTER ISLAND AKA RAPA NUI ISLA DE PASCUA
(AKA EASTER ISLAND, AKA RAPA NUI, AKA TE PITO TE HENUA OR BELLY BUTTON OF THE WORLD)

SATURDAY, FEBRUARY 13, 2010

My alarm went off just as it should at 7:30 a.m. this morning. I looked outside. Pitch black. This can't be 7:30, it just can't. I think to myself "Let's see, we're pretty far south of the equator and they have twelve hours of daylight. It's summer down here so we should get more daylight; it should be light already. Hmmmm." Then I decide to look at my computer time, which I know is correct because I set it last night. Yes, that's it – my phone time is off by two hours because it hasn't gotten a signal since I've been here. So now I have two more hours I can sleep. Except I can't sleep, it's too loud outside.

The neighbors just up the hill are having a party. Their property backs up to Te'Ora, the Bed & Breakfast where I'm staying. When I walked past their place on the way back from the market today there was already a big group of people there. And the music has been playing all day. But it didn't dawn on me that the music was from their place; I just thought that the owner here, Sharon, had a radio on. At least they like 80's music and not something like acid rock!

I was so tired last night that instead of getting completely ready for today and making sure my day–pack was all ready, I just laid down on the bed, head by the open window, breeze blowing in, and snoozed, music blaring in the background. My brain kept trying to get my body up. "You have to make a lunch, get your hat out, make sure you have batteries and memory cards packed. Get up!" My body just lay there. All of a sudden I looked outside and it was pitch dark. New moon.

This morning when I couldn't get back to sleep, I stepped outside to look up at the stars. All during this trip I've been thinking about the stars but haven't seen any. Oh my! It's like a black velvet carpet studded with diamonds. I've never seen so many stars all crowded together vying for room to shine. In the courtyard/patio area outside of my "casita" there's only a small space open to see the sky and I'm tempted to go out for an early morning wander, just across the road to the beach. Wow. They're pretty amazing. I love it when the Milky Way is so clear that it kind of looks the way it does in the books – with the darker streak in the middle of all milky star swaths on either side. It makes me feel so small. One night I'm going to drive out to a darker part of the island and look at these Southern Hemisphere stars. I'll take my camera and see if I can shoot some star trails.

This is my first morning on Rapa Nui. The party behind the house kept waking me up but I got the sleep I needed. I found out today that it was a celebration for a baptism – much more enthusiasm than we tend to have in the states. I'm not sure I can see my

Lutheran family up partying with music until 6 a.m. In fact, I know I can't! Since I slept away yesterday evening I got organized for my day–long tour this morning: downloaded and backed up photos, reformatted cards, caught up on my blog, email, etc. (Te'Ora has wi–fi – what a lovely thing!) Packed for the day. Packed camera, extra lens, battery, memory, flashlight (well, I would have brought it if the batteries hadn't corroded), raincoat, sandwich, water, and I put on sun tan lotion.

What a strange unexpected day. My guide Tuhee is beautiful and very knowledgeable about the island and its long and interesting history. We start off on the south west coast, where we see Ana Kakenga, the Cave of Two Windows which is a lava tube that goes underground, heading towards the ocean, and opens up in two places, just at the point of a cliff above the sea, like two windows overlooking the ocean. The opening is small at first and the ceiling is low but as you progress towards the ocean the room opens up.

The highlights of the day are the fifteen moai of Ahu Tongariki, lunch, and a visit to her auntie's house. The fifteen moai are cool because they're all in a row; only one has a top–knot and the sun is at a good position to emphasize the contours of the sculptures, particularly the deep eye sockets. And there are petroglyphs on large, flat rocks, of tuna being caught and of three bird–men and a turtle.

For lunch we stop at one of the sandy beaches; Tuhee invites me up the hill to eat with her. I'm not exactly sure what that means, but I follow. It is hot and I am tired, but follow anyway. Towards the top of the hill we veer off to the left onto a short narrow path, barely visible in the weeds. After about thirty feet we come to a small gate that is hanging open on its hinges. It leads into a small copse of trees, in the middle of which is a giant thick rope net strung up from tree to tree to tree, in a rough circle, to create a low canopy, kind of like a mix between a hammock on steroids and a trapeze artist's net. In the middle of it is a single mattress with sheets and blanket. Cool. This is like the ultimate long–term camping site. There's a fire made in some built up rocks so that the fire is about a meter off the ground. On the fire is a fish – a Barracuda, hot and ready to eat. Tuhee says that it's traditional to eat from the fire. She takes a large machete and chops off the head and it and part of the fish goes on a plate. And that's for "Momma." Another mystery. The rest she flips over so I can pick meat off the bones. The small bones go into the fire. This is the best fish I've ever tasted. So fresh; it was swimming this morning; just cleaned and tossed on the grill with a little salt. Fantastic. She hands me eggs from inside the fish. They don't look like fish eggs. They're in a shape of a smooth long flat tube the consistency of polenta but with even less texture. It doesn't taste bad. She gives me another. Then she hands me half the skin and asks if I've ever eaten fish skin before. I say no and try it. It's good. Good fats she says. It's crispy and reminds me of eating the crispy fat on the side of a pork chop. She says I'm adventurous for trying new things; that many of the people she takes on tours would just turn their head and say "yuck."

I ask if I can take a few photos, and I do, and then we take off back down the hill. I buy some fresh pineapple juice and we relax at a picnic table under a roof, and "Momma" gets her fish. I'm still not sure who Momma is, but she seems to run the beachside cafe. Perhaps she's my guide's grandmother.

After a few other stops along the way we pull up at her Auntie's house. There are several women, a few men, some babies, a couple of dogs, chickens and horses all roaming free. Yes, the men were roaming free as well. The house has a large covered porch in the front with side windows, open to let the breeze through. The walls are lined with cow or horse jawbones; jawbones hang on jawbones to form little abstract sculptures. The teeth look like carvings. A few carved moai sit in the corner of the room, leaning up against wooden beams. This porch looks like the main hang out spot for everyone. It's filled with a large wooden table and chairs which all balance on stepping–stones set in the dirt floor.

When we arrive, the men are picking at the vertebrae of some large animal looking for the last tasty scraps of meat. It was a cow I think. I'm offered some meat and some slightly yellow colored liquid. I declined the meat on grounds I was still full from lunch, but the liquid I accepted. It was pineapple juice with sugar – apparently my drink of the day. It's warm but good. Later I have a glass of rainwater.

Tuhee had mentioned earlier in the day that that her aunt makes art; rubbings of a sort, but I cannot picture how they are made. The petroglyph carvings found on rocks around the Island are not like the slabs in Edinburgh that you can hold paper up to in order to make a rubbing. These rocks are much more porous, and the carvings, aged and weathered. Auntie's "rubbings" are beautiful and must take a lot of time and effort to make. The Aunt explains their history and meanings, with Tuhee translating. They're too expensive for me ($200 for the 3x4 foot one) but they're beautiful and wonderful historical art pieces. She translates some of the things her aunt says but not all. One of the male relatives I can tell is either a little bit of a prankster, or is just being a guy, and he was saying things Tuhee wouldn't translate, but there were lots of smiles flying around me. I really must learn Spanish. Of course it's possible they were speaking Rapa Nui. I heard a little on the radio and I thought it sounded a little like Navajo. Perhaps it was the cadence of the speech.

Music with a good beat and a deep base starts to play somewhere from inside the house. The sound of the leaves rustling in the coastal wind is in the foreground. Dogs chase chickens around the yard. The men are outside now, sitting on the far side of the truck doing guy things. Most of the women are inside talking and smoking. Four or five horses and a colt graze nearby. On the island both cows and horses are all free range. And I suppose the chickens are too. They lay their eggs in the long grass, but Tuhee says that no one collects them.

Here in Rapa Nui is another example of non–native species being introduced to the detriment of native animals – in this case, hawks, to keep down the mice. However the hawks flourished and took over the territory of smaller native birds. So now the smaller birds have moved into the interior of the island and are not seen around the coast much. While out driving today I saw what must have been twenty or more hawks take off from someone's field. They are really abundant.

One of the places we visited is a magnetic rock thought to re-charge the power of the priests in ancient times, called Te Pito o TeHenua, meaning "the navel of the world." The rocks contain iron and have differing magnetic polarities. It is thought that these rocks were brought with the initial inhabitants from Hiva – the name for their ancestral home. Apparently this was in the Marquesas. Modern technology has shown that the Rapanui's (native islanders') genes are most like the people from the Marquesas. In that case, Thor Heyerdahl's theory of these people coming from South America would be incorrect.

All the moai standing around the island that have been "re-stored." There are two theories about how they were knocked down. One is that they all fell down during an earthquake or tsunami. The other is that they all had been knocked down during the civil war between the clans. The story goes, as told to me by Tuhee, that the Rapa Nui culture had peaked, the moai had gotten very large and the population was outstripping their own resources. This caused the Moai to stop believing in the statues that were supposed to look after them and bring prosperity. So each clan knocked down their own statues and many broke at the neck in the process. The eyes, thought to be important, were broken and thrown into the sea. At least one eye has been found and is in the museum here. It cannot be restored to any moai because there would be contention as to which tribe would get the power.

Easter Islanders have not had an easy time of it. They have a long sad history, which involves a lot of betrayal and exploitation.

In the 1800's whalers would stop at the island looking for fresh food and women. They left behind the special present of venereal disease and tuberculosis. In 1808, an American ship, the Nancy, kidnapped over 20 people from the island intending to make them slaves in the Juan Fernandez Islands. When the captain allowed the captives to come out of the hold, they jumped off the ship and started swimming away. The ship's efforts to recapture them failed and the Nancy sailed away, leaving the islanders to drown. This incident, of course, had its effect on how islanders treated arriving ships. Now suspicious of visitors, the islanders would often greet ships with hostility.

In the 1860's the Peruvian slave raids began. Peru was expriencing a shortage of labor and apparently saw the Pacific as a huge source of free labor. In December of 1862, over one-thousand Easter Islanders were captured and taken back to Peru to work in the guano–mines, where they were forced to work as slaves, overworked and poorly treated. Most died within one to two years of capture. Eventually the Bishop of Tahiti embarrassed Peru into letting the remaining Easter Islanders return home. Although seemingly a blessing, this turned out to be a curse. Most Islanders died on the way home as a result of a smallpox outbreak. The remaining fifteen arrived home only to spread the disease, which almost wiped out the remaining dwindling population.

In 1888 Chile annexed Easter Island. All the Islanders were confined to the one town, and Chile leased the rest of the Island to the British government who brought in sheep to raise until 1953. The sheep wandered the island and trod on the ahu (the platforms on which the moai stand) moving the rocks and disturbing the structures, causing further damage in addition to the eroding powers of wind, salt, and time.

During this time the islanders were not allowed to leave the settlement of Hanga Roa. Until that time the Rapa Nui had eaten a diet of fish with a high fat content, once a day, with many calories – about 8000 a day. Their very active lives called for a lot of calories.

Once confined and unable to leave the village to fish, they had to stop eating their normal diet, and so they became thin and sickly.

The British also thought they should wear clothes; their traditional outfit was simply a g–string type covering. The Rapa Nui had a tradition of covering their bodies with fat so when they were in the water their skin was protected. Clothes would have gotten wet.

The Chilean Navy managed the island until 1966. At that time Easter Islanders were granted Chilean citizenship.

Now cows and wild horses wander the countryside doing the same thing that the sheep did. They're mostly free range. The horses cause as much damage as the sheep did. Estimates are that there is about one horse for every person on this island. And the same goes for cars. My B&B owner, Sheila, said when she got her car seven or so years ago she was a novelty. On the same drive she did with us from the airport to the B&B she would have seen 4 cars. We must have seen 200 cars on the way to Te'Ora, sometimes they literally choke the roads. I don't think this town is large enough for the problem to be as bad as it is on some of the Caribbean islands I've seen, where it takes 20 minutes to drive down the main thoroughfare that is a football field in length, because half the cars are stopped to talk with friends.

Nowadays the major modes of transportation, besides walking, are cars, scooters, motorcycles, and horses. Although horses aren't the majority mode of transportation, I see quite a lot of people riding horses. It's not uncommon to be walking down the street and hear hoof beats coming up behind me. As I've driven around the island I've seen many guys on horseback on the side of the road. Sharon says it's mostly young men who think it looks cool to ride horses around bareback!

I've caught the end of the Tapati Rapa Nui Festival that celebrates the long days of summer. There is a stage painted by an artist that remains up for the two–week festival. This year's backdrop was spectacular – a blue and white ocean with a huge sea kayak and serpents adorning the front of the boat, which points into the full moon. On the other wall are moai with their backsides facing forward, and ahu and broken moai. Tonight was the crowning of the festival queen and the passing on of the crown from the old to the new queen. The dancing was inspired, and I was reminded of Polynesian dancing, lots of hip action and hand movements. The drums reverberated in my chest sending chills up and down my arms. The fireworks started and the night became a mixture of surreal and real. I could suddenly feel where I was; this isolated island in the middle of the Pacific, in the southern hemisphere, farther away from any other land mass than anywhere in the world. It was as if I could almost float up to the stratosphere and see this island, colored lights glowing, drum beats thrumming, and sending signals out into the vast expanse of ocean and sky.

CHURCH ON EASTER ISLAND
SUNDAY, FEBRUARY 14, 2010

I woke up this morning, much like I usually do on a Sunday – no alarm, and about 1/2 hour before church starts. I got ready in about 15 minutes and headed out the door. Once in the street I remembered, "Oh, a camera!" I dithered, wondering if I should go back. "Camera? Yes, well, I don't know. Maybe not. I'll just experience it. No, I should have it. What time is it – do I have time to go back?" I went back and I'm glad I did. The statues in the church were very beautiful and interesting. The Islanders have been able to find a way to combine their old traditions with their new faith – the mother Mary has a crown of a bird–man. The bird–man was the symbol of the cult of the same name, which became the main religion on the island after the cult of the moai started to fade out. The Birdman religion was still in practice on the island until 1866–67.

The church service, as far as I could tell- my Spanish is not good enough to understand much - pretty much followed the course of a Catholic service. There were songs, bible passages, the gospel, a sermon and communion. I tell you what; these folks know how to belt out a song! Everyone was singing with power and passion. There was no swaying or lifting up of hands, but they sang with conviction and what I only assume is a love of God and of singing. All these old souls; singing with voices of substance. When I closed my eyes I would have sworn there were a thousand or more people singing together. Looking around later it couldn't have been more than two hundred. How inspiring!

The music for the service was performed from the center of the church, right in the pews, about 4–5 people, mostly men with guitars, an accordion and perhaps one other instrument. When it was time to play for a song or a response, they would stand up to play. There was one prayer where everyone joined hands. All of a sudden I went from feeling like a stranger visiting, to part of their family. What a nice feeling, especially after having recently left my temporary Antarctic family and having to adjust to being a solo traveler again.

After church the music moved outside where there were dancers; teenagers in dresses and white pants, and a line of teenage musicians along the side. I watched for a while, and then wandered back down the hill toward my temporary home.

Today I got my car. It's so nice to have "wheels." What a difference it makes when thinking about going out somewhere. Now if I want to buy water, the weight and distance isn't a factor. So I went shopping. The artisans building was open today even if all the booths weren't. Perfect – business was slow and I could take my time looking at all the goods on display. I have a number of items on my list – things for specific people, gifts, and the standard: a spoon for Beth and postcards for me. I looked at the wooden masks but nothing really grabbed me except for one that was about $100. That's too much for something that's just going to hang on my wall. Maybe the artist was serious about giving a good price "just for me." I'll have to visit him later in the week.

Then I went down to the little fishing boats harbor, where there are little rowboats with motors on the back. They're all tied up in a row down the street from here, and they're colorful. I enjoyed wandering around their prows looking for a good angle for a picture. At the end of the little spit of land I found a few simple covered shelters; nice places to sit in the shade and look out at the ocean. The dark blue of the sky contrasted nicely with the white puffy clouds that the island tends to favor, the water a lovely emerald green.

Next stop, the stage from last night, the one used for the festival. Now that the festival is finished, I could drive down into the area where all the people were standing last night. The stage was still erect and photos of the painting close up was what I was after. Onstage was one door through which most of the performers onstage came through last night. From my new perspective I could see that the builders had built it around a moai, which was just on the other side of the wall, looking through the doorway, as if wondering if he'd missed his queue to come on stage. It made me chuckle.

Then on to the cemetery, just down the road. This cemetery is fairly new – begun sometime in the mid-1950s. The graves are a mixture of headstones carved as crosses on the front and with moai on the back, and just a plain headstone with handwritten letters. One cross, struck me in particular. A roughly square headstone with what looked like two quick brushstrokes of white, which had been allowed to run, forming a rough cross. As if the family member had painted it quickly in his grief, eager to get away.

Last stop was to check out a few carvings, some left over from the parade, and others as permanent installations in inhabitant's yards. There are moai statues everywhere on this island it seems, and not just in the landscape. They're for sale in shops of course, but also to be found in people's houses, adorning their gardens, hung as necklaces or keychains, used outside doorways much like bears are in Colorado, with signs that say "Welcome." (I haven't actually seen any moai welcome signs...but that's what it reminds me of.)

The last thing I did was to drive around in search of Edmundo's house. I'm invited for dinner but have no directions. A Lindblad group, a small subset of the folks who were with me on the National Geographic Explorer in the Antarctic, is here on an Easter Island post–trip, and is having dinner there tonight. Asking the folks I passed, 5 out of 6 of them knew where he lived. It kind of became a game to figure out how close I could get and still not find it. I did find some other unique homes and a cultural center that looked like it was closed for the weekend. The last man said something along the lines of "You're looking at it," when asked – the blue house just up the hill I believe is the one I'm aiming for tonight. We'll soon see! Looking forward to dinner and breaking bread with some "old friends." It's almost time to go.

LAURA VAE GATZ

DINNER AT EDMUNDO'S
MONDAY, FEBRUARY 15, 2010

It was a late night. As I mentioned before, Edmundo had invited to me to dinner with the rest of the Lindblad folks, at his home, up the hill, just outside of town. I'm on my own on the Island, and the other folks are on a Lindblad–led post–trip. I was standing at the rail with a pisco sour when the bus containing my friends drove up. Pisco is a brandy distilled from white muscat grapes grown in two main regions of South America: the area around Pisco, Peru and the Valle del río Elqui in central Chile. Chilean's are very proud of their pisco sour, and after tasting one, I understand why. It's delicious! I waved and smiled and held up my glass. How exciting to see them all again. As they wandered in the door, greeted by Edmundo, I greeted them next with a hug or a kiss on the cheek, a habit we all seem to have picked up somewhere over the last few weeks. Smiles all around. It was like being the long lost sister finally come home.

We ate at a lovely long wooden table out on the balcony overlooking the land below. A nice breeze was free to blow in and out and around. Pisco sours and appetizers for everyone – some sort of soft herbed cheese and an amazing salami. We all talked, caught up, and then sat down to dinner. There were several different kinds of salad – beets (which I stayed away from....traumatized as a small child to fear the very sight of them), tomatoes, and a lettuce salad with a homemade salad dressing. Wine was a choice of red or white. And the main dishes were beef and pork, rice and potato salad. Everything was fantastic. All homemade, and all so very welcome to my new "island diet" of eggs, melon, pineapple and yogurt.

Edmundo sat on the opposite side of the table from me and had the most interesting and funny stories to tell. He seems to have seen and done it all. Being the "primero" archeologist on the island, he often is asked to be a consultant for a film or some other project. When Kevin Costner came to shoot the movie "Rapa Nui," Edmundo was asked by the film crew to be a technical advisor. He asked them, "What do I do?" and they said "Nothing, unless we call you, But you have to be available." For the money they were offering he thought that sounded like a pretty good deal.

One day during the shooting of the movie he saw a guy with a necklace of horse teeth. Edmundo said that there hadn't been any horses on the island during the period this movie was set in. Apparently they didn't care. That made us all laugh.

The movie directors were bound and determined to get a specific bird in their shot and they needed the migrating birds to come to the island earlier than they normally do. Edmundo said there was nothing he could do about that. But they wanted the birds anyway; several ideas were considered. One was to purchase eggs, have Edmundo incubate and hatch them. The idea they went with was to visit the island the birds were currently on, with a ship, and toss out food behind the ship as it sailed back to Easter Island. It worked! About 100 birds followed them back to Easter Island where they continued to feed them. So the birds stayed until they were able to get the shot. I tell you, no problem is too big for Hollywood to try to overcome.

Apparently they also wanted an iceberg and couldn't understand why one was not able to be brought to the island. They kept saying, "We only want to shoot a very short piece with it – about 5 minutes." When asked what they were going to do with it they said, "Oh, we want to put people on it, in loin cloths. But it will be for a very short time." Finally understanding that it wasn't going to be possible to get an iceberg here they thought, well, why not go to the icebergs? Unfortunately it was May, which is early winter in the Antarctic. Once again they failed to understand why you couldn't go down there around that time of year. I have yet to find out if they ever did solve their iceberg problem; maybe I'll have to rent the movie to find out! Apparently it's a solid "B" film.

Later in the evening, during dessert, the men were telling stories of families who ship their elderly parents off on cruises, well past the time when they should be traveling. Edmundo told the story of one man from a Lindblad tour group whom he found knocking on his door in the middle of the night. This man had a long grey pointy beard, and a mustache with pointy ends. He had a black beret on his head, but nothing else on. When asked if he could be helped, the man said that he'd been in the bathroom in his cabin and went out the wrong door, ending up in the corridor, and now could not remember his cabin number. Edmundo called the front office and said he had a man who was lost and needed to find his cabin. "What's his name?" they asked. That was the other problem; the man couldn't remember his name. When Edmundo told them this, they said "Oh, yes, we know who he is, we'll come help him back to his cabin." Edmundo had given the man a towel to cover himself. When the staff woman showed up, the man handed the towel back to Edmundo, saying, "Well, if I'm going back to my cabin I don't need this. Thanks!" When the ship called this man's sister to tell them he was being flown home, she said, "I'm leaving the house and I won't be home to pick him up. Can't you just throw him overboard? I bet he'd like that."

Each person who had worked on passenger ships had their own story to tell of older people who were encouraged by their families to travel. One elderly man was flying home with his wife when he had a heart attack and died in his seat. The lady eventually told the crew he had died. When the plane landed, the lady got off the plane telling the crew to "Just ship him to me," that she couldn't stay, she had a connection to make. Unbelievable.

Another lady with no family who traveled with Lindblad most of the year, was traveling on board ship when she died in her cabin while they were in port. Not wanting to make a stink with the port authorities, the crew was asked to put her in the freezer. So she was tossed in. They knew that she would have liked a sea burial, so they started to make a casket. When they went to the freezer to measure the body, they found that she had frozen with her arms straight out from her sides. Well, it would be awfully difficult to make a casket that large. One of the crewmembers walked up with an axe and said that he'd take care of it. When it was about time for the ceremony, the crewmember walked on deck with a box about 2'x2'x2'. Knowing that would never fly with the passengers, he was asked to make normal shaped casket and stick this box inside of it. With that fixed, the ceremony continued. They hoisted her up, and off she slid, into the water, except the casket just sailed out to sea, and didn't sink. Apparently, even though anchor chains had been placed in the casket, not enough holes were drilled through the wood to let the water in. Eventually, though, enough water leaked in and down she went. Whew!

My alarm went off awfully early this morning. I rolled over and turned it off, but sat up and padded into the bathroom. Must get up and photograph cool things! The sunrise is about 7:30, and I left here about 7:00 for good measure. The drive to Ahu Tongariki took an awfully long time. As I drove around each sweeping curve of the coast, the hills in the distance never seemed to move or grow closer. The road out there is probably the road in the best repair on the island. The potholes have mostly been filled in, making it easy to go the posted speed limit of 60 km/hr. In the end I made it with time to spare. A handful of folks were already there, all in place to take photographs. One couple was just waking up, and having slept on the grass in front of the line of moai they were folding up their sleeping bags and re–rolling their foam mats. Eventually the sun made its way above the horizon, initially blocked by clouds. First the edge of the clouds turned golden and bright, like velvet rimmed in a halo of light. Then the sun broke through and I could hear the sound of shutters opening and closing. Then, ever so slowly, almost imperceptibly, the colors of the clouds started to change from grey to pink, to orange. Torn between taking one long movie of the sunset and capturing photographs, I chose the photographs, telling myself I had at least 3 more days to capture the sunrise.

Once in town, I hit the post office, asking to have an official Easter Island stamp put in my passport, and for 6 postcard stamps. Postcards are written, and now just need to be posted, but first a nap, at least until the heat of the day drains away.

On the way back into town I saw a horrible site coming over

the horizon – a cruise ship!! Duh duh (think "Jaws" theme) du duh du duh du duh.....I suppose not everyone can fly here. "Oh no," I thought, "that's just E–vile!" It sailed around the end of the island heading for town. The town has no dock, so it anchored in the little bay on my end of town. By the time I made it home, after visiting the post office, little orange tenders had appeared on the water, heading for shore. Made me think of an invasion. Perhaps I'd join the islanders and eat the interlopers, taking their orange boats and cute little Gucci purses. I took a nap instead. By the time I got up, the ship's horn was blaring, signaling its departure. Must be time for their dinner. Hard to believe they only had 8 hours here. That's hardly enough time to get out of town and see a few of the major sites.

Easter Island is growing in population. It's gone from 1100 to estimates of 5000 within less than ten years. Chileans come over from the mainland. It is easier to earn $20 a day here, versus $5 on the mainland for similar work. The way things tend to go are: first the man in a family comes to work, and rents a room. If he decides to stay, the rest of the family comes over, and now they need a house. Houses and hotels are being built. The population is exceeding the infrastructure. Sometimes the power needs exceed the supply and the power goes down, as it did just before my nap in the middle of my website sync. Sometimes the water pressure disappears, as it did at the end of my shower yesterday (good timing!). It is possible to bring additional resources to the island, but upgrading infrastructure takes time and money. The effects of the poor economy have hit here as well. Edmundo said that there are usually over 20 National Geographic charter flights that come through here in a year. This year it was only 6 or 8. The island has its own cargo ship, but it's been sitting at anchor since I arrived. FedEx used to have a pickup here, but no longer. If islanders want to have something shipped to them it can be difficult to get it. Some items get caught up in customs. The easiest way to get things to the island is to have an individual bring them.

LAURA VAE GATZ

EXCURSION WITH EDMUNDO
TUESDAY, FEBRUARY 16, 2010

This morning was time for an excursion with Edmundo. I drove out to his home to pick him up. The first thing I learned was that the Lindblad folks were not able to leave the Island yesterday – they were to have flown out sometime midday on Monday. Apparently they boarded their plane, and then were on the taxiway for several hours before being brought back to the terminal (probably all of 200 feet). That time on the plane wouldn't have been bad if they were in business class...

The plane had some sort of mechanical issue. Mechanics were working on it all day. And the passengers waited at the airport. Patricia, Lindblad's consultant on the island, took them all out for lunch and then brought them back to the airport. When it became apparent that the plane wasn't going to take off on Monday they started to call around for hotel rooms. Everything was booked solid. They called one more place and they had 7 rooms, the exact number needed for the group, but they could only stay one night because all the rooms were booked for the following night.

The next morning – today – Edmundo and I saw a second plane at the airport, when there weren't supposed to be any planes there at all. At lunchtime when we returned to town and saw the second plane was no longer there, we found out that our people had gotten off the island around 11:00 a.m. If I'd found out they hadn't left I was going to visit them and see if I could take their mind off their travel woes. I know one of the couples had several connections, from here to the U.S., to London and then on to Israel. That will be a challenge to rebook.

This morning we went around the north east side of the island

and Edmundo showed me a few toppled moai that I hadn't seen before. The light on their features was lovely. He also explained how new ahu (stone platforms) were built on old ahu. As the clan grew, they would need to provide new statues for them. If the ancestors in the moai were too far removed from the current generation, they wouldn't care about them and therefore wouldn't provide abundance for them. So the line of moai increased as the descendants did.

After a lovely extended nap (coma) in the heat of the day (from 2:00–6:00 p.m.), I drove back up to pick up Edmundo for the second half of our day. We ventured back out to the big crater where many of the moai were carved, and to Tongariki for the golden light and sunset.

Once again the light was spectacular. The clouds on this trip have just been magnificent. Clouds add so much to photographs – especially to sunsets or sunrises. They're so expressive, textural and colorful – changing by the minute.

I'd seen the moai on the outer slopes of the crater in the morning light, when there was no one to charge me for going in, and now I understand why they weren't there – the light in the late afternoon and early evening is much better. This time I had to pay, 5 mill – which means 5000 pesos – which equals $10. In March, the price of admission goes up to $60 USD – so I'm getting in just under the wire. And they gave me the lecture about not losing my receipt or I would have to pay again at the other crater. This receipt gets you into both locations. Secretly I wonder what they'd do if I took a photograph of the receipt with a time and date stamp, would they still let me in?? Don't think I'll be finding out. My car gets returned in the morning and I won't be making it to the other crater – which requires quite a walk in (hike) to get there.

The wild horses at the crater are so abundant and run all over the place. They like it there because inside the crater they have access to fresh water. There is a year–round lake there. So the horses climb up the side of the crater and cross to the inside to hang out and drink. While I was inside the crater I even saw horses taking a bath – completely covered with water except for their heads, and splashing around. Funny. I've never seen that before. The horses, as I've mentioned before, are destructive forces on the moai. They like to scratch themselves on the rock, and their hard hooves also make a negative impact when they walk on petroglyphs.

After capturing the nice light on the moai at the crater, we headed towards the coast and Tongariki. The sun was quickly setting just off to the south of the crater and it seemed as if we only had a few minutes to take advantage of the light on the faces of the moai. Edmundo headed off in one direction to take some photos he didn't have (having been around the island for so many years, and being an archeologist, he's gotten thousands of photos – but needed another perspective at this time of day), and I headed off in another. There were very few people around. This site is known for it's sunrise "photo op," not the sunset – however, the light on the faces at sunset is very nice.

Remembering Chris's and Mike's words from Antarctica, I intentionally put my camera down, sat down on the ground, facing the moai, and just watched. They had both told me that sometimes you need to put the camera down and not have a "filter" through which you're experiencing life. I watched the color in the clouds change, watched them drift across this amazing scene, watched the light start to fade, and just enjoyed the cool breeze on the my face and the sensation of almost being cold. What a change from the heat of the day. When the last of the good light had faded I headed off to find Edmundo who was sitting on a rock changing lenses. We sat and talked for a few minutes and then got back in the car to head home. I noticed the tiny sliver of moon as we got in the car. It was over the crater, surrounded by lovely dark clouds. On the ride home we stopped to take some photographs from an advantageous high point in the landscape. Lovely. I told Edmundo it was nice to have someone to hang out with to enjoy the evening.

Earlier in the day he gave me a tip. He said, that I should slow the car down on the dirt roads if I saw any locals. They don't enjoy getting a "dusting" and might throw a rock at my car, not caring if they break the windshield or not. Good to know. Then he added, "Of course, you don't see many locals walking any more." They almost all have a car and like to use it.

When we were almost at his house he offered me dinner or some wine. With such a hearty lunch not so many hours ago I was still full, but took him up on his offer of a glass of wine. Once home he went out to his bar to select a bottle and a few glasses and brought them back to the kitchen where we sat around the large kitchen table and talked. Oh, he has good stories. I wish I could remember them all!

We sat in the kitchen and talked like old friends. He told me of his years on the island, of political challenges and changes, his childhood, and of the funny stories that inevitably happen when living on a small island where rumor and gossip are some of the best entertainment around.

One of the stories was about our captain on board the Explorer, in his earlier days. Boy, I'm going to have to sail with him again just so I can give this man a hard time. Maybe this incident is far enough in the past that he'll find it funny now and tell me his own version of it.

So, according to Edmundo, this man was captain of a tourist ship going through the Pacific, and was taking the ship through a passage where a lot of ships had sunk, when a long metallic scraping sound reverberated through the ship. Edmundo was on board with his wife. His wife had gone upstairs to look out over the channel. Edmundo was below deck catching up on the ship's logs on his computer. Edmundo thought, well, it can't be too big a deal, until the door to his cabin swung open. When he didn't see anyone outside he realized that the ship was listing to one side and the door had swung open because of it. So he thought he'd go see what was going on and grabbed two life vests just in case, before heading out into the corridor. There was a ladder just outside his door and the crew was climbing up it quickly yelling, "we're sinking!" Not thinking that they could be sinking that quickly he started to head back to his room to grab a few essentials, like the cash he'd brought with to purchase several engines for boats back on Easter Island, and a pair of shoes. Well, their cabin was at the end of a corridor and there was a bulkhead just past the cabin – they were at the end of a hallway. He noticed water starting to swirl around his ankles. Before he could duck into his room, the wall at the end of the hallway gave way, and a gush of water as well as all the Filipino crewmembers burst through, and carried Edmundo by sheer force, upstairs.

There were under a hundred passengers on board, and four lifeboats, which could hold over a hundred passengers each. Edmundo and his wife were scheduled to be in lifeboat 2. The first lifeboat was lowered into the water and everyone rushed to get in it. The same thing happened when the second lifeboat was lowered. Doing the math, Edmundo decided they would wait until the 3rd or 4th lifeboat, and the ship was still well above water. Once in the water they headed for shore, which was only a few miles away.

When they arrived there was a man on the shore to meet them. "Welcome," he said sounding happy and pleased to have them as guests on the island, "Would you like a Coke or something to eat?" When told how the ship had sunk the man said, "I know, three ships have sunk on that same rock in the last few years." Of course he was asked why there was no marking on the rock to warn ships. He said, "Bad for business!"

Not knowing how long they would be on the island, Edmundo and the ship's doctor decided to go back to the Zodiacs to gather up the medical equipment that had been brought, and the emergency supplies, but the zodiacs were empty. After looking around they saw other zodiacs walking themselves up the surrounding hills, as if carried by little ants. And indeed they were. Little "ants" from the tribe on the other side of the island had come and made quick work of liberating what they'd found on the shore.

Word came that another ship was in the area that could pick them up. Some crewmembers went back to the sunken/wrecked ship to reclaim as much of the passengers' luggage as they could. The ship ended up on some rocks just off shore and many of the cabins were still above water. Although Edmundo wanted to go back to the ship to gather up some of his things – clothes, his watertight camera cases, and his bag of money – the captain wouldn't let him back on because it was dangerous and because his room was under water. Edmundo said he'd just get some of the scuba gear – which was still above water – and go in. Captain wouldn't hear of it.

Edmundo was in the zodiac with some of the crewmembers, when they went to go check out the arriving ship. The ship was a coconut and copra (the brown outer husk of a coconut) carrier, so it reeked of rancid coconut. When they looked below with a flashlight, where the coconut was usually stored, Edmundo couldn't quite make out what he was seeing at first. It looked like black and white moving clouds. He shone the flashlight again. The black faded to white and then back to black. Upon closer inspection he discovered millions upon millions of cockroaches, each about one inch long, reacting to the flashlight by moving away in a circular pattern, then moving back. Eeeww!

Although the passengers got on that ship that day, they all stayed up on deck. It was eventually ruled that the captain was not at fault for the sinking. The coral damage would not have been enough to sink the ship. The main problem was that some of the crewmembers had had their portholes open. So when the ship started to list to one side, the water just came pouring in the windows. If they'd been shut, the watertight doors would have stopped the flooding.

From what Edmundo said, it sounds like this and a few other experiences had an impact on the Captain. He has quite a sense of humor these days.

Another story was of a man we saw in the morning. "He's crazy," Edmundo exclaimed, "Every time I talk with him he's another person." Most recently he's declared himself the king of the entire island. And he had a brother, who I think was more crafty and smart, than crazy. This man would head out to one of the caves on the island that the tourists visit with his headdress of feathers and a cape, and tell the islanders that he lived there – that this cave had been in his family for generations and that his great, great, great grandfather had lived in the cave as well. Well, of course the tourists all wanted a photo with him. And he brought carvings with him that his brothers or cousins had carved, telling the tourists that he carved them all, and having one in his hand that he was "finishing," and that this was how he supported himself. If they wanted a photo with him that was $2, and photos of anything else in the cave was an additional fee. You can imagine with over 300 tourists passing through each day that he made quite a good living. After all the visitors for the day had come through he'd head back home, and didn't need to be back until around 10am the next day because the tours didn't show up until then. He would take about half the year and travel around the world on his earnings. Sounds like a pretty good life to me even if it does involve some underhandedness and skullduggery! It certainly made good stories for the tourists. So they all got something out of it.

When I asked about the Eucalyptus trees being introduced to the Island, Edmundo told me how they're dangerous. Not only do they use a lot of water, but they also grow very fast, and because the bedrock isn't very far under the soil, their roots spread out horizontally but don't go down very far. So when the winter winds come through after the rains, a stiff breeze can knock them down.

Years ago Edmundo was building his current house, and while they were building, they camped for about six months in a grove of Eucalyptus trees. One day they all decided to go into town to get cleaned up, take showers, wash their clothes and do a number of things they couldn't do at their camp-site. When they returned to their campsite at the end of the day there was nothing left. A huge branch had fallen on their tent, squashing everything in sight. Edmundo thinks he was lucky; I think that he's probably meant to be around for a while longer...

All week I've been thinking that I leave on a flight out of here at 7:30 p.m. I just checked my itinerary and it's a 12:15 p.m. flight. That's good news. Lying in bed this morning, before figuring that out, I was wondering what I would do with my entire day if I had to check out of my room by midday and not leave until evening. Excellent – so glad I checked on the departure time; however, I shouldn't feel too smug or my flight won't leave...don't need karma coming back on me. So the drill is that the airport opens around 9:30 in the morning, and flights are always overbooked this time of year, so we'll go in first thing in the morning to check in and get my boarding pass and check in luggage. That way I'm checked in first before all the extra people they booked. Then I have a few hours to do whatever I want. We'll head back to the airport when the plane lands. From the B&B we'll be able to hear it as it approaches. It has to be on the ground for at least an hour, and it takes five minutes to get there from the B&B. Small airports are great! I have one more full day before I leave.

LAST DAY ON THE LAND OF THE MOAI
WEDNESDAY, FEBRUARY 17, 2010

Packing day. Better get to it before the hottest part of the day hits...

I washed the salt stains out of the bottom of my jeans today. I was strangely attached to them. They kind of signified Antarctica to me on some level. Although I only wore jeans on the ship, not on shore, those stains remind me of going out on deck, getting wet, seeing the snow drift in the corners of the ship, and dragging my jean hems through the water, wicking water as well as salt several inches up my pant legs. Those crunchy little salt stains are a souvenir, and are now just a memory. Bye, bye crunchy little salt stains! I hope to have you again some day. Maybe in the Russian Arctic in a year or two!

Packing, packing, stuffing stuff back into little bags. It always reminds me of a jack in the box. When Jack is in the box he fits, but it's not always easy to get him back in. What do I really need? How warm is 72 degrees Fahrenheit really? Humid or dry, windy or calm, overcast or sunny? Hmmm. Expandable luggage is always a bonus. You can pack with the suitcase expanded, zip it closed and then magically, zip the expandable section closed. It's like a mini compressor. My bag to send home is all packed. I'm shipping it to Arizona – to Dad. Hey Dad, don't forget you can open it up and do my laundry! Tee hee. At least open it up and air it out...don't want those things fermenting for too long.

Looking forward to getting on the plane. Living on Easter Island has been like camping. I like camping. It's great fun to get dirty and then it's fun to get clean again. I'm ready to get clean again, to wash the red dirt stains off my hands, out of my white socks (I think they were white socks), and to have a temperature controlled airplane cabin for a few hours. One of the things I'll miss is the humidity. Although humidity can make the temperature feel warmer than it actually is, it's good for the skin. I'll also miss the sunrises and sunsets, which have just oozed color.

It's criminal to be ready to move on, but I'm ready. I thoroughly enjoyed my time here, completely different from Antarctica. I'm sure New Zealand will be different as well. All I've heard about it is positive – everyone loves their time in New Zealand. The British couple staying in the room next to me will be visiting there after a week in Tahiti. They're renting a minivan to stay in and will be driving around both islands for a month, after having been on the road 9 months.

During the day Edmundo dropped by his friends' home to check in on how their work was going. They've been commissioned to create the seven panels that will go in the museum in the new fancy hotel being built across the street from Te'Ora. They need to create and figure out what each panel is going to relate. This museum is a "virtual" museum and will not have any relics or historical artifacts in it. It will be more of a verbal journey with the Rapa Nui through time, and include their migration to the island.

This evening Edmundo and I went up to the south crater – Orongo. This is the site where the Rapa Nui held a yearly competition during the cult of the bird–man. This site is way up on a sheer cliff face, overlooking the ocean and two small islands, about a mile off shore. Orongo is a large volcanic crater. Its interior walls are much steeper than the other crater where the moai were carved. Down at the bottom is a lake, but it looks different than the lake at the other crater. It's filled with tiny grass islands, or rafts. The grass grows, creates a little "raft" and eventually it will sink to the bottom. Then a new raft of grass will grow. The spaces in between the grass rafts are where grass has already sunk down to the bottom. It looks like what I imagine the view looks like from a low plane ride over parts of Africa during the wet season.

A little farther up the road are round houses that Edmundo's friends reconstructed several years ago, and some weathered petroglyphs. The petroglyphs were hard to see in the light – they're easier to see at sunset in December, because the sun is farther to the south. Edmundo said the best way to see them these days is at night with a flashlight shining flat across their face, to create the most dramatic shadows. However, they close the crater at night, for what I assume must be safety reasons.

Back to the competition at the Orongo crater; during the age of the bird–man cult, the chief, once a year, would choose representatives for this competition. They didn't have to perform the feat themselves; each one could appoint a person to do it in his stead. Many of these men (and they were all men – no women were allowed at the crater during this competition) were older, with lots of land and prestige, and they weren't about to complete "the task." So they would choose who would go in their place. Whoever was chosen would walk to the top of the crater and live in the houses there on the edge of the cliff. People would bring them food to eat and they would collect reeds, which they would drop at the foot of the cliff, to later build into a raft. The goal of the competition was to be the first person to find an egg of the Sooty Tern that was laid on the island one mile off the coast. So these guys had to wait until the migration of birds arrived at the island, then they had to climb down the cliff, put together the reeds they'd collected to form a raft, and take their own water with them. They would use gourds to put water in, putting them at the base of the cliff a day or so before they made their way to the island. Edmundo said that you don't want water to be in gourds for too long or it gets – well – very smelly. Once on the island the men would sleep in caves and look for the eggs every day. The first man to find the egg would yell the name of the man for whom he was competing, across the channel, to the elders on the shore.

This is where it gets interesting. The man they were competing for would become highly honored for that year. He would become almost a deity and could not be looked upon by anyone for the entire year. He would live in seclusion, having an assistant who would cook and sew and clean for him. He couldn't come out of his hiding spot during daylight hours but could come out at night. This man could be heard, but not seen. His head would be shaved and painted with red ochre as a symbol of his power. During this year the man could not bath, or cut his hair or nails. I'm thinking that this doesn't sound like a good deal. Seclusion and no bathing? After the year was up he would come out and the first thing he would do was swim in the ocean. Water washes away the power, and a year's worth of grime...and then he would go back to his normal life.

Now, the guy who actually got the egg, gets a better deal. The hand that picked up the egg is painted red, and this man cannot do any work for a whole year. People must bring him food. And this applies to his entire family. So they get the royal treatment, and they don't have to go into seclusion.

The last year they held this competition in the traditional way was 1863.

LAURA VAE GATZ

III.

NEW ZEALAND
& AUSTRALIA

SO LONG, FAREWELL
FRIDAY, FEBRUARY 19, 2010

I've checked in at the airport, checked one piece of luggage (I am carrying my green duffle bag on), and gotten my boarding passes through to Auckland. Now I wait; about an hour to an hour and a half, at the B&B. And wait to see if the officials have any problem with my carry ons....la la la. Travel days aren't my favorite, however they are necessary to get from one place to another.

I like small airports. They're so easy to navigate. This airport has one check in counter – LAN. It has one security line and one gate. It opens just before flights come in, and closes when everyone has gotten picked up after getting their luggage. They have a scanner for checked luggage, but they don't turn it on until the LAN counter opens in the morning. Even if their schedule say they open at 8:30

a.m., it doesn't necessarily mean 8:30 a.m., it might be closer to 9:00 a.m. There is only one runway. Inside the airport there are three–dimensional mock–ups of a new airport. I wonder if they're really going to build it or if it's just a dream. There's probably contention on the island as to whether they need paved roads or an airport more. There's some thought that paving the roads would destroy the ambiance of the island. The locals think it would make their cars last a lot longer and minimize the effects of dust.

The dust is something else. I know I've mentioned it before, but it's really crazy. The car I rented already had a layer of dust over the dashboard and on the seats and steering wheel when I first picked it up. Dust layers your skin by the end of the day, making you think you've got a better tan than reality. Dust creeps onto my computer, in between the keys of the keyboard, and on the screen. It creeps into my ears, nose and under my fingernails. It covers my socks. Sometimes when taking a big breath outside all I smell is dust. Sometimes I smell the eucalyptus or the sea air, but sometimes only dust.

One of the things I like to do then traveling is to take very small glass vials with plastic stoppers and collect sand from the different islands that I visit. I have them all lined up on a shelf in my bath-room, labeled according to where they're from. It's just amazing how many varieties and colors and textures there are. Some you can see are made from crushed rocks and others from crushed shells. Some are very fine and others are larger particles. I enjoy looking over them when I'm home, remembering all the places I've been. They're like little bottles of memories, all in a row. Now I have several vials from this trip. I think about three from Easter Island – two of sand, one black and the other white, and one of dust, just because. (My vial of dust was confiscated in New Zealand due to their strict non–contamination laws.)

There were announcements in the Rapa Nui airport in Spanish. As most airport announcements usually are, they were a bit muffled. That, combined with my extreme minimal Spanish vocabulary meant I didn't understand a word. And they were not repeated in English. Although I did imagine what they night be saying, taking into account where I was... "Ladies and gentlemen, if you're here for a flight you already know where you're going and you're all going the same place – surprise! This is the only flight today. Since there are people waiting in line to go through customs you can tell that your plane has already arrived."

As I was waiting to board the plane I saw several children playing. One little boy was squatting in the dirt, throwing pebbles into a puddle. A five or six year–old girl with black hair made up into two braids, was skipping around barefoot, with a beaded ankle bracelet on one ankle below a white cotton sundress, one thin strap falling off her tanned shoulder. It looked like she didn't have a care in the world. I thought about how none of this would probably be seen in an airport in the U.S. First of all there wouldn't be much access to the outside and second I'm not sure barefoot children would be allowed in the airport – however that one is more within the realm of possibility. I guess I have seen barefoot children in airports occasionally – but not often.

I like getting on a plane for a long trip – well, at least if I'm traveling in Business. It's just a little like moving into a new hotel room (just a little). You come in, stow away your bags, getting out the things you're going to need immediately, arranging them in a way that it will be easy to access. I need my camera; you never know

when the clouds are going to be spectacular. Need my iPhone, laptop, power and earphones.

Feeling settled, I sit back and watch passengers board, happy to
be on a clean, non–dusty air conditioned plane, when a man and his
son come by asking if I'd mind changing seats with one of them
so they could sit together. I ask which seat. 3C, no problem. Both
he and his son say "thank you" in English and I say "de nada." My
new seat is one row back and off to the side instead of in the middle row. I feel more grounded on the sides and not so exposed, so I
like my new seat a little better. I move my vest and fanny pack and
then go back to get my bags so it's easy to get off the plane when we
land. One of the men helps me, exclaiming, "Do you have a moai in
here?" because it's so heavy. Another gives me one of his shell and
seed necklaces. It's hefty and beautiful, the kind of piece I would
have admired at a craft market but not bought for myself. But to
receive it as a thank you is a true gift.

I received another gift at the airport as Sharon, Te'Ora's owner,
and I were saying our goodbyes. It was a necklace; very simple – a
shell with feathers coming off the end. She said it's for me to take
a little of the island with me, a little part that wants to come back
to become part of the island again one day, and if I ever return, to
bring it with me and to toss the shell back into the ocean. The feathers are for safe flights. She even said that if I wanted to take another
sabbatical from work, I could come run her hotel while she goes
to visit her grandchild back in the U.S. for six months. Interesting
offer!

Taxiing down to the end of the runway I'm happy, simply and
completely happy. Two great adventures down, two to go. We turn
the plane around at the end of the runway, the engines rev and our
wheels leave the ground. Ahhh, takeoff! "Time to get out the Cheetos!" I think to myself. But I don't have any today. Cheetos are an

old tradition of my sister's and mine. When traveling together we would pack individual grab bags of Cheetos and pack them in our carryon bag. Once we'd taken off and were in the air on our last flight of the day, for at least a few minutes, we knew that we were really on the way to our destination and that chances were we'd actually get there. We were past all the hurdles – ticketing, checking bags, security, weather, mechanical issues, etc. But we didn't have our little Cheeto celebration until the last flight was in the air. We knew from experience that even taxiing down the runway isn't a sure guarantee of takeoff.

On our way to St. Lucia several years ago we were flying through San Juan and experienced such an instance. We were on the plane. I was all smiles and Lisa says to me, "We haven't taken off yet, don't get too happy." I pooh–poohed her, thinking she was being paranoid. We taxied down the runway, full speed, moments from the wheels leaving the ground, and...the captain cut the engines. We looked at each other. I think one of us said, "Well, that's not good," and the other, "That's not what you want to hear." And we pulled off the runway. We spent several tense hours at the San Juan airport, with a few tearful calls to Mom for help. We knew there was just one flight a day and that the flights were all fully booked. If they cancelled our flight, who knew how long we would be stranded in San Juan? At that point, Jimmy Buffett's song that has the line in it, "Don't want to go to no San Juan airport, don't want to go to Nashville, Tennessee," sprang into my head.

So, it's Cheeto time, sans Cheetos. I take off my boots. As I untie the laces, a puff of dust rises out of the fibers and I get what I hope is my last whiff of dust for a while. The island is sighing its last hurrah from out of my boots. Goodbye Rapa Nui!

The kid I swapped places with is one row ahead of me. I can see his television screen. He's watching "Happy Feet," the movie with the animated penguins. "Aww," I think, "I should watch that." We'd discussed that on board the National Geographic Explorer, how it would be fun to watch the movie, now that we'd seen some of these penguins in real life and observed their behavior. How fun to see just how many true–to–life things they got right.

Ohh, hot towel time! My favorite! I'll just bet that these particular hot towels have to be washed in bleach when they get to Santiago. This is one flight where they actually go back dirty. No matter how clean you are when you leave the house, I do not think it is possible to arrive to the airport dust free. My hands actually look clean for the first time in a week. Yeah clean!!

I am sooo happy to be on a clean plane! Have I mentioned that? Sitting on clean seats, listening to classical music as I type. Belly full of lamb, potatoes and salad and some sort of custardy flan thing that had a crème Brulee–like top. On this flight, business class is entirely full. I expect a full flight to Auckland too. According to the One World folks I've spoken with, the Santiago–Auckland flight is very busy and sold out quite a number of months ahead of time.

The lounge in Santiago was nice, but not the best I've seen. They had all manner of juices, wines, liquor, and soft drinks and water. I stuck with water. Good to be hydrated; good for the immune system and for avoiding blood clots. There were also crackers and cheeses, cookies, little white bread sandwiches with the crusts cut off, stuffed mushrooms, sushi, and various coffee drinks from a machine. Free wi–fi was a bonus. The seats were comfortable. The best feature by far was the showers. What a wonderful thing to take a shower in the middle of a long travel day. True, I had taken a shower this morning already, but I was still hot, a bit dusty still, and felt as if I'd been traveling for a while.

In order to use the shower you had to request the use of one, then a person would come unlock the door. Each room held one shower, sink, toilet and a place to hang clothes and sit. Floors, walls and countertops were all black and white granite, with glass and chrome shower doors and faucets. The amenities provided were just perfect – razor and shaving cream, shampoo, shower cap, hand lotion, soap, shower gel, comb, toothbrush and toothpaste.

Before I knew it, it was time to board the plane. Although I headed down to the gate before the posted boarding time, I got there after general boarding had begun, so I walked through the line and over to the "preferred passenger" line which was empty. How odd to be a "preferred passenger." Nice, but odd.

Time check: an hour and 15 minutes before I land. The flight from Easter Island to Santiago was four and a half hours, then I had a four–hour layover, and now I'm on a twelve and a half hour flight to Auckland. And we flew across the International Date Line, so I lost a day. Once I get there I'll have 3 hours until Mom flies in; then we have an errand to run, to FedEx. I am shipping one piece of luggage to Dad in Arizona. It's the suitcase with all my Antarctic gear in it. I'll be curious to see how well the suitcase travels...if it's still all in once piece with all its zipper pulls, etc. It's already sustained some damage from a zipper pull getting caught in the luggage conveyor belt in Santiago. When I tried to lift if off the belt it wouldn't move because the pull was under a metal lip on the conveyor belt. I had to ask for help from some nearby man, who nicely separated it from the belt, and also from a few of its seams. So, let's cross our fingers that my luggage shows up. I want to say "Hello, luggage!" and then quickly turn around and say, "Goodbye, luggage! Have a nice trip!"

All in all, the trip across the Pacific hasn't been bad. I probably slept on and off for about 7 or 8 hours, getting up to walk and stretch throughout. No matter how often I fly it's easy to forget just how dry the air is on planes. After sleeping on a plane, when I wake up I feel as if I've been put in a dehydrator. It's a good thing they give you a bottle of water before naptime. I wonder how the flight attendants deal with so much dryness.

Almost time to start getting things prepped to get off the plane — making sure everything is put back, that I haven't left anything laying around like my scarf, sweater, iPhone, face mask, etc. After long flights it's easy to forget what you got out during the night.

KIWI-LAND!
SATURDAY, FEBRUARY 20, 2010

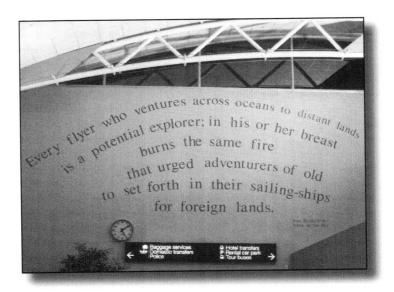

I am through immigration and the Bio–Police at the Auckland airport. That was fun. Immigration wanted to know a few things, like how long I'd been in South America, and why. What I did on Easter Island and what that was like. The immigration officer was good looking and tired. I asked him what time he has to get here in the morning and he said he'd been here all night. When I stopped to explain my answers on the Biohazard/Declaration/Customs form, I had to explain some of my answers to the Biohazard officials. Like the fact that I'd marked down "soil, sand, wood, and feathers." I explained how I have these very small glass vials with plastic stoppers and that I collect sand from around the world because it's cool to see all the different colors and textures. And that on Easter Island I decided to collect some dust because it is such a part of life there. They made a clear distinction between sand and dirt. If it was dirt, I think, things could be living in it, but if it's more like sand, it's more likely to be bug free.

They asked if I had any other boots. I have my Antarctic boots, which took me a minute to remember. Then I said "Oh, yes, I was in the Antarctic, and there might be penguin guano residue on them." They were taken off to be treated, then brought back wet and smelling clean and sanitized. My farewell necklace was a casualty. I could either pay $20 to have it sterilized because of the feathers, or they could take the feathers off. "Feathers off," I said. Hey, the feathers were for a safe flight, and I had that, so I don't need them any more, right?

They looked at all my wood products – two masks, a wooden "crèche" and my shells and rocks from different places. All of that was fine. Even my vials of sand were fine. But my vial of Easter Island dust ended up in the rubbish bin. My necklace gift from the plane was fine. Then I could pack up and move on to have things x–rayed. Sweating a little bit because of the high humidity, I got through and wandered beyond the frosted glass doors to the folks waiting to meet arriving friends and family. There are an awful lot of planes that arrive here early in the morning, more than 20 between 5:00–7:00 a.m. - from all over the place: Los Angeles, Singapore, Sydney, Kuala Lumpur, Papeete, Shanghai, Osaka, just to name a few.

All the stores are open. I certainly would not want to have a job in one of them. Can't imagine what their hours must be! I've already bought a few things. Thought it would be a good idea to change some money. And, well, I have to say that Mom was right about something. She thought that the power outlets here were different than the ones in South America. And she's right. I didn't think they would be, but they have the two prongs that are angled, and then the "ground" prong is straight. It's like our plugs in the U.S. except that the two prongs are angled. I don't think I have an adapter like that one. So I bought one.

Just got off the phone with the Duxton hotel, the place where we're spending our first night in Auckland. Manisha is the one with whom I've been emailing back and forth. I checked to make sure we have a reservation (we do) and to make sure our pick up is arranged for 8:30 this morning. They're picking us up at the FedEx location. I think finding a taxi that will take us there might be the bigger issue. The taxis here have to queue up here for passengers the way they do in the states, and no one wants such a short fare. However, there are shuttles that take a number of individuals going in roughly the same direction. They're pretty economical compared to a taxi. Typically they're large vans with an extra, wheeled attachment on the back for all the luggage. We convinced a shuttle to take us the short ride to the FedEx station for about $8US. Not bad compared to the quote of $30 we'd gotten from a taxi driver.

As we were landing I wondered what stores and restaurants would be open at this time in the morning, and then I absently wondered if there would be a McDonalds. Not because I want one, just because they're all over the place. They do have one. And they have some interesting food. The item I found the funniest is something called "the hungry man" or "the gut buster:" that is two slices of cheese, two sausage patties and an egg on an English muffin. That would be something I think would only be found in the U.S.!

Mom came through the arrival doors, escorted in her two–wheeled chariot by a lovely woman who helped us figure out how to get to the FedEx station without spending a fortune.

We didn't really say a good hello until we were at the FedEx station waiting for it to open. Once we were all squared away and had some time to stop and say hello. We're good about attending to details first. I think we'd both be good in a crisis.

The FedEx station opened at 8:30 a.m. instead of 8:00. I called the Duxton back and changed the time of our pick up, asking to be connected to the taxi service again so I could explain. The first time I'd talked with them I explained where we wanted to be picked up. When I said it was next to the Caltex truck wash they knew exactly where it was. When you see the Caltex truck wash you understand why it's a landmark. It's a very large, bright yellow building.

Before leaving home I'd started a commercial invoice, listing out the items I already knew would be in the suitcase when I sent it home – basically all the Antarctic gear – parka, long johns, waterproof pants, hat, mittens, boots, etc. Then, when packing it on the ship to leave, I listed out all the additional items I'd added – you know, the trinkets and souvenirs I'd bought: a penguin figurine, postcards, presents for cat sitter and friends, wooden carvings, etc. I'd even filled out the shipping label ahead of time with all the shipping information. All that pre–work made the whole process go very quickly. While we were waiting on the curb outside for the office to open, a few FedEx employees stopped to make sure we were ok. When I told them I worked for FedEx it was smiles all around. They seemed to know FedEx Services and that there were offices in Dallas. Nice to know the company you work for has employees all over the world. Makes the world seem a little smaller, and like, if you were in a bind, that one of them would help you out.

When we arrived at Auckland's Duxton Hotel, we were told there was a room available immediately for us to check into. How nice! We went upstairs, and I plopped down on the bed wanting nothing more than to cease to exist for a few hours, the hours of travel piling up on me all of a sudden now that I'd stopped moving. Even though the time difference is something like 4 hours from where I was, it's a day and 4 hours. Somehow the body knows; I don't know how, but it knows. And, after adding up the number of travel hours, it makes sense that I'd be tired; 26 hours from takeoff to Mom's pickup.

Mom and I decided on a one–hour nap. A little present to ourselves for making it to New Zealand and meeting up with each other. Mom got all ready, putting in earplugs, arranging pillows around herself and tying her scarf around her head to keep the light out of her eyes. Somehow her facemasks had scattered like the wind. Where did they all go? After an hour I made myself get up and wake Mom up. We decided to sleep one more hour.

Everywhere we went Mom found someone to talk to and was able to finagle a deal, two of her very favorite things. We met a lovely couple at Starbucks, up from the south, bringing their daughter to University. We talked with them for about a half an hour. We talked with the antique shop lady for about 15 minutes about story–book dolls and accents. She'd heard me trying to pronounce the name written on one of the spoons and pronounced it for me and told us where it was. So we walked into the shop and started talking. We also talked with the mini–mart shop man from whom Mom got a deal on bottled water. We saw some great little water bottles, ideal for carrying water around in during the day – not too big in diameter, not too tall. You know how each fanny pack takes just the right size water bottle to fit into it without falling out?

We wandered down a few roads, not too far from the hotel, peeking into shops as we walked along. One coffee bar was in a lovely long thin building with high round vaulted ceilings, so elegant with a hint of Art Deco. It almost seemed like a building that had been made out of a passageway between two other buildings. One of the ladies sitting with a cup of coffee said it used to be the entrance to a theater.

Everyone is nice and seems willing to talk. Mom is fearless. She'll walk up to a stranger and start a conversation. Mom's friend, Nancy, says Mom can talk to wallpaper. We got a coffee that was a little too large – mostly because I didn't drink my share, and Mom wandered around the Starbucks until she found someone who wanted to take it off our hands. She hadn't drunk out of it because she'd gotten a smaller cup to pour some into to cool it off faster. I tend to be fearless in other ways, but can be quite shy when it comes to talking with people.

TOUR TIME
SUNDAY, FEBRUARY 21, 2010

While Mom was getting ready this morning I made up breakfast in our room from the food I'd bought at the convenience store down the road: plain yogurt, an orange and an apple, sparkling water and an interesting looking yogurt covered musli bar. It was good and much less expensive than eating at the hotel. Such a deal! However, it was a little too much food so there were leftovers. Mom said, "Here's a zip–lock bag to package up your vegetables (meaning fruit)." That made me laugh. She and I have the same problem – not saying exactly what we mean. We're thinking the right thing, but our brains just choose a word that lives close to the word we actually want. Like fruits and vegetables probably are stored close together in the brain.

Mom saying "vegetables" reminded me of traveling with my sister Lisa. We were staying on St. John in the Caribbean at Maho Bay – the rooms were actually individual permanent tents built on high wooden platforms. We were going to go to the showers and I said "Just a minute, let me grab my vegetables," meaning "let me grab my vitamins first." From then on we liked to call our vitamins vegetables.

Last night we did laundry. Well, I suppose, more specifically, I started laundry and Mom finished it. The washing machine in our room was a washer and a dryer. There was a whole page of instructions written out, step by step, how to use it. This machine took special laundry soap provided by the hotel – soap that was "low sudsing." The wording in the front of the laundry soap packet said, "uber clean laundry soap," which made us both laugh. After an hour Mom wondered why the washer was still going. After an hour and a half she called the front desk and they came up to help. We must have had a faulty washer because it never went into the drying cycle – the water just kept coming in, even when the dial said it was supposed to be drying the clothes at that point. So, while I was passed out sleeping Mom hung up the clothes and they dried before morning.

Before I left home I made two 11x17 inch copies of calendars - one for February and one for March. Nice to know that I've still got over a week left in February and haven't started the March calendar yet! Although from experience, I know that at the beginning of trips time seems to slow down, and the further you get into a trip, the more time seems to speed up. The same goes for life. As a child it seem forever until we grow up, and then once you're out of school life just starts to speed by. Before you know it, ten and twenty years have gone by and it seems like just a few. That's part of why I'm here. Carpe Diem! Seize the day. If you don't seize it, life will just slip on past you like a ghost in the night and disappear into so much vapor.

All my Lindblad friends – I miss you! I think about our time on the Explorer every day and miss the excitement of getting ready for a trip in the zodiac or ashore. Looking through my photographs again has been so much fun. That time seems to be fading quickly into the background – but I know I've gained some fantastic friends from that time. What a privilege it was to sail with all of you! When asked what part of my life I'd like to live through again I've always said my semester in Germany while in college – I think our time in Antarctica is giving that answer a run for its money!

We've met all the folks on our tour now. Everyone is very nice, and all from the U.S. Of course, I am the youngest, by far, which is ok. I've always liked hanging out with people older than myself. When I was a kid I preferred to be with the adults instead of the kids. Three of the couples here are from places I used to live – Loveland and Windsor, Colorado and from Santa Barbara, California. It's been fun to reminisce about some of my old hangouts.

From 12:30 p.m. until about 4:00 p.m. we took a walk and headed across the water from Auckland to an island called Davenport. Seems like a cute little island; lots of tourists and locals go there on day trips. The Food and Wine Festival was in full swing while we were there. There was a charge to go in, so we simply walked around the edge of it and looked in. People were walking around with really good smelling food and little glasses of wine.

We had dinner at a local restaurant back on the mainland right in the harbor area, just a few minutes walk from the hotel. Service was quite slow, but we've heard that is normal, and it was quite a small restaurant, so I think 17 people were quite a feat to feed all at once. They were so busy that we were supposed to keep our silverware because there wasn't any more that was clean. But I didn't know that when I piled our salad plates together along with our silverware, so when they came by to pick it up and asked us to keep the silverware, we didn't know whose was whose. There was probably about a half an hour between courses during which I went out scouting for silverware – specifically for forks – but there were none to be had. Good to know for future reference that it might be a good idea to hang onto the fork you're given at the start! Mom and I both had the salmon, which is locally caught and very fresh. It was very good. For dessert we had New Zealand's Hokey Pokey ice cream – which is vanilla with little toffee balls inside, and apparently is New Zealander's favorite ice cream flavor after vanilla.

Afterwards we walked slowly home through the lighted streets. Some of the wrought iron railings along the harbor area had bright blue lights lighting up the ironwork. It was very nice, blue and glowy. I must have gone right to sleep as soon as I got home. So amazing to crawl into a clean, cool bed of white sheets at the end of a long, hot, tiring day. Ahhhhh. Goodnight!

HOLY HIKOI!

MONDAY, FEBRUARY 22, 2010

I woke up early and laid in bed thinking about stuff. Stuff like "What on earth are we going to do today?" How silly that we're in Auckland with a free afternoon and we don't know how we're going to spend the afternoon. Just before breakfast I downloaded an "Auckland tourism" app for my iPhone that lists attractions and things to do around the area. After looking through all our options there were only a few things that looked like good options – a hot air balloon ride and a historical living museum. The balloon ride was a little too expensive for us, and the historical place looked like a cross between Williamsburg and Springfield, IL.

Our group took the "Link" bus down the road a few miles to St. Mary's Cathedral, which was the site of Sir Edmund Hillary's funeral. This cathedral was originally built across the street from

where the building currently is. They moved it as an entire building, by closing down the street, raising it up on rollers, and rolling
it across the street, finally turning it ninety degrees from its original
orientation. It's a lovely building; very Episcopal looking. It's in an
area called Parnell, which is a cute little neighborhood with gingerbread–trimmed homes and little antique and boutique shops sitting
next to modern housewares, furniture, and bathroom fixture stores.
This neighborhood feels a little like perhaps we're not in the U.S., in
contrast to Queen Street in central Auckland, which feels just like
being in any large town in America. Parnell has some great character. Lovely, giant, old trees, well attended gardens, beautiful flowers,
and homes that look like they could be in a cute English village.

Then we met our guide, Afina, who is Maori. She gave us some
Maori history and cultural information as we walked around the
grounds of the museum. Our guide, Graham, had taught us the
word used for greetings in Maori which is pronounced "key–ora."
So when we met her we tried out our new word. That reminded

one of our folks of a call she'd gotten from her grandson when he was visiting Australia. He said, "Grandma, I can speak Australian!" When asked what he could say, he said, "G'day mate!" with a perfect Australian accent.

Afina told us that the Maori came originally from Tahiti. They left because of warfare. Originally they came to New Zealand, looked around, and left a few people behind to start a new community. They came in canoes, one family per canoe. Only the strongest, those most able to survive, and those most able to reproduce originally came. With them they brought dogs for breeding, for food and for their skins.

The settling of New Zealand by the Maori was much like the settling of the west in America. If you found a place you liked, you stuck your stake in the ground and claimed it as yours. That's what the Maori did. If they landed on a beach and saw that a stake was in the ground, they knew it was already claimed. However, they didn't always play by the rules. Sometimes they'd take out another stake and put in their own, a distance further inland – making sure to ensure their stake looked really old so they could claim their stake was in the ground first.

Afina talked about how family units live together and that it's typically the grandparents' role to bring up the children. The older you get the more "Mana" you have. Mana is knowledge and power. This is a word I heard on Easter Island, used with the same meaning. Family and ancestry is very important to the Maori. The same is true with the Rapa Nui. As Maori introduce themselves they tell who they are by who their family is – their father and mother and their grandfathers and grandmothers. When meeting a Maori in the traditional way you may never find out what their name is. It would appear rude to walk up and ask them what their name is. What is important in the culture is who the family is.

When a Maori became a Christian, he or she would take the name of the missionary who baptized them. So there are a lot of families now with the names of Kendall, Hall and Thompson, a few of the missionaries in New Zealand in the 1800's.

After our Hikoi we paid $5NZ admission to the Auckland museum. I believe the official name is The Auckland War Memorial Museum. One of the floors is dedicated to information about the wars. This museum reminded me of the Museum of Science and Industry in Chicago. What a lot of fantastic displays they have. On the first floor, which is called the Ground Level, are all kinds of artifacts from all over the South Pacific islands – places like Samoa, Niue, Salomon Islands, Tahiti, Society Islands and I could go on and on. Easy to forget what a huge number of Islands are in this part of the world. When thinking about sailing around the world, it would be easy to take a year just to sail around the South Pacific islands. We saw the most ornate shell and whale tooth necklaces. Breastplates made out of shells and bone, tools made out of obsidian, bone and wood, detailed and slightly creepy masks.

Both the museum restaurant and store were very nice. The restaurant had great healthy and fresh food choices. I opted for a Greek salad and Mom got a ham and cheese pastry which came with mincemeat sauce, which was surprisingly good. How interesting that a little sweet can add dimension and flavor to a dish. It was a little like chutney, I suppose.

Mom was trying to get cash from the ATM at the museum, but it didn't accept her type of card. We were just turning away when we heard my name being called by a male voice. I turned around and it was Mark and Sam from Easter Island – the couple from Britain who stayed in the room next to me at Te'Ora! Wow!! "They're not supposed to be here yet," I thought to myself. I introduced them to Mom and had to ask Mark's name, one more time. Why is it that some people's names just don't stick in my head? I don't know what that is. I asked how Tahiti was and they said, "We don't know. We only got to see the airport." The airline had cancelled their flight out and so they could either fly right back out and on to Auckland or they could extend their stay and stay longer than planned. Since they had reservations for a mini–van they couldn't pick it up late. What a wonderful surprise to see them and so unexpected! We talked for about 15 minutes and then went our separate ways. They have four weeks here in New Zealand, five in Australia and a short stay in Singapore before flying home.

One the way back we saw a Thai restaurant called "Siam I Am." Punny (funny and a pun)!

Laundry time! The laundry is on the 2nd floor and we're on the 6th floor, $2NZ per load and the same to dry. Not bad. The last laundry washing was taken care by Mom so this one is my turn. Time to wash the jeans. How fantastic. Clean jeans. My college roommate, from my semester in Germany, would be appalled, if we went back in time, by how long those jeans have been worn before being washed. I remember she would wear a pair of jeans once, then wash them, and then iron them. As I remember, that habit didn't last for the whole semester, she eventually started to wear them more than once between washings.

Sitting on my bed, air conditioner on as well as the television, I'm taking an Olympic break. I'm so happy to have a little ice–skating and hockey watching time. It's USA against Canada. The U.S. is up by one goal with 12 minutes left. Wait, now we're up by 2. Whoo hoo! But nothing will ever match the U.S. against the Russians all those years ago in the Olympics. Now 5 to 3. What a great game. I wonder if this is live or if it's pre recorded?? We win!! Ahh, there's nothing like a little winter Olympics. Four years ago I was a little busy and don't think I watched any of the Olympics. This is a much better year. Whenever I watch high–speed sports like downhill skiing I always hear the music in my head and the television spot where the announcer says "The thrill of victory and the agony of defeat," which is accompanied by wonderful thrilling footage of incredible ski wipeouts. Gee, that's from a long time ago – I was a kid when that was on TV – although it was on TV for many, many years.

Here are a few examples of signs I found interesting or funny. I love some of the phraseology here. Found on an antique shop's front door - "Back in a tick" is a great way to say "back in a minute." And then we saw some sweets in a middle eastern shop. The signs under them indicated they were called "barfi." Mmmmm, mango barfi. Yum! They had lots of flavored barfi – fig and almond and a bunch I can't remember. Barfi is a confection from India that is made from condensed milk and sugar. From this base many flavors can be added. Barfi is derived from the Hindi word "baraf" which means "snow." Plain barfi can look similar to ice or snow. The barfi reminds me of a brand of sweet Mexican snacks found in shops in Texas, called "Bimbo." Tee hee. I know it's childish, but that label makes me giggle every time I see it.

LAURA VAE GATZ

ON TO ROTORUA
TUESDAY, FEBRUARY 23, 2010

For some reason I wake up early here. Perhaps it's because I get tired so early and go to bed by about 9:00 p.m. Waking up around 4:45 or 5:00 a.m., I then lie in bed and my brain starts to think. The best plan of action is to get up, grab my computer and do a little writing. Otherwise I'm just lying there thinking – and you know a woman lying around thinking is never a good thing!

It's a good thing I like the temperature in my room. Although there is a remote to control the AC, which is located high above the main door, I can't get the unit to respond. Oh, I know I could call the front counter, but it's not such a big deal the way it is. These air conditioning units are the same ones as in the Caribbean. They're usually attached to a wall, placed up high, and are operated only by remote. And they're very effective. I don't think I've ever seen this kind in the U.S.

In the elevator your key must be inserted into a slot in order to go to your floor. That's a security feature used since the elevator is accessible to the public, being just down an open "alley" off Queen Street. And in each room, there's a slot to stick your room key into, just inside the door. That's the "key" to turn on the lights and electricity. The other "key" is to remember to take your room key with you when you leave the room! You'd almost think it would be easier to remember if it's always in the same place, but it doesn't seem to work that way.

I'm all packed up and ready to go this morning, although I'm having difficulty getting everything to fit into my one remaining piece of luggage. I've weeded through all the extraneous paper and tossed out what I can. Oh, I do dislike traveling with so much stuff! Half my things are "just in case" items. Although they might not be necessary here in the city, because they could be bought easily, they might be needed while I'm in Africa. So they stay with me, for the most part. There are a few things that have been ejected – an almost empty hair product bottle, a map, a folder that takes up too much space, and a spray bottle taking up too much room that hasn't been touched since it was originally packed.

We did a lot on our way to Rotorua today. Many of the stops were surprises, which was nice. If you don't know exactly what you're going to be doing, then when you find out, often it's a pleasant surprise.

First we took a drive through some of the swanky areas of Auckland – up on a hill overlooking the bay. The homes were beautiful, some old ones with gingerbread trimming, some new ones, which were very modern and were a definite contrast with the older homes. Then we headed out of the city.

Man, the traffic is something else. The streets in Auckland just aren't that big. We passed very long lines of cars, all in a single line, waiting to get through stoplights. If you live outside of the city you can expect a 2–3 hour commute time into the city. There is public transportation in the form of trains, but it is an older system that hasn't been updated – and the lines are the same ones they had 40 years ago. Our guide mentioned that there is a negative sentiment regarding using public transportation. I suppose that's the same in the U.S., except for the movement to be green and limit the burning of fossil fuels.

One of the common birds in the city seems to be the Pukeko, also known as a Purple Swamp Hen. It's a large bird that walks around on the lawns and in fields. I would say it's about the size of a small Canada goose. It has long whitish legs and a black body highlighted by a dark blue chest and a red beak and front of the head. It's very beautiful.

Approximately three months ago (November 2009), cell phone use while driving was completely banned in New Zealand, although there have been a few sightings by our group of folks not abiding by this new law. One of our folks saw a young guy driving a motor scooter with both his hands off the handlebars – texting away.

One of our fun unexpected stops was at a kiwi farm. I think the most appropriate terminology from the way it looked, even if it's not technically correct, is a "kiwi vineyard." There are several kinds of kiwis – the two main kinds being, Hayward, the kind we get in the States, the fuzzy ones, and the Golden kiwi, which does not have a fuzzy outside. The kiwi was originally known as the Chinese gooseberry until New Zealanders started exporting it and renamed it kiwifruit. The vineyard we stopped at was so interesting. Because it's important that the fruit does not touch anything while it is grow- ing, it is grown up short fences and then across on trellises, forming a low long corridor of kiwi plants. I totally enjoy seeing where my food comes from!

On another kiwi note, I seem to be over my irrational fear of kiwis. It's not as if I thought one was hiding under my bed at night, it's more like they just seemed a little creepy. Is it a banana, or a strawberry, and what's up with the little black seeds inside of an otherwise very smooth fruit? The kiwis here are fantastic. So fresh, and the seeds don't seem to be an issue for me any more. Also, I figured out how to eat one – cut it in half diagonally and scoop it out with a spoon much like you would with an avocado.

Our group had an exciting day yesterday. My staying home "ill" was the least of the excitement. During a hike along the edge of the volcano, Mt. Tarawera, part of the group decided to go down into the crater and down what they call "the scree," which is a steep slope of very small light porous volcanic rocks. As you can imagine, its a little like going down a large sand dune, and each step carries you several feet. Although walking sticks were provided, one group member lost her balance and started to roll down the slope. It was about another 400 feet to the bottom. She was rolling down, bouncing and screaming, which alerted the guide who was not very close to her. Folks on the hike said they'd never seen anyone take such large flying steps and move so fast. He got over to her and planted himself in her path to stop the rolling, which worked. She did stop, but not before getting some bruises and scrapes on her face, palms and arms, and badly bruising the guide's sternum. She was fine to walk out of the crater but was taken to the health care center to be checked out. Many cinders were removed from her face and hands. I'm so glad she's ok. She's a bit sore today but in good spirits and I daresay feeling better than I am.

Mom encouraged me to get dressed and go into town with her once she returned from the volcano. I'd been up already, showered and stretched, and so it was a relatively easy thing to get ready in a few minutes. We went to the Rotorua Museum, which used to be a spa for people coming from all over to "take the cure." Rotorua sits on a very thin crust of earth, much like areas of Yellowstone National Park. Our hotel, in fact, was right on the edge of some of the hot springs and geyser activity. At night with the window open I could hear the boiling mud in the mud pool just outside my window. I could also smell the sulfurous emissions, but that's another story!

The historic Government house, which is now a museum, reminded Mom and me of Jumer's Castle Lodge, the German restaurant and hotel in Urbana, Illinois. The building is black and white with German "Fachwerk" timbering. In front of the building is a large area of fields for various sports, also known as the Government Gardens. The only sports we could identify were croquette and lawn bowling, which looks a lot like Bocci Ball. When we asked one of the gentlemen decked out entirely in white if that's what it was, he mumbled something to his comrade about us probably being American. He asked where we were from, and then started to discuss some of the differences. We both have several large balls and one small one. And the goal of the game is to get the large balls closest to the small ball. One of the differences is that their large balls are not spheres. They are squished so as to not be symmetrical. If you were to create a perfectly round ball, then take your palms, one on each side and push in, pushing the opposite side flatter than the other sides, that would be the shape of ball they use. So, the way you hold it for pitching or rolling makes all the difference in where it goes. Many of the rolls were intentionally rolled out to the side so that at the end they would curve back in towards the little white ball. Fascinating.

Another interesting aspect was both their clothes and their manners. Players were dressed entirely in white from their shoes and socks to their hats. And they seemed to act as if what they were doing was high society and very posh. Perhaps it is considered just that in New Zealand! As if they were at the country club, and not just anyone could play. "Tup, tup. Jolly good of you to play today ol' chap. Charlie's whites seem to be a bit dingy today. "

✦✈✦✈✦✈✦

Yesterday evening was a fantastic experience at Te Puia. Te Puia is a little bit like the Irish Medieval feast my friend Beth and I attended a few years ago in Ireland. This one has a Maori focus to it. We had a guide for several hours that took us through the park, showing us information on the migration of Maori people from their homeland, explaining how they lived and showing us replicas of a village. Then we had a little tea out on a terrace surrounded by steaming pools of hot sulfurous water. Our corn had been cooked in one of these pools, in large woven baskets of flat plant fiber. This must have been a real benefit to the Maori that lived here in the past. They wouldn't have had to always build a fire in order to cook their food. And just like our food doesn't taste like gas if cooked on a gas stove, this food didn't taste like sulfur. We had a lovely meal of fresh breads with lovely dipping sauces, corn on the cob, prawns and oysters, and our choice of wine, beer or kiwi juice. I stuck with water.

After, we had a little trolley ride around the thermal area. Cement slabs have been built to sit and lie on that are over a hot area. This heats up the cement and makes it like one big heating pad. Good for the back! I was tempted to lie down on my stomach and see if the heat would make my stomach feel better.

While we were there, the geysers erupted, blowing more water into the air than normal. Once the hot steam hits the cooler air, it turns into rain and mist, covering any unsuspecting visitors in a fine shower. Around the corner from the mist, water cascaded down into a river, over years and years worth of mineral deposits, white, tan and orange. Some of the blowholes were lined with a coating of pure pastel yellow sulfur.

Te Puia is also a school for carving and weaving. Each year they select a small number of students to study the carving techniques of their ancestors so that knowledge is not lost.

The evening portion of our time there started with a traditional Maori welcome, with the Maori warriors coming out of their meetinghouse to greet us. It was a mixture of tribal dance, posturing, intimidation, and welcome. A random man from our group was chosen to be our chief. He was the one who walked forward to accept the leaf thrown at his feet as a sign of welcome. Then the group went into the meeting hall. All in all there were probably about 150 of us. Next we were treated to some traditional dances, songs, and dances. The men wore short, heavy swinging, grass skirts; the one man with an upper leg tattoo, had some of the grass strands broken off on the side where his tattoo was, for better viewing I think. And he didn't have a badly shaped thigh either...The women wore woven tops and cummerbunds with long straight skirts; some had feather trimming on the bottom. In one of my favorite dances four long wooden sticks were used to make tapping sounds and then were thrown from one dancer to the next.

Dinner was very tasty. Probably the best food I've had since arriving on New Zealand. The starter was smoked salmon on top of mushroom risotto. My entree was stuffed chicken over a sweet potato patty with watercress. And dessert was some mango ice cream in a sugar cup with a beautiful chocolate "tiara" sticking out of the top. My meal was a little different than everyone else's, being gluten free, but just as good. My dessert was a gluten free orange and poppy seed pound cake. Yum! Mom wanted to get the recipe to take home.

The first time I've thought about wanting to be home is within the last day when my stomach was having an attack. There would be nothing better than to be in my own bed, cat curled up under the covers by my side, and heating pad on my tummy. Oh, the comforts of home. However, I haven't had that thought except when I'm feeling poorly. It's not that I don't like my life at home, I do. It's fantastic. Awesome job, friends, house...but I like to be traveling and seeing new things, taking photographs of places and things I've never seen, experiencing new cultures and writing about it all.

Throughout my travels I find that native people tend to get cheated out of their lands. It's not an exclusively American thing. Australia, New Zealand, all over South America, the same thing happened over and over again. The natives always seem to get the short end of the stick. While that makes me feel just a little bit less guilty to be an American, it kind of changes my faith in mankind as a whole. We have a tendency to be greedy and take advantage of people.

LAURA VAE GATZ

ON TO QUEENSTOWN
THURSDAY, FEBRUARY 25, 2010

The New Zealand Air flight to Queenstown went from Rotorua through Christchurch and then on to Queenstown. We had about a half an hour layover where we had to get off the plane. "Take your boarding pass with you," they said. It's not always easy to figure out where we put them, but both Mom and I found ours. Mom was on a mission to call a friend who is studying in town, and I was on a mission to find some food because I was starving. First I bought a banana and then talked Mom into calling her friend after we got settled at the hotel, and then we found the bathroom.

On both flights the flight attendants came through with little prepackaged cups of water. Those things crack me up. They're so small; it must be only 4 ounces of water. And they're packaged up like pudding, with the clear plastic bottom and the aluminum foil peel away top. We also got "biscuits" (cookies), and a "sweet" (hard candy). The slightly different words they have for things are so much fun to hear. Overhead bins are overhead lockers.

We had a two and a half hour break once we checked into Millbrook, during which time I broke open one of those air activated heating pads and lay down on the bed to take a little snooze for about a half an hour. Then it was time to get ready. Shower. Hairwash. Ahhhh, lovely. Then over to Mom's room and up to reception to wait for our ride into the cute little village we're right outside of Arrowtown, which reminds me a little of Grand Lake in Colorado – a cute little main street and not much else but residences. Raised walkways and cute little shops, even an old–fashioned candy store with all the candy in jars in the window.

A little grocery store was open. It wasn't a full grocery store but it was certainly larger than a convenience store. Our entire group of sixteen found it and were like kids in a candy store. You'd think we hadn't had access to shopping or food in a week. A lot of the women were gathered around the top–opening freezer with the sliding glass doors deciding which Magnum ice cream bar to buy. Magnum is my favorite ice cream bar when I'm traveling outside of the U.S. It's just a good quality, solid bar with great chocolate on the outside. Yum! I headed straight for the produce section, which was small. Just when I thought they weren't going to have any bananas, I spotted them around the corner. They didn't look very fresh, but I think they'd just been in the fridge, which turns them brown.

I spotted Mom's favorite licorice, which is hard to find in the States, and although she wanted to buy some, she didn't have anywhere to put it – our suitcases are both bursting at the seams. She and I are the only ones that have one small roll aboard suitcase as our only suitcase. Everyone else has one large suitcase, you know, the kind that always weighs at least 50 lbs, no matter how lightly you try to pack, the kind in which a small person could fit. The kind you wouldn't want to try to lift fully loaded.

LAURA VAE GATZ

TREK TO MILFORD SOUND
FRIDAY, FEBRUARY 26, 2010

The golf resort where we are staying, Millbrook, is fantastic, and SO much better than the place we stayed in Rotorua. It's just on a different level. It has rooms in small buildings that make them look and feel like little cottages. Many rooms look out onto the golf course. The grounds are nicely landscaped, and nicely paved pathways lead you across bridges spanning streams, and around the golf course. This place not only has hand soap, but shampoo, conditioner, body soap, shoe shine, sewing kit and bubble bath.

Oh, I slept so well; I don't even remember sleeping...except that when the alarm went off I was in another world, having a dream. Waking up on this tour is interesting. We change hotels often enough that I'm briefly disoriented upon waking up. As soon as the light is on I remember, but it's an interesting feeling not knowing exactly what is around me...and what configuration it's in. You know, most of our lives we're in the same place, doing the same things, and can make it to the bathroom or the kitchen with our eyes closed, knowing where each piece of furniture and door frame is.

An interesting story was told to us about when President Clinton came to stay at Milbrook. The Secret Service had arrived ahead of time and thoroughly checked everything out. The first morning after the president arrived gun shots were heard ringing out. Everything was quickly "locked-down" until the Secret Service discovered that it was opening day for duck hunting!

Our bus driver for the day was Ben. He said there is a tribe hiding out in the bush so if he's hauled off the bus, there is a medical kit somewhere under the front seat. Also we need to pay attention to where the emergency exits are. There are little red hammers to smash our way out of the bus if it comes to that. We all laughed. He said, "you won't be laughing if you need to use them!" So we laughed again.

Mom was able to get the front seat behind the driver, which is a good thing because she needs to be able to see out the front window so she doesn't get motion sickness. It was an interesting day sitting up front. I was able to talk with the driver and ask him questions when I missed some of the facts and stories he was telling us. Ben has published a book as well, and it was for sale at the dock we sailed from around Milford Sound. Ben was very entertaining, telling interesting stories about growing up on a farm in the area and about how things were back then and how things have changed. At the beginning of our trip he recommended that we go into this trip today with a sense of adventure and humor – a good recommendation, as the day was a long and exciting one.

Today was a trip of contrasts. We left the jagged schist rock and drove into a flat country of five rivers. Then past hard rock, steep and deep, that gets 10 times more rain than other areas. We had fantastic weather considering all the rain this area gets. We've been unbelievably lucky and blessed with good weather. Along the drive, Ben told of stories of the building of the road we were driving, the hardships of the workers, and how avalanches and rock slides plague the area during all times of the year.

One of the first lakes outside of Queenstown was Lake Wakatipu, where the water is 98% pure and apparently the other 2% is fish – trout, salmon and long finned eels that grow as large around as a fencepost and as long as two meters. If you went for a swim and saw one of them, you might figure out how to run on water, Ben said. At the end of the lake is Kingston, a small village. It used to be a big milling town but that industry has since died out here.

The towns in this area sprang up and grew quickly when gold was found in this area in the middle to late 1800's. The sheep here are merino sheep, an exceptionally soft wool, which is used for fine suits and other clothing. And, apparently also used in concrete!

This whole area was created and formed by the glaciers. Much of the area is a glacial moraine with large boulders scattered across the countryside. The lakes are where the glaciers carved out the land. Along with rocks and boulders, gold was brought down out of the hills. One farmer apparently mined his land and brought up over 50 million dollars of gold. The folks seriously started to consider building the Milford Sound road in order to more easily get the gold out of the area.

An interesting fiber combination sold here is lamb's wool and possum fur. It's very soft and warm. New Zealand has a huge possum problem. Because of their diet, they damage the local ecology, and so it's very nice that their fur can be used for clothing and accessories. The possums eat a lot of trees, so everyone is encouraged to buy possum. Their saying is "Buy possum, save a tree."

Back in the day, settlers would bring their favorite trees with them from their homeland, so today there is a great mixture of trees along the lakeshores. Along the road we see several things used to dissuade the possums from climbing the trees and power poles. Tin strips are put part way up the power poles to keep the possums' claws from being able to grip the poles. Open-ended metal barrels are place around the bottom of trees when they're planted and then the tree grows up protected, but eventually the trunk gets so thick that it bursts the barrel open.

Here are the facts. What we call a "possum" in the U.S. is actually an Opossum – Latin name of Didelphis viginiana. The main species in the U.S. is commonly called the Virginia Opossum. It is a marsupial and an omnivore. It will eat carrion, fruit, worms, frogs birds and snakes. The New Zealand possum is actually a possum, not an opossum. It's Latin name is Trichosurus velpecula, with a common name of the brushtail possum.

New Zealand used to export a lot of possum skins, which was the perfect industry for them; they got rid of their possum problem and made money from it. Then in the 1990's Sophia Loren started her successful "no natural fur" campaign and then the New Zealand fur trade went in the tank. I'm not sure if their wool/possum blend is exported, but it can be found in shops all over New Zealand and is really quite lovely.

Each strand of possum fur is a hollow shaft, like polar bear fur, which makes it exceptionally warm. It's also soft and light. The cloth that they have created is 60% Merino wool and 40% possum. Really lovely fur, and so incredibly warm. I found these very neat red leather and red fur gloves, which have just the thumb and the palms, without any fingers. They would have been perfect for the Antarctic. If Lindblad is able to arrange their "Russian Arctic" trip, maybe I'll bring them along for that trip!

The local organic ice cream company is called Orgasmic Ice Cream. The short story is that Peter and Glenys Williams were dairy farmers on the north island of New Zealand. After both being sick, they realized that their cows were also suffering from unhealthy conventional farming practices that are used at so many of our farms today. "There must be a better way!" they decided, and so moved their farm to the south island and changed the way they farmed. Becoming organic was a process, and in the year 2000 they achieved an international Organic status with Biogro, New Zealand's leading organic certification agency. After selling their produce at local farmer's markets, they also started to make and sell their own ice cream. With a growing demand and market for their ice cream, they realized that this was a little out of the realm of their main business, being farmers. So a search started for the right company to make it – and Deep South was the answer. Deep South worked with Peter and Glenys to create their brand of organic ice cream. Their current flavors are Virgin Vanilla, Kinky Karamel and Strawberry Seduction, Chocolate Climax.

Lots and lots of sheep dot the landscape. Sometimes they're so thick I find it hard to determine if they're really sheep or if they're rocks.

We just passed the booming town of Garston with its large post office – a red wooden paneled building about 6 feet by 8 feet. Just enough room for the postmistress to get inside and put the mail in the post office boxes, which are accessible by the public on the outside of the building. Such a quaint little building, just larger than a two–hole outhouse! Garston also has one hotel that is quite busy on Friday and Saturday nights, and two churches where the hotel guests can confess their sins on Sunday...

This area is big on taking tourists heli–skiing as well as heli–fishing. Talk about extreme sports! I had no idea there was "heli–fishing."

Our driver's father used to live and farm out here. He would light a fire on the railroad tracks when he wanted the train to stop and pick him up.

There are windmills on the hill to our left. Two of them are on the driver's nephew's land, which is funny because the driver's brother always was pounded by the wind during chores and now he's getting a small compensation from the company that owns the windmills. So he's had the last laugh on the wind.

Flax plants are interesting and useful. They have long flat fronds much like a very tall grass with shoots of seeds sticking up around three to four feet. The plant was and is used for many things. As our guide at Te Puia showed us it can be used for skirts or ropes, capes and fishing nets.

The Fiordland, which is the area aroundMilford Sound, can get up to 15 meters of rain per year, which is about 40 feet! Amazing.

Outside of Milford Sound is the Tasman Sea. There are many unique animals here – e.g., geckos, and the flightless Takahe bird - and also unique endemic plants. Manuka, also known as the tea tree, is a plant used for flavoring food; manuka honey is derived from this bush. This honey is used overseas for dressing wounds... it's one of those plants that you're not sure if you should have in your kitchen or bathroom.

The sheep here are shorn once a year in the shearing shed – a building open on all sides with a roof. Imagine. The shearers try to get through as many sheep as they can in a nine–hour period. The blood is flying, sweat dripping down hard–working backs and faces, dogs barking, flies buzzing. It's certainly not a sight for the faint hearted.

The latitude here is roughly the same in the southern hemisphere as Portland, Oregon, or Bangor Maine in the northern hemisphere. Interesting.

The road to Milford sound was constructed by men who were not paid very well, even though their jobs were incredibly difficult. They had to drain swamps, cut through stone and haul it out, and live up here during all that time in primitive conditions. Baths were in the river; washing clothes by hand. The road opened up in 1953. New Zealand knew that if they could get the road to Milford Sound open, that it would put New Zealand on the map for tourism. It more than did that; it's also brought film crews and car companies. Car companies such as BMW, Mercedes and Jaguar like to film automobile commercials here because of the fantastic scenery and curving road.

We are on State Highway 94 (also known as the Milford Road). The tunnel we drove through is called Homer Tunnel. It is 1.3 km long (4/5 of a mile). It drops four hundred feet in elevation. And there's no lining, the inside of the tunnel is just bare unlined granite rock. Picks, crowbars, and drills were the only tools used to carve it out, starting in 1935. It took nine years of digging to get through. World War II interrupted the digging, and although the other side of the mountain was reached in 1940, an avalanche in 1945 destroyed the eastern entrance to the tunnel. Three people lost their lives in avalanches during the decades of construction. Although the tunnel is wide enough to allow for two vehicles, it's not quite big enough to allow for two tour busses to pass each other, so during the busy season the tunnel alternates directions. Depending on your luck in timing, you could drive right through or be in for a little bit of a wait. Once through the tunnel it's about a 10–15 minute drive to Milford Sound.

Rabbits were introduced as a gaming opportunity in the mid 1800's. Stoats and weasels were brought in the 1880's to keep the rabbit population under control. Stoats are mean little things about 6 inches long and 2–3 inches high and are related to the weasel, mink and ferret. They've been known to attack humans when being let out of traps or if a human gets between them and their dinner.

Although the introduced predators did kill some rabbits, which is the reason they were introduced into new Zealand, they seemed to prefer the flightless birds instead. They were easy to catch. The theory is that some of New Zealand's birds became flightless because they had no natural predators – no animal they needed to fly away from. They started to get into the habit of hanging out on the ground. Then after losing the will to fly they lost their ability to fly, with their wings turning into just vestigial wings and not wings that could actually help them fly. Then predators arrived on the scene and they were in trouble, unable to fly away. This is yet another good example of the introduction of non–native animals and the resulting unanticipated consequences, such as the hawks on Easter Island, or the Beavers in Ushuaia. Each time I hear of animals being intentionally introduced into an environment, a little voice in my head says, "Oh no, not again! Don't you know that's not going to work?"

Stoats have eliminated close to 100 species of birds in the south island. The stoats got even lazier than capturing birds; they found it extremely easy to eat the birds' eggs. One more thing about the stoats – they birth between five to twelve babies at once. Many females are already pregnant by the time they leave Mommy's nest.

No wonder they're all over the place.

As we're driving along, Ben makes random, interesting comments about local language, phrases, or manners. Road kill might be referred to as "squashums." New Zealanders may go out of their way to hit a possum. They feel like it's their national duty. In mountainous areas you might experience a "hill slip" or "running rocks" (rock slides and falling rocks). And in regard to manners of some of the other bus drivers in the country, they might be described as "having the manners of a hungry dog," meaning that there may be an occasion where we might need to stop quickly because another bus made a stupid move. When referring to the scenery, the bus driver might say that "this is a good valley to take some photos wildly out the side windows, but not an oil painting stop," meaning that we are not going to stop all the way, only slow down.

Mitre Peak is the big peak in Milford Fiord...the most photographed feature in NZ...

We had perfect, beautiful sunny weather for our Milford Sound cruise. We saw bottlenose dolphins off the port side of the boat, a pod of them about 7 or 8 strong. Feeling in my element, wind in my hair, rise and fall of the deck beneath my feet, I was camped out on the bow of the Sinbad, sitting cross–legged. Then I spied smaller animals porpoising out of the water in front of our ship – the little blue penguin, also previously known as the fairy penguin. At sixteen inches tall, these little guys weigh in at just over two pounds. They are often mistaken for ducks, on first glance.

We sailed past beautiful mountains, misty in the distance, the midday sun casting hazy rays past the edges, and deep shadows. Waterfalls cascaded from lofty peaks, sometimes evaporating before reaching the water below. Our boat stopped at one waterfall, pulling up close enough that the spray shrouded the bow in rainbows. The captain had given a warning on the loudspeaker, warning photographers to beware of the mist. I stayed on the bow with my camera out, capturing the falls, rainbows, mist and greenery until the last second when the wind caught the mist and blew it towards the boat. It was magical. The sound from the falling water drowned out any other sound; it was just us, and the waterfall. The rest of the world faded into nothingness.

DART RIVER JET BOAT
SATURDAY, FEBRUARY 27, 2010

After we got on the bus, as we were driving out of Queen-stown, the bus driver got a call on his cell phone to see if he'd pick up some newspapers that were on the side of the road and deliver them. Once he'd picked them up, he looked through the bunch that had addresses on them, putting them in order according to how we would drive past them. It was quite funny because he didn't slow down much to toss the newspapers out of the window. Many of them didn't land in a very good spot. One actually landed in the middle of the road. I'm sure those farmers have to hunt each day to find their newspaper if today was any indication of the normal state of things.

We drove past Rees station, which is one of the largest farms in the area. They have sheep and cattle. The sheep stay up in the surrounding mountains until the snow starts to fall in the autumn. Around October the owners fire up the helicopter, toss in the sheep dogs and head up to the mountains. The dogs get off and do their work, bringing the sheep down the mountain for their once–a–year shearing.

We just stopped at a sign on the side of the road that said "Paradise," and under that, on the same sign it said "no exit." I just had to get off the bus to take a photograph. How funny!

As we were coming up on the river just past the town of Glenorchry, we approached some lovely land with beautiful views where many commercials and movies are made. Most of the crews don't actually stay there overnight; most of them stay in Queenstown. We stopped the bus just off the road where a film crew was doing some work. Apparently they haven't divulged what they're working on. They've leased the land for a few months and also some of the farmer's cows, which they are apparently training to carry saddles.

Some of the reasons so many movies are made here are: the strong U.S. dollar vs. the New Zealand dollar, the infrastructure here, the small number of crew strikes, and the seasons being opposite from the northern hemisphere, which allows American companies to shoot a month before the release of a commercial instead of a year.

Some of the movies that had scenes shot in this area are the forest scenes from the Narnia movies, The Lovely Bones, and Vertical Limit.

The jet boat we went on sat about 20–25 people. A jet boat is just like a jet ski. The motor takes in water from the front and expels it very quickly out the back. I didn't understand our driver 100% of the time about the physics of it, but let's just say that a lot of water is pumped very quickly underneath the boat. This is what makes it so fast. These boats can go up to about 80 miles per hour, I understand. Before getting onto the boat we were first given life preservers, then long black raincoats, with hoods, and Velcro clasps to keep them closed. Although good for keeping us dry, they did get a bit hot when the boat stopped and the sun beat down on us, heating up the black material. We drove up the river only about three kilometers, but down about thirty. This river, the Dart River, is a constantly changing river. It is a glacial melt water river, so it is very silty because the water constantly brings the rocks and silt down out of the mountains. The area of Glenorchy has been able to reclaim quite a bit of land over the last few decades because of all the silt. The silt builds up to a point that where there used to be river, there is now land that can be used as farmland.

This river is called a "braided river" which means that the water doesn't flow through just one channel, it flows through many, ever–changing channels. So it's not actually possible for the guides to memorize or learn the river because every time it rains or there is an increased flow of water from the glaciers, the river changes again. Each day is new. The drivers are trained to be able to figure out if the channel should be safe to go through. I think the rule must be "if there is water flowing down it, chances are that it's deep enough, and that it's not a dead end." The jet boats, once they're going fast, only draw four inches of water. And it doesn't matter if the boat goes over some rocks; the hull is very strong and won't get a hole in it unless terribly abused.

One of the most exciting times on the river was when we would do 360's, you know, donuts, on the water. The driver would give us a warning, by putting his hand up in the air, circle his finger, and give us several seconds to put our cameras away and prepare. To prepare we were told to hang on to the rails in front of us. I also found it helpful to spread my feet out wide for stability. What fun! The driver seems to be able to control the spin enough to choose whether or not he placed us in or outside of the spraying wall of water. We only got wet once or twice. I was tempted to keep my camera out once to see if I could capture a video, but I wasn't confident in my ability to put it away quickly enough if I saw a wall of water coming towards me.

I slept great that night until Dad, calling from the U.S., woke me up at 3:00 a.m. with news about the Santiago earthquake and Tsunami Warning, wondering where exactly we were in New Zealand. We are in the center of the south island, south, but not near a coast, so we're fine. But it did make me stop and look at Google Earth to figure out where we are exactly, and where we are going. Today we are headed north and west, so we won't be affected by any Tsunami. Christchurch would have been affected if it had not been low tide at the time the wave reached land.

LAURA VAE GATZ

PINOT NOIR COUNTRY
SUNDAY, FEBRUARY 28, 2010

B ungee jumping. The first jump "ever" was done from the Eiffel Tower, and of course the jumper was arrested. New Zealand was the first country that really "took up" the sport. The bridge we visited today was a bridge that was used in the old gold mining days to haul the gold across the chasm that stands between the hills and the road. That is where the bungee jump is. It is forty-three feet high. They used to let you jump for free if you jumped naked, but so many kids were going naked that they stopped that practice. The price board inside the building said one jump is 175NZ. The operators could adjust the bungee so that you could either just touch the water on your way down or be halfway immersed. No thank you!

The valley we are driving through is a big wine area known for its Pinot Noir. This is such a good growing area because the summers are hot and the winters are crisp. The soil structure is different from other areas of New Zealand, and has a large percentage of mica, which is good for drainage. Rose plants grow along the side of the road. These rose plants attract the same kinds of bugs that the grape vines do. So if the rose bushes get diseased, there is a good chance that the vines would be too. They're the vineyards "early warning system." It's kind of like the canary in the mine, but without the instant results.

New Zealand's wine is world renowned. One is called Persnickety Pinot Noir. In 2008 New Zealand's wine production grew 38%. Only in the last few years has New Zealand's production exceeded internal consumption, meaning that wine is just starting to be exported.

We just stopped at Mrs. Jones's Fruit Stand. We are on route 6, outside of Arrowtown about 45 minutes and heading north. What an amazing selection of fruits, honey, nuts, dried and chocolate covered fruits. I haven't seen this variety of fruits since arriving in New Zealand. All of us swarmed over the stalls, tasted some of the dried fruits and plums on offer as samples, and then wandered out to the beautiful rose garden just beyond the fruit stand. Mrs. Jones's Fruit stand reminds me of the Fruit Basket in Beulah, Michigan, just next to the Cherry Hut. Both are really great places and make you stop to rest for a moment, remember what fresh produce is really like, and smile because there are still quaint little farm stands on the side of the road.

Phil and Kath are the proprietors of The Big Picture winery that we visited. What an interesting place. Starting in the "smelling room" we were told how to proceed through the room. In a horseshoe shape were about 45 different snifter sniffers to twirl around and sniff. Each one was an attribute that wine can have, from raspberry to licorice, smoke, plum, honey, etc. This room was designed to awaken our smelling buds and prepare them for the next room, the tasting room, in which we had a flight of six different Pinot Noirs to taste. The room was nicely designed with room for about fifty tasters at once. We were left to ourselves while a movie, with history, information on some of the local vineyards, and tasting instructions, played for about 25 minutes. We went on a "virtual flight" across all the regions on the southern island where wine is produced, viewing from a helicopter's point of view the vineyards and how they're situated in the land. When the helicopter approached a vineyard of one of the wines we were going to taste, we would be virtually introduced to the owners or vintners who would talk about what we were going to taste and take us through looking at the color, smell and taste of the wine. It was a very interesting time. Now we're all tired as an after-effect of the wine. It might be time for a little nap once we get on the bus...

There's something about the movement of the bus, rolling and swaying as it goes around curves, that is just like a sleeping pill to me, and I have to fight to keep my eyes open. I'm interested to find that I can sleep sitting up in a bus. Amazing! I'd thought only men could do that. In the distance I hear our tour guide say, "You're going to want to open your eyes, the scenery is getting quite fantastic." I struggle to open my eyes. My brain has an internal struggle with my body; I feel as if I've been drugged. My eyes open to numerous waterfalls breaking through the lush green forest. "Ahhh, yes, this is beautiful," I think, perking up for a moment. And then my eyes get heavy again and I'm doing the bobbing–head–nap–dance. That's certainly a workout on the neck. Mom is swaying in her seat as well and I know that she's sleeping next to me. As we go around a particularly curvy bend, I hang onto her arm to keep her from falling into the aisle, which I don't think she'd actually do, but it's for good measure, just in case.

Just before arriving at the Franz Josef Hotel we make a beach stop. The trees we've been seeing along the coast are fantastic; old, gnarled, and blown permanently sideways, they're a testament to the ever-present force of the winds in this area.

As we're wrapping up dinner our guide asks if any of us are interested in seeing glow-worms. Yes, yes! We meet a half an hour later at reception, where we head out into the darkness with "torches" (flashlights), walking through town and then into the woods. We walk single file, torches placed strategically throughout the small group of nine. Instructed to hold the flashlights so they're illuminating only the ground, we walk slowly, making sure not to trip on rocks or run into tree trunks. After walking for about five minutes we start to see little fairy lights along the side of the path. It's as if stars have fallen into the forest, and are lying on the ground, glowing. Along the right side is a little copse about ten feet high. The glow worms have a little convention going on in there, and it's just beautiful. Taking turns walking close to them, wondering at their tiny little lights, we silently rotate in and out of the copse. Glow worms are sensitive to light and noise. When we shine lights in their direction they shut off theirs. What a magical experience - otherworldly, really. We turn around and slowly walk back out of the woods, sad to leave the little lights behind, but glad to have the experience. Our beds are calling.

BIG BLUE GLACIER
MONDAY, MARCH 1, 2010

T he luggage gnomes have already been by our rooms to take our luggage to the bus. What a lovely thing to put luggage outside the room and have it automatically vamoosed! We don't have to worry about it until tonight where it automatically appears in our rooms.

From the bus we can see that the weather has closed in and we won't be going on our helicopter ride up to Franz Josef Glacier, but the upside is that the misty weather makes the mountains surrounding us just beautiful. Franz Josef Glacier is on the south island, about in the middle, north to south, and on the west coast, located within Westland National Park. It is 12 kilometers long, and terminates 19 kilometers from the Tasman Sea.

This morning we take a walk along the glacial riverbed up towards the Franz Josef Glacier. It will be a wet morning so we're dressed appropriately with raincoats and umbrellas. The drive to the glacier was only a few minutes from our hotel. Then we walked up the bed of the river, which is mostly rocks, large and small, composed mostly of schist and quartz. Many of the rocks have very thin layers of these two alternating which makes for a great pattern and a beautiful rock. I found it hard to keep walking. Being a natural beachcomber, I wanted to stop and look at all the rocks, which would be impossible, because it's ALL rocks! Mom and I did come up with some really nice specimens. When heading home with my luggage, and someone asks why it's so heavy and inquires as to whether there are rocks inside, I can say "yes" and it will be a true statement.

Our hike started out in a rain forest, which eventually gave way to the glacial moraine of the riverbed. This is one of the few places where a rainforest runs right up to a glacier. One of the other places where you'll find that is in Patagonia, in South America. The green went right up to the edge of the glacier. The forest is so lush and green, with many types of ferns, growing tall, growing small, with complicated or simple fronds, and fronds growing in a circular pattern. All so beautiful! And in the middle of all this are some birds. One is green and white and is a local pigeon, the Kereru that looks like a large parrot. Another is a fantail bird, probably the New Zealand Fantail, and I'm sure there are some sparrows flitting around here as well.

The walk from where we started walking on the riverbed, to the foot of the glacier, was longer than it initially looked to be. The size of the glacier and its distance was easy to misjudge. Other groups had gone before us and we could see them winding their way down the path. They kept getting smaller and smaller until they looked like a long line of ants, and they still weren't at the glacier. Perspective, or the lack of it, is a funny thing. One thing I've started to get more of a grip on during my trip is perspective – you need to change location very often in order to get better perspective, and that's what I've been getting. It's almost as if by flying around the world, my life is coming into focus.

At the "end of the line" (i.e. as far as Mom and I went) there was a little area along the river where we could walk closer to the melt water river to get a great vantage point of the ice cave through which the water was flowing. Intriguing. Secretly, I wondered what it would look like inside, with smooth, undulating blue ice walls. I could almost imagine wading upstream and into the cave, camera at hand, taking photographs and trying to catch my breath while at the same time struggling to keep my balance. Ah well, I can't always be "Adventure Girl," much as I would like to be.

Too much time on the bus. Mom and I have developed a case of "bus butt." I suppose that's better than "cadaver butt," which is the condition resulting from sitting on very cold stone or snow for extended periods of time. Bus butt is a subtle ache in the posterior region from squashing the gluteus maximus muscles flat, draining them of blood and sensation, instead of using them.

A related disease is "bus–nap neck", which results from taking naps sitting up on the bus. You nod off, your neck muscles relax, and then the bus jerks or sways and your neck extends in a way it was not meant to. Ouch!

One of the nice things about the OAT (Overseas Adventure Travel) tours is that the tour guide has the latitude to customize the itinerary a little bit. Each guide has his or her own little secrets and special treats that they like to introduce to their group; and they don't necessarily share that information with the other guides. Much like photographers may develop special places they like to shoot, they won't divulge the exact location of where a photo was taken. Our guide took us to a glow worm convention last night. That's one of his secrets. While sitting in the front seat one day we could hear the driver and our guide discussing where to take us next. I like knowing that the day's itinerary isn't set in stone. There's something about having the itinerary flexible that makes a trip more of an adventure.

We all just took a little breather at the historic Empire Hotel in the little town of Ross. Apparently it's for sale, as I learned when I walked in and said "Wow!" then looked over at the proprietress who said "Hey, it's for sale. You could buy it and say that every day." It's an old hotel, bar and restaurant with a lovely old wood burning stove. Antique trinkets litter the mantle; old posters paper the wall; money, business cards and matchboxes speckle the ceiling and wooden ceiling trusses. A group of us played darts, having fun seeing who could get the most number of points or just who could get the darts closest to the middle. Then the jukebox started to play "I Fell into a Burning Ring of Fire" and it all turned a bit surreal. How odd to be in a little bar, playing darts with a group of new friends, on the secluded west coast of New Zealand with Johnny

Cash playing in the background. How cool. What a memory. What a picturesque little place.

After our hotel stop we had a presentation on Pounamu, also known as greenstone, which is a treasured stone by the Maori in the same way that Europeans value gold. It is found in the south island and the Maori used it for weapons. Greenstone is a very hard stone and required very hard and sharp utensils to cut through it. They believe it is not a stone you buy for yourself – only for a friend or loved one. They also believe that the stone is blessed with a spirit. Tradition says that if lost, the stone can find its way back to its owner.

SICK
TUESDAY, MARCH 2, 2010

My body decided it was time for a day off, after being driven hard for four weeks. I stayed "home" today at the hotel in Greymouth. We are at the Ashley Hotel, which is quite nice, and close to the beach. The food and customer service are fantastic.

My cold descended upon me disguised as allergies. Others in our group got sick about the same time with the same symptoms, leading me to believe I did not have allergies. Sneezing, watery, itchy eyes, nose doing an imitation of a faucet – you can understand why I thought it was allergies. I am just about past the faucet stage, thank goodness. How uncomfortable to have a constantly running nose. So, I used the age–old solution of scrunching up little pieces of Kleenex to act as nose corks. Such a fashion statement! But when you're sick you don't care about fashion, especially in the comfort of your own room.

We are ten days into our New Zealand tour and the following mishaps and illnesses have occurred: one bad stomach, one fall in a volcano crater, one infected big toe and six or more colds. Not bad, I suppose, for a group of sixteen people mostly above age sixty. And two of those items belong to me – the youngest one! However, no one else has been traveling as long as I have.

Today went kind of fast. I slept until Mom brought me breakfast, then watched part of a strange depressing movie on "Sky TV" after which I decided that just because I'm sick doesn't mean that I'm an invalid, so I took a short walk down to the beach, did a little photo work and beach combing, and brought back several really nice rocks. Rocks are so cool. If it were possible, I would ship home a lot of them to decorate my yard. Yesterday we saw some wonderful usable art, which utilized smooth rounded beach rocks glued to thick spongy pads to be used as a welcome mat.

The beach here is a rocky beach with rocks as far as the eye can reach. The Tasman Sea reaches from the west coast of New Zealand over to Australia. Waves upon rolls of waves line the shore, smaller waves near the shore, larger four foot waves one hundred feet out. While I was there the tide started to come in, and some of the wave action caught me by surprise as I was playing with the rocks, arranging some of the curved ones into a circle for a photograph. All of a sudden I heard the sound of the water surging very close by with the sound of rocks moving with the force. I moved out of the way just in the nick of time.

Then I took a five hour nap, sinking into a blissful unaware peace, only to wake up later to remember that I'm sick. However, I think everyone's prayers are working, once again, and I am already feeling better. Thank you to all my prayer warriors back home!!! Especially all of Beth's 4th graders. I know that your prayers have kept me safe throughout my travels and have helped me to heal faster when I have gotten sick.

I'm glad that Mom's here. Not only does she have some of the drugs with her I should have brought, but also it's nice to have "Mommy" here, because no matter how old you are you always want your Mommy when you're sick.

If I were to go back in time, there are some things I'd change regarding what I packed. However, it's almost impossible to know what you're really going to need. I have too many of some things, like electrical plug adapters. I haven't needed as many pairs of underwear or socks as I brought. A few items I took out at the last minute would have been helpful. Perhaps the guidelines to follow should be "If it's going to be easy to procure an item where you're going, perhaps you don't need to bring it. And conversely, if it is going to be hard or impossible to get an item where you're traveling then bring it." Some of the most important things are medicines. You might think, "Oh, I won't get sick," but you really don't know. There's a whole world of germs out there and traveling can take its toll on your immune system because of what you eat, time zone differences, long days and busy schedules. When packing, I like to err on the side of "what if" when it comes to medicines.

Water in New Zealand is so good. Out of the tap. Yeah, I know! That's just about unheard of. The first time I turned on the tap to fill up my water bottle I hesitated just a little. It seemed unnatural. And then I tasted it and the water was great. And I've been filling up my water bottles from the taps here ever since. Strange how something so simple like not using tap water becomes such a habit and makes you question the safety of water. Here we are, in the U.S., worrying about the health of our tap water when it has got to be thousands of times cleaner and healthier than water many people from around the world drink on a daily basis.

LAURA VAE GATZ

ON TO CHRISTCHURCH
WEDNESDAY, MARCH 3, 2010

I'm amazed at just how much I take breathing through my nose for granted. It's something most people don't think much about on a daily basis. And then you can't because you have a cold, and then you think, "Gosh, I miss that!" Oh well, at least my nose has stopped running. Now I'm battling stuffiness and plugged up ears. This will pass, no matter how much it feels like I'm going to be sick forever.

Tours. They're just really not for me. Yes, sometimes they're necessary, and they do have their benefits, but I really prefer to be on my own. Lindblad was fine – that was different. That was the only way to get to the Antarctic – because that's not a place you can really go on your own without a lot of equipment, money, and know-how. But tours just frustrate me as an inquisitive curious person and as a photographer. I like to be able to explore in my own time, not on a deadline. Sometimes we'll get a five–minute stop some-where. That's a nice break from the bus and does allow me to get a few shots that aren't through the bus window, but five minutes is not a sufficient amount of time for good photography. One thing it does do, though, is to force me to be ready and shoot quickly under pressure. It's not the ideal situation; it's more like journalistic photography – shooting what you can get, in the time and situation you're in. Much like shooting from the deck of the National Geo-graphic Explorer. The ship is moving and you only have a second to capture the scene because you're moving through it. Capture it quickly or that perspective is gone forever...unless you can convince the captain to circle back for you!

The sixteen of us just spent a few hours at Flock Hill Station, which is a sheep and cattle ranch. We were treated to several sheep dog demonstrations and learned a bit about the sheep. In New Zealand, in order for meat to be considered "lamb," the sheep has to be killed before it's bottom teeth start to come in, any older than that and it becomes "mutton." I think that what we get in the U.S. when we buy lamb must often be "mutton," because it has such a different, gamier flavor. Here in New Zealand, when you order lamb you can count on it being superb.

What fun it was to watch the sheep dogs do their work. Each one works a little differently. One will get close to the sheep and stare them down, another will back off a little and get into a crouch, and others run around and bark. It's quite something to see how much control the sheep dogs have.

The gentleman we met and one of his shepherds both wore fleece jackets and very short shorts and had very tan, well-toned legs. I imagine they spend a lot of time outside.

One of the sheep had been raised as a pet by one of the owner's daughters and it walked along with us, right in the middle of the group, pretending to be a human. It reminded me of a dog as it wandered around looking for attention. That made me laugh as we walked farther on in the pasture, with the sheep slightly out in front as if leading us on, as if we had become the sheep. One of its offspring came to join us as well. By the end of our time with the sheep, we had a third generation walking around with us, a very cute little sheeplet.

After watching the dogs herd the sheep around, we went into the sheering shed to learn a bit about how wool is graded and to find out who buys it. Wool is graded according to how thick one fiber is. It's measured in microns, even down to the quarter micron. The smaller in diameter the strand, the more the wool is worth. Typical merino wool here at Flock Hill is about 17–17 1/2 microns. A mixed breed (merino with a non–merino) jumps to about 30–35 microns. It's not necessarily a bad thing to have a thicker diameter. Flock Hill has a contract with Smart Wool, a Colorado company that makes hiking socks (I wear them almost every day, all year 'round). Smart Wool is interested in the mixed breed wool and so Flock Hill is working to produce more of that kind of wool. I believe the man we talked to said this was the only station in New Zealand that Smart Wool buys their wool from.

The sheep dogs were sweet. One of them likes to stand between people's legs. I don't know if it makes him feel safe, or if it's just a really good place to stand out of the sun. But when the whistle blows or they hear a command, they're off; it doesn't matter if you're in the middle of petting or scratching them. They're off like a shot; they have work to do. And it's work that they love. Sheep dogs are natural herders. I've seen them playing in a dog park and they often will try to herd the other dogs together.

Once we got on the east side of the mountains, or at least on the east side of the first stretch of mountains (because we're still in the mountains), the weather changed. The weather went from overcast and rainy to breezy and sunny – delightful weather, about 70 degrees, like a fantastic Colorado spring day. The hills in the background are a palette of different greens mixed with the grey of rockslides; the valleys below hold meandering streams and thick waving grasses, and the farms we pass are chock full of sheep, horses, cows and deer. Yes, deer – venison! They raise deer here just like we would raise chickens or hogs back in the States.

The bus rocks gently from side to side, putting us all to sleep after a large lunch of chicken, lamb, roasted potatoes, and pavlova. The bus is quiet as people stare out the window at the natural beauty, review the day in their minds, or nod off for a short afternoon nap before we reach our destination for the day – Christchurch.

Pavlova is an interesting dessert, apparently named after the Russian ballet dancer Anna Pavlova in honor of one of her tours to New Zealand and Australia in the 1920's. Of course, being natural rivals, Australia and New Zealand argue over which country actually created the confection. This dessert is similar to meringue, but has a slightly different consistency than the meringue that might be found on top of a lemon meringue pie. The addition of cornstarch, and a long, slow baking temperature, renders the egg white, sugar, vinegar and cornstarch mix into a crispy outer shell, with a soft, moist interior. Traditionally it's topped with fruit, such as strawberries and kiwis, and whipped crème.

LAURA VAE GATZ

BAHHH!
THURSDAY, MARCH 4, 2010

Dolphins!! Specifically, the Hectors Dolphin. We drove to Akaroa today which was about an hour away, stopped at a really cool art gallery on the way, to do a little "retail therapy" as our guide likes to call it, then took a cruise out of Akaroa to see dolphins, seals, and the little blue penguins. They're the smallest penguins in the world, and are totally cute. When they're resting in the water they float on the surface. We saw some at the Antarctic center yesterday, but that was like seeing them at the zoo – this was in the wild.

Our group had a little fun with our guide today. It actually started yesterday. He had bought a stuffed toy sheep that "baahs" when you squeeze it. We'd seen a lot of sheep over the last few days, along the side of the road and at the sheep ranch we'd visited. SO our guide bought the sheep, brought it back on the bus and said that he'd be giving it to someone with one condition, that person had to promise to make the sheep "baah" once an hour on the hour on the flight on the way back to LA. Well, in the minds of our group, that was just an invitation to swipe the sheep and hold him hostage. At first the sheep was quietly sheep–napped, until our tour guide decided to mention to us that he noticed it was gone. Then there was a bunch of "baahing" on the bus. Here a baah, there a baah, you get the idea. Once in a while whoever happened to have the sheep would make it baah on the bus and we could all giggle and baah. Today the sheep started to change hands. When our guide wasn't looking the sheep would fly through the bus, landing in someone's lap. Then it would quickly get stuffed somewhere out of sight. Eventually he saw the flying sheep, and it was given back. It was very funny. Our group has really gelled well, and has pulled a few pranks on our guide. We give as good as we get...and vice versa.

WALK AROUND CHRISTCHURCH
FRIDAY, MARCH 5, 2010

Today we had a laid back day – leaving the hotel on a walking tour of Christchurch at 8:45 a.m. – which is a good thing, because I had a hard time getting to sleep last night. I can't tell you why, I was just thinking too much. About what? Oh, this and that, my trip, people I've met, how the time is ticking away bringing me closer to when I must go back to work and go back to "normal." Normal. Not sure what that is any more. My normal will be different when I get back. I want more out of life now. And I have some ideas on how to accomplish that. The key is going to be remembering those ideas when I get home at the end of a long, busy day at work and want to sit on the couch and stare blankly at the walls, imagining I'm looking at a really large, really white iceberg.

Our first stop was at a shop named Eyris Pearls where we were given a mimosa and a presentation on the unique Blue Pearl, found only in New Zealand. The blue pearl come from the abalone species Haliotic Iris. There are over a hundred species of abalone around the world. The species found here in the waters off the New Zealand coast, Haliotis Iris, or "paua," have an incredible range of color and are the only abalone that has successfully been able to be farmed for pearls. Each pearl must grow within the shell for three years, growing in their home waters. So, although they are farmed, much of their environment stays the same – their diet, the water and temperature. They are kept in protective baskets to protect them from predators. Only approximately 10,000 pearls are harvested each year, and only 1000 of those are graded as top–grade quality.

As we walked into the shop, we were asked to select a ticket for a drawing later. After our guide selected two different numbers, which turned out to be numbers that no one had selected, they selected the winning number. Mine!! My prize was a very lovely paua shell necklace in a sterling silver setting. There were about 10 different ones to choose from. Each shell had a different pattern, look and feel. I beckoned Mom over to help me choose one. What a fun decision to make! (photo is not my necklace, but a nice example of what a blue pearl looks like)

The botanic gardens in Christchurch we've heard are amongst the top 10 best gardens in the world, according to whom, I'm not sure, but they certainly are amazing, expansive and beautiful. 150 year–old trees, fantastic Jurassic sequoias, rose gardens that make the air smell like roses, towering hedges of hydrangeas, lush green lawns littered with relaxing couples, mothers in small groups with strollers laden with children, kids climbing on statues and laughing, dripping ice cream cones covering tiny faces, birds begging food from visitors on park benches, the wind gently blowing limbs of trees that have been growing for longer than I've been alive. Lovely, relaxing, and the perfect weather for a morning stroll. Cool and breezy in the shade, slightly warm in the sun. An Arcadia, Michigan day. A spring day. The perfect, happy day in the park. Ahh, life is good! Go God!

This afternoon was free time – time to do whatever we wanted – napping, shopping, wandering – or, as we did – meeting friends! The daughter of one of our long–time family friends is spending a college semester here in Christchurch. So she came downtown to hang out with us at Starbucks for a few hours. Hearing about her time here made me fondly remember my time in Germany during my junior year in college. Oh, how much fun to be in college and overseas!! It was one of the best times of my life.

Mom and I walked down to the local mall – the South City mall – yesterday, looking for a suitcase. We'd recently found out that we are allowed to check one more piece of luggage than we originally thought possible, without penalty. As both our small roll–aboards are bulging at the seams, I wanted to buy an extra piece of luggage so that I could purge some of the items I've packed that I don't need any more or that I haven't needed. For instance I have too many cold weather clothes. From here on out I'm going to be in weather that varies from 100 degrees to, oh, maybe a little more, or maybe a little less. Whew, it's going to be warm! Who knows, by the time I get home, my new "hottest hot" may change from Aruba and Thailand to Africa. Time and experience will tell!

I'm finding it hard to believe that I've been on the road for 5 weeks. It's effortless. I could do this forever. Which leads me to believe that I'd be very happy traveling, writing and photographing for a living....or sailing around the world. Well, ok, it's not completely effortless, but it's certainly enjoyable. It is hard work keeping up with everything like photographs and writing AND traveling, and certainly is very tiring, which is why I think I got sick, but so much of the time it is easier than every day life with chores and bills and cats acting up. And the fact that I love every moment of it makes all the hard work enjoyable.

But before I come home I want to make a few commitments to myself. It's like making a list before the weekend so that when the weekend comes I actually get done what needs to get done. Maybe that's what I need – a list! Yes, I'm the consummate list maker. Lists are motivators for me. If a task makes it to a list, it gets done. If a task is simply floating around in my head, strangely, it never gets done...

So sad to leave these people who have become my travel family! Eleven of us are continuing on to OZ (Australia – because OZ sounds like the first syllable of Australia...) with our tour company, and a few others are continuing on to Australia on their own. So, the group is breaking up. It's the end of an era (picture a melodramatic scene, my head tilted back, back of my hand across my forehead...)!

We had a lovely farewell dinner. The food was great too. One couple created a little limerick, to read aloud that was very cute. Someone bought a nice card that we all signed. Our guide had some nice words he said about our group. There were several sheep jokes, and a few Kiwi jokes. It was very touching and made me sad to think we wouldn't all be traveling together come tomorrow.

ON TO OZ
SATURDAY, MARCH 6, 2010

S itting in my hotel room at the Grand Chancellor Hotel, my television is on the Movie Preview channel. I'm amazed that I have it on. At home I discontinued my cable service after my trip to Asia in March of 2009. When I returned from my trip, the commercials were so annoying that I picked up the phone my first day home and told them to "turn it off!" The woman at the cable company must have heard the seriousness in my voice because she didn't even attempt to talk me out of it, but she did repeat what I'd said, as a question, to ensure she'd heard me correctly.

One movie preview that I've noticed and that captures my attention is Julie and Julia about Julia Child and Julie, who starts a blog about cooking her way through Julia's French cook book, Mastering The Art of French Cooking. When that movie came out I saw it in a movie theater and was inspired. It continues to inspire me. The further I get in my travels, the more people I meet with interesting ideas, new perspectives, and with knowledge about the areas I'm interested in pursuing. It feels as if my passions are a jigsaw puzzle to which I'm starting to find more and more pieces, and I'm finally getting to the place where I've put enough of the pieces together to start to see what the picture looks like. Right now I feel like I have those pieces in my possession and I can't wait to get home to spend some concentrated time putting them together.

I've done it!!!! I've gotten more business cards. Although I brought some with me from home, I've already run out. I guess I met more people I want to keep in contact with than anticipated. You wouldn't believe how much time I've spent wandering around town trying to find a place that could print business cards for me while I waited. There are lots of places that have photo kiosks, but none of them have business card templates and none of them allow you to add text to your own photographs. How frustrating! And for some reason Adobe InDesign won't allow me to turn my file into a PDF at the moment. You'd think, being in Technology, and being a former technology manager, that I'd be able to figure it out. C'mon, I used to TEACH team members how to make PDFs for goodness sake. Argh! The graphic design gods are against me. So, instead, I recreated my cards in Microsoft Word – which took like 20 minutes because Word doesn't like my large photo file sizes, and turned THAT into a PDF and put it onto a USB drive...and then we found a place with a Kodak photo kiosk. Although the guy working there directed us to two other stores, those stores didn't work out for one reason or another (one had moved out and the other wasn't open on Saturday); we kept coming back to his store. So I won him over and had him working on our side to figure out the best way to produce what I wanted. Yeah! So, now I have these adorable little miniature waterproof business cards. They're very cute.

Once again, all our luggage has been collected and is sitting downstairs in the lobby, in a line, all connected together by a rather long, thick chain. Mom's and my luggage looks out of place. Everyone else has large suitcases and we both have roll-aboard sizes. It's like they're Lilliputians in a sea of Brobdingnagians – Munchkins in a land of humans – or perhaps Hobbits in a sea of tall trees.

Time to move on. Twelve hours of travel to the hot, hot land of

Australia's north east coast. From the weather reports, we're looking at temperatures soaring just above one hundred. Time to put away the scarves and cardigans; the possum fur gloves and jeans. Time to get out shorts and sleeveless shirts and slather on the sun tan lotion. And time to go snorkeling on the Great Barrier Reef!! A whole new world – just a day away. We fly from Christchurch through Sydney and on to Cairns (we were told to pronounce it "cans" but have heard people pronounce it three different ways: Cans, Cairns and Can). And lastly, a bus ferries us on to Port Douglas where we'll stay at the Sea Temple.

Some airplane flights are just the luck of the draw. Some are perfect, half full, and quiet, with no turbulence and interesting seat mates. And then there are the others; those that seem like purgatory. The ones that make you want to voluntarily jump off the plane, with or without a parachute. This one is somewhere in between. We're surrounded. Kids under the age of 5 surround us on all sides. One is crying and peering over the seat at me, one is sick with a fever, and one is running up and down the aisle like a little banshee. My head is covered like I came to the party as a mummy. Germs, you know. Full face mask, and my scarf up over my head. Yes, it's a bit much but hey, it makes for a good humidity factory inside, and hey, I look like Mom, except she doesn't have a scarf – and she has a much more hip face mask. Mine is an industrial one with a one–way breathing valve, which makes it easy to exhale. Mom's is one I bought in Vietnam that the locals wear on the way to work. Hers is blue plaid and hooks behind the ears. The positive side is that there is only a half an hour left of this flight, and then we will be off this plane and waiting for our next connection. Woo hoo! Perhaps this purgatory won't last quite so long.

Koalas, Kookaburras and Kangaroos, Oh My!
Sunday, March 7, 2010

Aaakkk, attack of the swarming ants! Last night I saw a few ants in my room and thought, "Well, what are you going to do, we are in a rainforest. As long as they're not in my bed I'm fine." But this morning they'd decided that there was something tasty in my butt pack. And later they were after something inside my photo backpack. I applied liberal amounts of bug spray to both items, after removing sensitive items such as cameras and lenses, Kleenex and other absorbent items. These ants are very, very tiny, and seem to love the sugar coating on the Advil and have wormed their way inside the plastic Cold-Eeze wrappers.

We visited birds, koalas, crocs, kookaburras, kangaroos, and other interesting Australian animals today at the Rainforest Habitat Wildlife Park here in Port Douglas. This park is extremely nice, well laid out, with interesting and knowledgeable guides. Whew wheeee, it was hot and humid! We were damp and sweating as we walked around the different habitats.

There was an area for the different kangaroos in the Grasslands area. I had no idea there were so many different kinds – all different colors and sizes. One of them looked like a body builder. It's a kangaroo that lives in a hilly, rocky area so it needs a lot of strength in its front arms and chest, but doesn't need so much in the way of speed.

Kangaroo mothers can have one baby in their pouch, and be

pregnant as well. When the second baby is born, another nipple appears in the pouch, with milk specifically for that baby, because each nipple has a different kind of milk. Each one has the correct nutritional value for the age of the baby.

Another section of the wildlife sanctuary was the Rainforest Habitat, which was inside a high net, to keep in the birds. The walk took us through the forested area on a raised wooden walkway, taking us past many bird species, each brightly colored in its own way. We saw a variety of parrots: Red Winged, Electus, and Double–eyed Fig. During lunch a man came around with a Rainbow Lorikeet. I saw Kookaburras and a Papuan Frogmouth. The frogmouth looked like a medium sized owl to me. It was sitting on a log, hardly moving. In fact, I thought it was a statue and not a real bird at all until someone walked too close to it and it raised its head into the air and opened its beak wide.

One of the most stunning and exciting birds to see was the Cassowary, which the 2007 Guinness Book of World Records lists as the most dangerous bird in the world. There are many internet entries claiming that they can disembowel a human with one swift kick, using their extra long second toe claw to slice through the gut.

In this bird species it is the female that is the bigger and brighter of the two genders. Adult females can stand one and a half to almost two meters tall (that's four and a half to almost six feet). The only other taller birds are the Ostrich and Emu. Their bodies are mostly covered in black feathers. It is their bright blue neck and bright red wattle that are brightly colored. Two distinctive features are the "casque," or pointy aqua crest on the head, which can be as tall as seven inches, and their extremely thick (for a bird) legs, which end in three rather large toes. Sometimes I think the prototype for this bird must have been a children's rendering of a scary nighttime horror out of a dream. It doesn't look like any other animal I've ever seen. It almost looks kike a caricature of itself.

Another highlight was seeing a koala. They really are just as cute as you think they are going to be. The one we saw was larger than my cat Max, solid and heavy like a solid, well-muscled dog, and soft, with long front "fingers." Koalas actually have a double thumb, which aids them in gripping tree trunks more securely. One other odd factoid about koalas is that they are the only animals to have individual fingerprints, like humans.

Before we entered the exhibit I'd had in my mind that I wanted to have a photograph of Mom holding the koala. Once we got there the cost kind of changed my mind. However, once one of the couples in our group decided to do it, I decided that it would be worth it. What a cool photo to have. What an amazing experience. I can still feel the heft of that furry little guy in my arms.

Once back at the hotel, while walking to reception, we came across creepy rain forest ants with long legs. You know, the ones that are like leaf cutter ants; ants from movies, with sand colored bodies and runway model long legs. And they're all in a line, like they're trying to make a bridge with their bodies. Those kinds of ants are cool on television but not necessarily so when you're trying to go to your room and they're standing in the doorway. They're so small and yet I feel as if they're so well connected to each other, that if I pissed one off, word would spread around the world to all the different ant communities, and I would be on the ants' "black list." Wherever I went, ants would seek to harass me. And so, I walk gingerly around the creepy ants, being careful not to disturb them.

A friend of mine and I pulled off a coup. We figured out how to meet up in Port Douglas. She and I met in Ecuador in the Galapagos Islands two and a half years ago and have kept in touch through email and Facebook. Although she lives in Melbourne, she's been working in Christchurch. We missed her there by a day. Then when she heard we were flying into Cairns and staying in Port Douglas, she said "I'll book a room there too," not knowing exactly where we were staying. When she got back into cell phone range yesterday after being up in the Daintree area north of here, she called and said that she was booked at the Sea Temple – which is where Mom and

I are staying! There are so many places here it's just wild that she picked the one we were staying at. And it's so swanky, I'd never have believed that we were booked here!

So we met at the pool about 20 minutes after my friends arrived at the hotel. Seems like just a few months ago that we were in the Galapagos together. Unbelievable to meet up here! How amazing. Yeah!!

GREAT BARRIER REEF - TRULY GREAT!
MONDAY MARCH 8TH

This morning was a bit rough for me. Something had a complete disagreement with my stomach and decided it didn't want to be on speaking terms with it. As soon as I got back to my room from breakfast I laid down on the bed for about a minute before I was sprinting for the bathroom, with a little voice in my head asking, "You're not REALLY going to throw up, are you?" Well, yes I was. Not only once, but 4 times. And breakfast had been so good, too. There aren't a whole lot of breakfast foods you want to see once you've consumed them. We'll leave it at that. I wonder what herb and vitamins I left in the toilet. My thought is that I did not follow the instructions on my anti–malarial medicine, meaning I did not take it on an empty stomach 1 hour before or 2–3 hours after a meal. I also took it with antacids. Yeah. Just not following directions. Won't do that again. So, it's evening and I'm taking it again, before the evening meal. We'll see how this goes. If for some reason I've developed an allergic reaction to it or have become susceptible to one of the side effects, I kind of need to know in the next day or so, so I can get an alternative prescription, and have it filled, before heading off into Africa. Believe I should know the answer to that in less than a half an hour.

The Great Barrier Reef was indeed "Great" today — sunny, light breezes and flat water with a slight ripple. Fantastic! Mom did great snorkeling. She felt very comfortable in the water, and we took it easy while swimming around. The company we went with was Aristocat, and the boat we were on was the Aristocat as well. The area of the reef we visited were the Agincourt Reefs, north of Port

Douglas, and to the east of Cape Tribulation. Some of the reef was even sticking out of the water at the last spot we stopped. Our trip started around 8:30 a.m. and got us back to our hotel by around 5:00 p.m. There were three snorkel stops, and diving was also an option. The trip included lunch, which we ate after the second snorkel stop.

The colors of the coral were brilliant — blue and pink and purple. The water was clear and, because the sun was shining, the colors on the fish were vivid. Some color combinations I'd never seen before —pink and aqua and sky blue; salmon with aquamarine. Lime green, lemon and sage. Giant clams with glowing, light blue eyes. Fish with eyes that took up most their head, sergeant majors on patrol, parrot fish head butting the coral and ripping off chunks to eat. Although our boat could hold up to 100 passengers, there were only about 60 on board.

They have very strict safety protocols, which I appreciate. The movie (I think it's called) Left Behind flashed into my head a few times – the one where a couple is left behind on the Great Barrier

Reef, and no one really knows what happened to them. As we got on the ship they recorded our presence by taking a photo of each person, and having us "sign in." At the end of the trip we "signed out." And after every snorkel/dive, we were asked to stand still as every crewmember walked through the boat to count us, ensuring they had the correct complement of guests before leaving for the next stop. Also there were always two lookouts when anyone was in the water, ready to render assistance if needed. Everyone went through a safety briefing before snorkeling/diving for the first time, learning the signals for "I'm ok," "I'm ok, but tired and need help," and "Help, help, help!"

It's a little different experience snorkeling with Mom – having someone besides myself that I have to make sure is ok. We checked on each other several times a minute and only briefly lost each other a few times when Mom went swimming after a pretty fish. That was pretty funny when I told her "she'd left me," and asked her why. "I was following a pretty fish," was her answer. Hmmph. Sounds like something I'd say! I think she's learning things from me! Mom pointed out some really amazing animals. She spotted a beautiful manta ray with bright blue spots, and some really large beautiful parrot fish. She would often spot things before I saw them.

This was my first real practice with my underwater housing for my little Canon 990 PowerShot. I got the housing for this trip - well, specifically, for today! I thought there might have been an opportunity to use it in the Antarctic, but I never found a good time to use it. The exceptionally cold water was enough of a deterrent to keep my hand out of it! How exciting to finally have some decent underwater shots! Taking photos underwater is not the easiest thing in the world. I think it's the next step higher in the difficulty scale, next to taking photos of icebergs and penguins from a moving zodiac. In the water the fish are moving, you're moving, the waves or water action is moving you unpredictably, the fish are swimming in and out of focus and in several directions, not just up and down, but on all planes. And the underwater housing combined with the snorkel mask makes it difficult to find the subject you're looking for. It's almost like trying to use binoculars for the first time. "I can see the bird, but I can't find it with the binoculars. Am I not pointing this thing in the right direction?" Today the fish always seemed to be a little higher than I thought they should have been. Some fish must have built—in radar that knows when a camera is being pointed in its direction because they seem to scatter as soon as my camera is in front of my face. I know it's more likely the movement of my arms and hands, but still!

Oh my, did we run into a character on the bus on our way to dinner! This gentleman must have been living in the heat too long because I believe it's gone to his head. Picture this: an older gentleman, thick white shock of hair, white leisure shoes, white pants and a white shirt. White hat. Shirt unbuttoned all the way to his belly button with thick white chest hair seeking escape through his open shirtfront. He walks on the bus and greets us, saying "Hello! I'm an Austraaalian. I live here!" But it's not just what he said, but how he said it, and that he continued to repeat it, incessantly, for the next 6 minutes. He would pull back his lips so as to show all of his teeth in a sort of smile, keep his teeth together, edge to edge, and talk around his teeth. And he did this all with a flamboyant flourish. Mom talked with him for a little while, but gave up when she realized she could only understand part of what he was saying. So then it fell to me to talk with him, as he clearly wasn't going to stop talking.

"I'm an Australian, I LIVE here!" Uhh huhh. He babbled on asking, "Do you know who I am? Everyone knows who I am. I was on television. I know everyone!" Ending with, "I'm Australian, I live here." The bus made a stop. The man in white stood up and got off, with a flourish, as if welcoming the world to stand by and bask in the glow of his fabulousness, arms held out wide, graciously welcoming the city of Port Douglas, as if looking for a way to hug it. Mom and I couldn't wait to talk with the bus driver.

"Do you know him? Does he ride this bus often?" Apparently the answer was yes. The bus driver said that he never talks with the man because if he does, the guy never stops talking. He's like a pale albino energizer bunny, in a creepy sort of way. So the joke between Mom and I today was "Hello, I'm an Australian! I LIVE here!" The other would just dissolve into giggles, which was a little dangerous when we were snorkeling. Giggles tend to let water into your snorkel.

Tonight I took my second anti–malarial medication. It immediately made my stomach hurt. Thinking this through a little I decided to call Mom and she suggested I call reception to see what our options were. Thinking it would be a good idea to have an alternative anti–malarial, the front desk had the local doctor call my room. He said if we could make it there in 1/2 hour, he'd still be there. We made it with no time to spare, catching a taxi from our hotel.

This poor doctor looked as if he'd had a long day and was completely ready to go home. He was out of words for the day and beyond being interested in enunciating. When we couldn't think of the name of our hotel that was enough to confound him. Mom explained that we change hotels every few days and sometimes it's hard to remember the name of the hotel because we're always changing and we didn't book any of them ourselves. He wrote me a prescription for an alternative anti–malarial that would work in the area I'm going to. Doxycycline, the current medication I have, tends to be hard on stomachs. The one I got as a replacement tends to have psychotic side effects – Malarone. Whoo hoo! That could get interesting. Maybe I'll be telling the lions and giraffes, "Hello! I'm an Austraaalian, I LIVE here," from my safari vehicle.

SKYPING BETH'S
4TH GRADE CLASS
TUESDAY, MARCH 9, 2010

I Skyped with my friend, Beth's, 4th Grade class this morning. The time difference is fun to figure out. They're one day behind, but 6 hours later. We Skyped at 7 a.m., Tuesday my time, which was the Monday, at 1 p.m., Denver time.

Beth has been keeping her class up to date on my travels, and has been weaving my destinations into her lessons. National Geographic made a series of videos for kids called Really Wild Animals. They watched the Polar Prowl when I was in Antarctica, Wonders Down Under while I was in New Zealand, and to end National Lutheran Schools' Week, they watched Swinging Safari, on Friday the 12th, while praying for my safe travels to Africa.

Where applicable, Beth also shared some of my blog. The kids were tickled pink when she read them a passage where I thanked them for their prayers of safe-keeping.

Before I connected to Skype, I have to say I was a little nervous. I knew that my face was going to peer out of the big electonric whiteboard in Beth's classroom; larger than life. I also knew there were going to be 24 eager 4th graders staring at me, eager to ask their question. What if I didn't have an answer?

It's funny, when we grow up, and reach our dreams, so often we become a bit nonchalant about what we're doing, because, while we're in the middle of it, it seems like normal life. I took a deep breath, and tried to put myself in the mind of a 10 year old. When I was in 4th grade, anyone taking a trip around the world would have been a superhero to me. So, I smiled and hit the green call button, that looks like a phone, on the Mac. They answered on the third ring. There was Beth's smiling face in the middle of the screen, her class clustered around the camera like a choir, some standing, others sitting on chairs and yet others sitting cross-legged on the floor. I said hello, told them I was in Sydney, Australia. Then I recounted some of the highlights from my trip so far; seeing penguins and whiles in Antarctica, the huge moai on Easter Island, and traveling around New Zealand with my mom.

One boy asked a question about where I slept in Antarctica, and I explained that, for the most part, no one lives down there, with the exception of researchers; there are no towns, no McDonalds, and no hotels. I explained that some of the ice is a deep blue, and explained the science behind it, and talked about how the ship's scuba diver would go on daily dives and would show us short videos of what he'd found that day, such as interesting fish that have anti-freeze running in their veins so they don't freeze.

The experssions on the kid's faces were priceless. Some of my answers or comments even elicited exclamations of "Ohhh!" and "Ahhh," or "Wow!" Once I got over my worry that I wouldn't have enough to say, I really had a good time. After about 40 minutes it was time to go. The kids had another lesson to get to, and I had to get ready to go on a tour around the city. We signed off - the kids waving their goodbyes, and I thanked them once again for all their prayers, happy to know I had 24 little prayer warriors all asking God to keep me safe.

SYDNEY – CITY OF SAILS
WEDNESDAY, MARCH 10, 2010

I can't believe I haven't written since we've gotten to Sydney. To-day was the day I broke down and took a nap when we got back to the hotel late this afternoon. Don't think I've ever been quite so tired. Think my nap was about 3 hours. So of course, now I'm up. It's time to start weeding through all my stuff so that only the things I really need in the next two weeks come with me to Johannesburg. It was also laundry day. That might seem like a small accomplishment, but it feels so good to wash the clothes I've worn just about every day for the last two weeks.

Sydney is a very cool town; I might even go so far as to say I like it better than San Francisco or Chicago – and that's something, because I really love Chicago. Sydney has a law in place that keeps historic buildings from being knocked down or "hurt." So all over the city there are beautiful old building facades with modern insides. A lot of developers will go into an old building and completely gut it, while keeping the front original. The historic building fronts really add to the charm of the city.

The land here is fairly hilly, and the hills slope gently down to the bay. There are many hillsides where every house has a great view of the bay because of the elevation change. Sydney harbor is really large, with a fairly small opening to the ocean – just a few kilometers or less across. Although Sydney is a really huge city, it has a small town feel because of the small cozy neighborhoods they have. Many buildings have little alleyways between them that remind me of the alleys in Edinburgh, Scotland, which are called "closes," like Mary King's Close.

Darling Harbor is one of the harbors not very far from our hotel (Rydges – in World Square). Rydges is in a great location because so much is within walking distance. In fact, we even walked back from the Sydney Opera house today. Darling Harbor is a hot spot for hanging out and eating in the evenings; most of the eateries have outdoor seating that overlooks the water. Right in this area are also the Aquarium and the Naval Museum.

The Sydney Opera House is impressive, both from the outside and the inside. When we first saw it this morning I experienced one of those Moments where I can picture myself on a world map exactly where I'm standing. One of those "Ahhhh!" moments; the, "I'm really here!" moments. Very cool! I knew there was a large flight of stairs on one side because my friend Sherry, in Denver, visited a few years ago and told me about sitting on the stairs. The inside is full of local Australian wood used on the walls (brush box and white birch), the ceiling, and floors in different areas.

To decide on a design for the Opera house a competition was held. Many architects went in traditional directions, envisioning square buildings with ninety-degree angles. One architect, Jorn Ut-zon, literally thought outside the box and designed the form that is reality today. The funny thing is that although it was a beautiful design, the architect really had no idea how to actually construct it. Construction started on the foundation before the building plans were figured out, but it eventually all came together.

While walking around inside the Opera house, we were able to duck into one of the performance halls where an orchestra was rehearsing. The sound coming from them was unimaginable – so hard to describe. It was loud, but crystal clear. The force of the music carried with it emotion and feelings. The hair on my arms stood up, and I couldn't tear myself away. The base of the cello reverberated in my chest. The violins carried angels on their melody. I almost felt as if I'd been swallowed by Walt Disney's "The Sorcerer's Apprentice" movie and was trapped inside where the music was alive. I could sense everyone else in our group leaving the room, and a little voice in my head said, "What are they going to do to you if you stay a little longer?" So I stayed, until someone tapped me on the arm and said it was time to move on. Those few minutes made an impression on me. I can still feel that music shocking my system, almost making feel as if I've never been awake.

Another stop for our senses was an opal store where I viewed the most amazing colors trapped inside rocks that seemed alive; the colors in each opal change as your perspective changes. We learned a little about the different kinds of opals mined in Australia. There are black, fire, and boulder opals. Then there are opals called doublets and triplets that describe the final jewelry product. Black opals are called that because of the black rock in which they are found. Fire opals are the ones you and I are probably most familiar with – sometimes called milky or cloudy opals. As you can imagine, the opal people don't like those two particular descriptive words "milky" and "cloudy." And we learned boulder opals always have a portion of the rock face left on the back of the opal.

Prices are much higher on the opals than I thought they would be. Although some pieces were affordable, for the most part those pieces were ones I wasn't interested in. The ones I liked were around $20,000! Time to leave the pretty rocks, Laura.

LAURA VAE GATZ

MOTHER IN BOLLYWOOD
THURSDAY, MARCH 11, 2010

Mom and I got up early, had breakfast, and then a nap. Ah, what a life. What a great start to a great day! That IS the first time we've done that on this trip. I think it's deserved after a long three weeks of traveling together. And what a great three weeks it's been. Again, I can't believe we're just about on the other side of it. After our nap we ran a few errands, to ensure I have all the drugs I might possibly need out in the African bush.... because there's no pharmacist around the corner there – and if there is one, it might be a witch doctor.

After dropping off our purchases, we walked around Hyde Park, which is a lovely park in the middle of town. We sat and watched school kids taking their lunch break, dressed in uniforms consisting of black pants and blue dress shirts. Some of the kids were wearing long black shorts with knee socks, probably because of the warm day. They were all dressed alike, even down to their black dress shoes.

On our way out of the park we stopped to watch some construction workers playing a little lunchtime rugby. Then it was on to St. Mary's cathedral, just a block or so away. The approach to the cathedral is lovely, landscaped with water features including a fountain and man-made ponds with water lilies and lily pads. Mass was being held as we walked into the church, so we sat down and took part, sitting fairly close to the back. We caught the last 1/3 of the service, which basically consisted of communion. Although we missed part of the service, it was still nice to catch at least part of it. The church was lovely, with very long middle and side aisles, long wooden pews with padded kneelers, wooden beams high up in the ceiling, and dark intricate stained glass windows.

As we exited church after mass, a group of people started to arrive, carrying a lot of equipment including a movie camera, large light reflectors, and carts full of equipment. Mom and I sat down on the cathedral steps to see what was going to happen next. Mom stopped one of the guys to ask what they were filming. He said "An Indian movie." Then he told us the basic plot – an Indian man comes to Australia with this girlfriend, attends an Australian wedding, and is so moved by the love he sees, that he asks his girlfriend to marry him.

A little later, after talking with more of the staff, we learned that Indian movies have more than one director – there is one director each for the action, fighting, and dancing sequences. Each director has control over his individual parts of the movie.

The scene they were shooting was a bride and groom coming out of the church with three bridesmaids. The first few takes they were all being directed to laugh – so they were laughing, but the bride wasn't looking at the groom, it looked as if she was laughing with her girlfriends, not reveling in the joy of being just married. Mom, being Mom, thought she should say something. So, playing "director," she asked one of the directors if she could say something. He said yes, so she mentioned she thought the bride should be looking at the groom and showing how in love she is. He actually went up to the actors and told them to change what they were doing, taking Mom's suggestion. The next takes were so much better – instead of looking like she was just having fun with her bridesmaids, she looked like she was in love and happy to be married. Now the magic is set for the proposal that is about to happen.

It was so much fun to watch all the filmmakers work. First they did some test shots, then got the "real" huge camera out to shoot, using a tape measure to measure how far away the subjects were from the camera (I'm assuming for focusing purposes).

Later I asked what the working title of the movie was. It's called "Orange." Wonder if we'll be able to find it in a year or two. They have 5 more weeks of shooting in Australia, and then they go back to India for 5 weeks, and end up with another 8 weeks in Australia. After the church scene they were headed down to the Rocks area to Mrs. Macquarie's Chair, which is right on the harbor.

Our next mission was to find Darrell Lee's Chocolates, a local chocolatier. They were having a licorice sale – a large bag for $1 each! Mom is a big licorice fan. Wherever I travel or shop I'm always looking for new or interesting licorice. Until we walked into the shop I'd almost forgotten that Easter is right around the corner.

There were chocolate Easter eggs, large solid chocolate bunnies, and little woven baskets with colored cellophane Easter grass holding a bounty of wonderful looking Easter chocolate goodness.

Next we found our way "home," - back to our hotel. I've finally given up on trying to remember my room number; I just know where it is in relation to Mom's room. Every few days there is a new room number to remember. The first morning I wake up in a new hotel it takes a few moments to remember the layout of the room and where the bathroom is. It's really only a problem in the middle of the night when it's still dark. However, it's kind of a fun mental challenge. Just picture it: I wake up. I'm groggy but have a full bladder. I've really got to go, but first I have to figure out where I am. The challenge begins. Can she make it to the bathroom without running into any furniture? Without stubbing a toe? Without running face first into a door? On your marks, get set, go! Maybe I should just turn on a light…but then will I be able to get back to sleep?

So, I will be back on my own in about fourteen hours. I wonder if it will be a big adjustment? I've got a long day ahead with a lot of connections to make within the next 30 hours. Sydney to Johannesburg, airport pickup, dinner and sleep. Then a ride back to the airport and a plane ride to Maun, Botswana, where I catch a light aircraft to my first camp. Whoo hoo! I'll be seriously looking forward to getting settled in at my first of four safari camps. Maybe it's time to review the information about the first place I'm going to be staying. It will be good reading for the plane ride.

IV.

AFRICA

FLIGHT TO JOHANNESBURG – ON MY OWN AGAIN
FRIDAY MARCH 12, 2010

I'm at the Sydney airport again – and there is so much to do I don't know where to start. I've downloaded my latest batch of photos, but I still need to keyword and rank them all, and keep writing about my time in the great land of OZ. There are not enough hours in the day, and the more traveling I do the more tired I get. I'm just exhausted (yeah, I know "Oh, poor Laura – she's so tired. Too much travel, it's such a hardship...").

In the background there is light jazzy music surrounded by an undercurrent of people making lattes and other coffees, the clink of plates and cutlery, small murmurs of restless children and the occasional announcement for a flight that is boarding. And one woman who has swallowed something wrong. I think she might die. Not really, but she has been coughing for an inordinate amount of time. That is just the worst feeling. Sometimes you DO feel like you're going to die, to drown in the quarter cup full of coffee you just inhaled into your lungs. Oh, what a sad way to go that would be.

Once again I'm in the "business" world. It's soooo nice. Check in was lovely; they gave me all the information I needed without my having to ask. I got priority lines through customs and security, and now I'm sitting in the lounge with free wi–fi. Ahh, free wi–fi! It's so rare, like a white elephant. Is it rare or just a myth? Sometimes I almost start believing it's only a myth. FREE. It just rolls off my tongue, "F-R-E-E." Not much is free over here. However, Mom did manage to get my one-hour of internet for free at the last hotel. They'd charged it on my credit card and she said she preferred to pay cash – so they said it would be complimentary – which is great. I think they decided it was easier to forget it than go through the work to pay with cash. It's the least they could do for putting us all on a smoking floor when we arrived.

Now, smoking floors here are something to behold, not like in the states, well, at least at our Sydney hotel. The smoking floors actually appear to be smoking. You can almost see the smoke in the halls. These are some serious smokers on these floors. Many of them even keep their doors open to vent at least a little bit of their smoky rooms out into the halls. I know this because, 1) we were originally put on a smoking floor, and 2) the laundry facilities are on a smoking floor. What an interesting choice of place for the laundry. I would take one big breath of air before the elevator doors opened, and walk quickly to the laundry room and close the door. Whew. Smoke stinks.

Which takes me back to our original smoky experience. When we arrived at our hotel, the Rydges, each of us entered our rooms at roughly the same time. We were all on the same floor, mostly on the same corridor. I could hear all the doors close as everyone entered their room, and just as quickly I heard the doors open again and there was talking in the hall. "Hey, is your room smoky?" "Yeah!" "Mine too." We all started to try to figure out how to get moved. One person called the front counter; I tried to call Graham, our guide, on his cell. And eventually we all reassembled in the reception area for room reassignments. The only thing they did to compensate for their error was give us each a ticket for a complimentary drink. Mom and I never got around to using ours.

If I had to pick what my favorite things have been from the last three weeks in New Zealand and Australia, I would say 1) The Great Barrier Reef. All the fish, coral, colors and watching Mom having fun. 2) Holding a koala. 3) The waterfalls on Milford Sound. 4) The dolphins at Akaroa, NZ.

I just finished watching an in-flight movie and eating lunch. Both were great. New Moon – The Twilight Saga, and a red curry chicken with bok choy and eggplant. Lovely. Now it's about time for a nap. The time difference between Jo'burg (as the locals call it) and Sydney is about nine hours – Jo'burg is nine hours earlier. So instead of being 1:40 in the afternoon, it's 4:40 in the morning. Time for a little nap; then I'll work on getting into my new time zone.

This time I'm sitting in seat 17K, on a Boeing 747 which has an upstairs. I'm upstairs and in the window seat, which rocks because there is a lot of storage space between the seat and the window, due to the curvature of the plane body. This reminds me of the plane I took from Japan's Narita airport into Bangkok, Thailand. I sat upstairs as well, and there were huge bins to put things in. The bins I have today are about 2 feet deep, a foot wide and three feet long.

The stewards handed out our little business class kit that has all the normal items in it – a face mask, ear plugs, socks, tooth brush and paste, hand crème and lip balm. The case is the largest one I've seen yet. I'd keep it because it's cool, but the zipper is a real dud. After we got our kit they came through with sleep suits. I wonder if they were extras left over from first class. Both my seatmate and I changed into them right away. Lovely grey stretch cotton, very thin and soft, with a long sleeved teeshirt with a kangaroo on the front, which I believe is Qantas' logo. Wonder if I can keep it? My pants already have a hole in the seam, but I can sew that up. I can use it on my next long flight because I doubt I'll be getting a sleep suit on that one.

Yes, Mom, I've taken my Malarone – with lunch – and I had something with "fat" in it to increase the absorption rate (ice cream for dessert!).

This flight can be up to fourteen and a half hours long depending on the winds. Today they said it would be thirteen and a half hours. Out of Sydney the flight path is south past Melbourne, then passing south of Adelaide across the southern sea. Apparently this path is necessary in order to catch the correct winds. My seat mate, Janet, said that the flight back eastbound can be several hours shorter because of the winds – sometimes as short as ten and a half hours.

You'd think I'd write more on a thirteen and a half hour flight, wouldn't you?? It's really a long flight because it's all during the day. So my body isn't tired. I laid down for a bit but the guy in the row behind me had his window shade open (the only one on the upper deck) so it wasn't dark enough to sleep even with the eye shade on. I may have gotten a little shut-eye, but not a lot. We arrive at 3:30 p.m., which is like 12:30 in the morning to me. But I need to stay awake until about nine tonight to make the time change difference work. My flight tomorrow is midmorning, which isn't bad, meaning that although I'll have to get up fairly early; it won't be before the crack of dawn, more like right at the crack of dawn.

I'm starting to get a little nervous or excited. I'm not sure which. Although I can't wait and I know it's going to be totally cool, I've been living "in the moment" each step of this trip (except for those moments when I can't resist yearning to be back on the National Geographic Explorer again), that I haven't had a chance to think much about the safari part. Now it's almost upon me. Lions and tigers and bears, oh my! Well, ok, not bears, and not tigers…but lions, and I can't wait to see what else. Can't imagine how many photos I'll take! Once again my targets will be moving so I'll need to take photos on high speed, on my favorite setting of eight frames a second. That will give me lots to choose from and lots to toss out.

What I'm a little worried about is the heat and the mosquitoes. Two weeks without any possibility of air conditioning. I'll have to start a regimen of being slathered in bug repellant 24 hours a day. Time to get out the dryer sheets, which are purported to repel mosquitoes. I will find out if that is true and let you know. I've permethrined my clothes in an attempt to deter the pesky little biters. Not only do they carry malaria, but dengue fever and sleeping sickness (encephalitis). I'll be mostly protected from the first, but there is no prevention for the other two.

The practice I've heard for ensuring your sleeping space is "mozzie free," is to crawl into bed quickly through the mosquito netting, bringing with a can of bug spray. Then tuck the netting in under the mattress, making sure it's all good and tucked in. Next, kill all the mosquitoes on the inside. Then, and only then is it time to go to sleep. That brings to mind an interesting problem. I usually get up in the middle of the night to use the facilities. I'm either going to have to hold it, or go through the whole procedure each time I get out and then back into bed. And its very important to stay hydrated which could be difficult if not kept in the front of my mind, because the weather reports are for heat up around 100 degrees, getting down to the low 70's at night. At least it cools off for sleeping!

Also, I'm a little worried about the luggage I'm bringing with me on safari. Tonight I need to go through everything I brought with me and cull out the things not needed for the next two weeks – some clothes, including my jeans, and anything else I can find to make my duffle bag less full. The heavy piece, my photo backpack, is what worries me. It's about 20 pounds. This is one trip where I'll need to wear my photo vest, and fill it with heavy things. Now the question is, do I use my camera pouch that is worn around my waist? It would make my backpack lighter, but will make me look as if I'm carrying more.

Oh no!! I made a mistake in my itinerary. I thought that we arrived a day after leaving, but we're not going over the International Date Line, and we're flying during the day so we arrive the same day. That means that my pick-up isn't planning to pick me up for another day. I just made an attempt to contact him right now, on the plane, through my TV remote, which also doubles as a phone, text message, and email machine. It said it went through. We'll see. Just wanted to try to give him a little heads up just in case I could reach him. Wonder if I should try to text him too. Wonder if he receives texts on his cell. Think it would be worth it....maybe I'll try that too. Ok, the text sent as well as email, the only thing I haven't done is call him. My seatmate says there is a Woolworths upstairs if I need to sit around and wait for him. I'm going to call him as soon as the plane lands. I'm a dork. Well, this is the first mistake I've made. What a place to make it. *sigh.* I tell you what - I am not going into the arrivals hall until I know I have a pick-up. So, I have a free day in Jo'burg. Hmmm. Wonder what there is to do? I know there are some wildlife places pretty close in. Maybe Walter (my B&B host) has a suggestion. I do hope he's easy to get a hold of. He answered my last email pretty quickly. We're flying over Africa now. Never felt so unprepared to meet a continent before. I'll be fine. Time to remember the monk's mantra, "Everything will appear as it should."

As the plane lands I already have my iPhone in my lap. The wheels touch down and I pick it up, ready to turn it back on, and bring it back from airplane mode. I wait like I should, turning it back on only as we taxi off the runway. It seems to take forever to find the network. Searching...searching...searching. Aha, a signal! Ding, ding, ding, ding. Texts from Mom, arrive on my phone. She's so funny. More concerns about Africa and driving around Cape Town. Yes, I know it's on the other side of the road – I am very comfortable with that. No worries!

I punch in the numbers to call Walter; the phone rings. Good, I've gotten the right combination of numbers at the beginning of the phone number. He answers. "Walter?" I ask. "Laura?" he inquires back. "Yes!" Whew. Excellent. He laughs and I explain my mistake. He'd been out shopping when he got my message from the plane. So he adjusted his shopping list for dinner and ran home to change before heading to the airport to pick me up. Fantastic. I take a deep breath and exhale in a sigh of relief. I look heavenward and offer a little prayer of thanks.

Being in business class, I'm among the first 20 people to exit the plane. Walking with my seatmate, she explains that the immigration area is new in preparation for the World Cup which is in June. Unlike a few other places I've been in the last year, the line is short and moves quickly. When you are the first person in line, the immigration lady across the way takes your photograph, which requires you to take off your glasses. The image on the screen looks like a heat image reading. I wonder what they were doing – looking for weapons? I have no idea. Oh, I just asked Walter and he said it is a heat imaging scanner looking for evidence of Swine Flu.

I am at Impengele B&B, which is lovely, and very close to the airport, and across the street from a lake with hundreds of different bird species. Impengele is a native name for the numerous helmeted guinea fowl that live in this area. Walter is the owner of this lovely home, and has a large family of beautiful dogs, Rhodesian Ridgebacks, who are all being a bit shy with me at the moment. Dinner is at seven-ish so I have a few hours to relax and chill out. His friend Steve is coming over so it will be three for dinner.

JO'BURG
SATURDAY, MARCH 13, 2010

And so the battle against the mosquitoes commences. Humans 397, mosquitoes 0, I think. Last night Walter's friend came over for dinner and we all hung out on the patio until about dark. He first met Walter as a guest staying here. He now lives here and they're still friends, and quite funny. A great pair for dinner conversation.

Evening is the time for mosquitoes, and although there aren't a lot in Jo'burg, Walter's house is right across from the Korsman Bird Sanctuary, which is a large pond/lake and grassland, so because of the water there are more mosquitoes than in other parts of town.

When we discovered the little buggers were starting to swarm, we moved inside, but not before a whole micro-flock of them followed us inside. The next half an hour was a mosquito spraying party. The air inside became quite fragrant, and not necessarily in a good way. In order to take a deep breath I had to walk around to find a part of the downstairs that wasn't full of spray. But the spraying was indeed necessary. Little mosquito corpses started falling to the ground like little kamikaze pilots falling short of their goal.

Dinner was fabulous – steak, mashed potatoes, vegetables and salad. The vegetables he said were boiled and flavored with his "secret" spice. The steak was marinated in a secret marinade as well. Dessert was a kind of cheesecake–pastry, the perfect end to a great dinner.

Dinner conversation covered many topics, each flowing seamlessly from one to the next. I felt a little uncomfortable with my lack of knowledge about the history of this part of the world and asked a few questions to help my understanding. I admit I also Googled "Apartheid" and "Mandela" before dinner, which was helpful. Apartheid didn't end very long ago and is still fresh in many people's minds. The blacks here have definite opinions about outsiders. Race relations here are quite complicated. What was relayed to me last night was that foreign whites are tolerated better than foreign blacks. If you're going to be a taxi driver here, for example, you have to be a local black, not from another country, or you're not going to last very long. During Apartheid people were divided into groups: Black, White, Colored and Indian, and were further divided within each group. The blacks were divided into ten groups. Those groups still exist today in one form or another. And, like any country, people prefer others from their own group more than from another group. Understanding the issues and struggles between the groups is an important part of living here successfully. Always important to understand the local politics even if it has nothing to do with actual politics – just relationships between peoples.

For instance, a Zulu and a Xhosa (pronounsed "kosa") working in the same house, one as a maid and another as a gardener might tolerate each other in passing and for the sake of employment, but certainly not talk with each other. Zulus consider themselves superior to other groups, and a position inside a house is considered a higher position than one working outside the house. If the roles were reversed and a Zulu were to work as a gardener where a Xhosa was working inside the house, one would leave or there would be trouble.

Another topic was Americans and how some of us are naive when it comes to traveling. Sometimes we seem to have a different set of standards for the places we travel to, than we have at home. For instance you probably wouldn't walk around lots of places at home at night, but think that it should be safe to walk around in similar places at night while traveling. It's almost as if we're using a different measuring stick; as if the rest of the world should be safer than where we're from. Here, you don't go out at night. My B&B is in a safe neighborhood and the house is behind a tall fence topped with an electric fence; however, Walter said, "If you're going to go out at night, first, please tell me, and second, take a dog with you." He had a guest last week that went out without telling him and came back after dark. Walter was just about to go out looking for him when he came home.

We also talked about Soweto and how the media informs our thoughts and ideas about it. More than informs, really. It comes up with its own version of reality to distribute to the masses. When I've thought about Soweto, which isn't much, and certainly not in depth, I've thought about the African equivalent of the slum in India used for shooting Slum Dog Millionaire, which apparently Soweto is not. Sure, there is a slum area there, but it's not all slum. It is one of the settlements used by the government during Apartheid, with "matchbox" houses – rectangular 4-room houses, all with the same floorplan.

On our way to Soweto we ran into some lane closures. More lanes are closed on the weekend than during the week, making what should be an easy drive, into a very long, frustrating drive. As soon as Walter saw what was going on, he merged into the far left hand lane and swung a left handed U-turn to drive up the on-ramp to the highway (i.e. driving the wrong way). In order to make sure that I was correct in my assumption I said, "Now, this is an onramp to the highway, right? – It's one-way the other way?' And he said "Yeah, what's your point?" Followed by "You Americans, you need to learn to be more flexible." Which is true. However, in the U.S., there's no way you'd ever get away with that, except in an extreme situation like an oncoming hurricane. Normally the drivers going the other way wouldn't let you drive the wrong way up an on-ramp – they'd probably get in your way and make you turn around. U.S. drivers are not very flexible. I think that's one of the reasons many U.S. citizens find it extremely hard to drive in other countries. They expect too much— like if the sign says no U Turns, then no U turns. They expect people to stay in their lanes and can get freaked out if someone crosses the line. In many other countries I've been to, especially if they're developing countries, the rules of the road are just guidelines and it's important to stay flexible and go with the flow. The main thing is to stay a safe distance from all other vehicles. If you can master that then you've pretty much got it covered.

This is a coal-burning city. The cooling towers I usually associate with nuclear power are cooling stations for the coal plants.

Here, a major form of public transportation is the minibus taxi. They're everywhere, and seem to be every second or third vehicle on the road, which is a good thing, because it helps keep traffic congestion down. If I were to guess, I would say that will change in the next 7–8 years. More and more people will get their own cars and this will increase the traffic on the roads. These taxis stop anywhere someone is waiting on the side of the road. So it can take quite a long time to get any sort of distance. It looks like they do a bustling business - they're busy and bursting at the seams with people.

Competing with these taxis is the new bus system that has been put in place. The city took lanes from the middle of the roads and made them exclusively for buses. Not only do the buses drive down the middle of the road in their own lanes, the middle of the road is where passengers get on and off the buses. As you can imagine, the minibus taxis are not very happy about this new development. The transit system is called Rea Vaya, and is also known by the letters BRT – Bus Rapid Transit. Within the last year there have been attacks on these buses and bus drivers, some being shot, and other threats of bombing the stations.

The BARA (short for Baragwanath) Transport facility is a "taxi rank" – a central place for people to catch a taxi. This particular one is about a kilometer long and over 2000 taxis operate out of it. Can't say I've ever seen so many minivans in one area before – even at an auto dealer. It's as busy as an airport. There are so many people coming and going. It's a beehive of activity.

Soweto is short for South Western Township. Kind of like our Lodo in Denver is short for Lower Downtown. Soweto was created in the 40s and 50s but the name wasn't adopted until 1963. It's funny how western news media seems to portray Soweto, as a ghetto, which it isn't. It looks like any other suburb. Sure, there is a small shanty town, here called "Informal Housing," but it is a very small percentage of the Soweto area. Soweto probably houses about one million people, most all in single-family dwellings. Most homes are small, and built by the government, but tidy, built out of brick, and many have little gardens or small family-run businesses next to them.

Johannesburg is a crazy mixture of first world, and second and third world all strangely juxtaposed. I don't think I've ever seen such a mixture of different worlds all mixed up amongst each other, like commuters on an Indian train with no space in between them and hardly any room to breathe. In one block I might see a woman with a baby begging at the intersection, a storefront selling blankets with a metal pull down door for when they're closed, next to a bright and shiny BP gas station, with all new gas pumps and neon signs in the window.

Down the street is the traditional medicine market, the Kwa Mai–Mai market, housed in several small hard dirt packed alleyways lined with continuous brick buildings on either side, each business has a doorway with a small shop inside. Most shops look like they are just large enough to stand up in, arms straight out from your side, and spin around in, about 6x6ft or maybe 8x8ft. Each shop is dark, lit only by window light, so when the sun goes behind a cloud, interiors become even darker. Kind of appropriate, I thought, given the nature of what they are selling – potions and charms. Outside many shops were the dried goods of their trade. Bones, vertebrae, dried bird carcasses, animal horns, animal hides, hair of goat, snake skin, feathers, and drums made with sinew and rawhide. Inside the shops were Zulu shields, small vials of concoctions and animal parts in a preservative, herbs and ornate headdresses and other paraphernalia used in healing rituals. Fascinating. Odd. So, not 21st century. Like being in a time warp. We were the only "whities" wandering around there. I felt distinctly out of place and felt as if I was holding my breath and walking on eggshells, trying to act nonchalant and as if this was not a big deal. "Yeah, I do this all the time." As I stepped over disjointed paver tiles I felt as if I was a foreign war correspondent being taken into back alleyways in order to see the real life behind the front lines.

We drove through old downtown. Johannesburg has two down-towns, an old one and a new one. Nearly all commerce has moved to the new downtown, and the old one has been "left to the blacks," as Walter described it. Many buildings that were previously banks and trade houses are used for something else now. At one point many of the high rises there were empty. Now they are again full with businesses. There are also many apartment buildings in this area, all jam packed with people, many of whom are finding crea-tive ways to dry their clothes outside in the "fresh" air. Wash hangs drying from rooftops, outside on balconies, and over the edge of building roofs. It's a sea of drying laundry and blankets airing out.

Blankets are big here. People use them for more than blankets. They're something to sit on, they can be used to carry babies around on your back, they're for warmth in the winter and used overhead to keep the sun off you in the summer. Much like the Scots used to use capes as multipurpose garments – cape, towel, blanket, napkin.

We stopped at a small flea market where Walter sells some of his things once every few months, so he's a friend with many of the vendors. One of the staple foods for South Africans is something called pap. Pap is made from corn and is a smooth meal. Much like grits in the southern U.S., except the meal pap is made from is a finer texture than grits are. Also a lot like the Scot's "parritch" which is made from oats. Pap can be cooked, and then reheated. It can be eaten by itself or with other things – for instance I had it with a bean and carrot salad, which was slightly sweet, and added some contrasting flavor to the bland white pap, which looked a lot like the way I typically end up cooking Malt–O–Meal – a bit stiff and firm. I was given way more than I wanted to try. The plateful was the size of a whole meal. But, down it went - all of it. Good for me! I'm such a courteous guest.

Then we ambled along to the next table, another friend of Walters. She had used books. I bought two. One is full of short stories by South African writers, and the other is a travel novel about traveling around Africa and Botswana. Should be very interesting reading. I usually look for books by local authors written about the places I've traveled to. The books are a nice memento and something I can read after I return home and need a little something to remind me of my travels.

Next we drove through Parktown and Westcliff, which are two of the oldest suburbs, up on a ridge north of the city center, still home to mining "magnates." We entered one neighborhood, guarded by a gate and guard. He let us in when Walter told him we just wanted to drive through to look at the houses. The drive reminds me of a nice road through a rich area of Santa Barbara, CA, with twisty tree trunks on the side of the road, branches elegantly arching over the road. Ornate fences topped with electrical wire, English gardens competing with riots of native flowers. White Greek columns next to an English manor house. Mercedes and Jaguars parked on the paved driveways.

As a contrast to this area we proceeded on to Hillbrow, known for its dense population of foreign blacks, many from Nigeria. Being a Saturday, the streets and sidewalks were bustling with people, reminding me of a street in New York city, except these people were dressed much more brightly, many carrying large heavy items on their heads. I'm always amazed at what people can balance on their heads. Undoubtedly it is a superior way to carry things. Lugging things over your shoulders or in your arms quickly becomes exhausting. Neck muscles are strong and can support a lot of weight.

Our last two stops of the day consisted of a little shopping. First the Bruma market. Mostly a market for souvenirs, but nice ones. Reminds me of the market my aunt took me to in Antigua, Guatemala. It was full of textiles and crafts, hand made wooden items and baskets. Walter and I did not venture very far into this market, I knew what I was after and we stuck to that - a little something for Mom and Dad, and my masks. Although I tend to not buy much when I travel, I do like to buy one or two things that are locally made. I know that the masks here aren't from this part of Africa, but they're going to symbolize my first trip to Africa as a continent, so I'm ok with the fact they were made elsewhere and imported to this market. Oh, there were so many to choose from! I probably won't buy any others. So I wanted them to be special and say "Africa" to me when I looked at them. I found just the ones. A male and a female mask. And they have hair. Oh, not real hair, but cool braided grass hair. I can remember visiting homes of my parents' friends and seeing masks from other countries hanging on the wall. To me that symbolized being a world traveler. I've never forgotten it.

My home is a mishmash of different styles, all very "comfortable." I've combined the warm gold and deep sage green of my living room furniture with differing woods in my coffee and side table, banister bookshelves and an antique from my grandmother's cottage in Waupaca, Wisconsin. Nothing matches, but it all co-mingles nicely. Behind my couch hangs the first quilt my mother ever made. It's a big star. Over the fireplace, a photograph of a white Adirondack chair on the beach with an aqua sarong blowing from it in the breeze. You've probably seen this photograph at one time or other. The mantle holds a wooden sailboat with canvas sails, driftwood, treasures from many a beach combing, and a frame my mom made for me that is covered with beach rocks. The photograph is our Michigan cottage.

The bookshelves hold my treasured books: tomes of Harry Potter and Outlander in hardback, Twilight in softback (yes, I have to admit it, I love them!), travel guides from countries I've visited, and a good assortment of travel writing. From perusing the titles anyone could tell I'm fascinated with two topics: sailing around the world, and quitting my job to travel. In a high window I have more driftwood, glass fishing balls, a huge conch shell a friend found in the Caribbean, and an old paddle. In another window is a ship's steering wheel, and large Ball canning jars brimming with found seashells, corral and beach glass.

In my upstairs bathroom on a wall shelf I keep my little vials of sand, collected from beaches on my trips. I now have over 50, one-ounce vials, from beaches including the Caribbean, Baltic, South America, Galapagos, Africa, Europe, Taiwan, Vietnam, and New Zealand. They're right next to the photograph of my sister and I posing on either side of a face carved from a palm tree, and an oil pressure gauge from one of the Windjammer tenders, and a large yellow plastic hair ornament Lisa (my sister) wore in her hair during one Windjammer trip for our PPP Party (Pirates, Pimps and Prostitutes). The theme was anything starting with a "P." We went as a Pair of Polynesian Princesses. But back to the present. I'm in South Africa, on a tour of Johannesburg. You'd think I was homesick or something!

Next (and very last) was a stop to the ATM and grocery store. I needed a little South African Rand (South Africa's currency), and I needed a little something for lunch. And I wanted to buy some of the local mosquito repellant. Walter said that a lot of people show up here with mosquito repellant from the states and it doesn't work well. Walter says it's because "the mosquitoes don't know what it is" – that you have to use local stuff so the mosquitoes know to stay away. Tee hee. So I found just the right stuff, and bought a few bananas, a tomato, peach and yoghurt. Perfect!

Home again, home again, jiggity jig jig.

FLIGHT TO MAUN
SUNDAY MARCH 14, 2010

I'm off again. The last adventure of the trip, well kind of. I do have two days in Cape Town with a rental car after this. But this is the beginning of the "safari" portion. Hard to imagine what the next two weeks will hold for me. Think what I'm most worried about is being too hot and not being able to do anything about it. Well, heat and the mosquitoes, because mosquitoes all over the world seem to love me. I'm yummy to them. And the bites, now that I'm older, leave marks that don't go away, unlike the skin I had in my 20's that seems to heal any wound without leaving any sort of evidence.

Everything is going well. I've made it to Deception Valley Lodge, which is in the Central Kalahari. My flight from Johannesburg to Maun (not pronounced Mawn apparently, pronounced Moun, rhymes with town) was fine. The plane was an AT7 – which is the size plane I usually fly into Traverse City from Chicago. Two seats on a side, and about 20 rows. And the tiniest little bathroom you've ever seen in the rear of the plane. Well, at least there's a bathroom! However, you have to walk in and turn around to face the door before you shut it because there isn't room to turn around. Seriously.

I had Walter take me to the airport early because I was ready and didn't have anything else to do. I got there around 8:00 a.m. for a 10:30am flight. He thought I was crazy to go so early. But I'd rather be early than have to rush. I'm a firm believer in avoiding any stress than can be easily avoided. There were already about 10 people in line ahead of me and check-in had begun. The line moved quickly, and I observed that they were not weighing carry on luggage. Bonus! I breathed a sigh of relief and mentally checked off one worry from my list. I checked my green duffle bag, wondering if I would see it in Maun and if anything would be missing from it.

Onboard we were served a little lunch in a box – a roast beef and cheese sandwich on ciabatta bread with a granola bar. Not bad for a two hour flight. Out the window there wasn't much to see. Lots of scrub trees and wide-open spaces. Clouds moved in, or maybe it is better to say we moved into the clouds. I had no seat mate so could stretch out a little. I talked myself into taking out the big camera and taking a few photos. Sometimes it's funny how difficult it is to make myself do that. Can't tell you what it is – laziness? The sense of "Oh, I've seen this before," or "this is nothing special," or "I just don't want to move?" I do not know. Perhaps it's the fact that I've been traveling for too long and things have ceased to surprise me.

Upon landing, after making my way through immigration and collecting my luggage without incident (although for the life of me I can't figure out where the new stamp in my passport is), I headed through the double doors that lead to the arrival hall, walking slowly and scanning the crowd for a man holding a sign with my name on it. Bingo! There he was. I walked up to him, introduced myself and he took my luggage, shook my hand and we walked across the street to a small office where a woman told me that there was a message for me, from Sun Safaris. Mapula Lodge is flooded and so they are changing one of my safari camps to a different one. Ok. Good to know. Nothing I can do about it. It might be a blessing in disguise. I do believe I've gotten into the flow of just going with the flow.

We walk back to the building we'd just come out of, under the brilliant sun, through the scorching heat, then through security, lickity split, and outside again back into the blinding heat. You didn't know heat could be blinding did you? Colors fade in the bright sunshine. Although breezy, the breeze doesn't cool so much as blow furnace-like air into your face, drying out your eyeballs. Blink, blink. Oh, it's hot. This is what I was worried about. It's 40 degrees Celsius, that's 104 in fahrenheit. We walk past a squadron of four-seater planes. I notice that all the wings are narrow, not deep enough to store any luggage, and think to myself, "luggage gets stored in the wings, my booty it does!" That's the first notion I arrived with that has been incorrect. Maybe somewhere the luggage gets stored in the wings, but it's not on any of these planes. Also these planes are smaller than I thought they'd be. These hold a pilot, and three passengers. From the safety diagram it looks as if a second row of seats could be added, but then there wouldn't be any room for luggage. My luggage gets tossed in the plane directly behind my seat. I am reminded of flying with my friend Doug from Fort Collins, Colorado, in his little two-seater. This plane is larger, but only just.

Steve, my pilot says, "There's nothing to see except trees on the way there. We'll be there in about 20 minutes." I don't believe him, but it's true. Lots of bushes and trees, a few dirt tracks, roads I presume, and the occasional farm with a few dozen cows standing around in a dirt lot, probably thinking, "Yeah, there's nothing to see around here."

Staring out of the window feeling a bit underwhelmed I remembered that I meant to download the sound track to "Out of Africa" to play on my earphones while flying at low altitudes over Africa. Not feeling inclined to discover if I'd actually done that or not I simply hummed the theme song to myself, not loud enough for anyone to hear above the din of the engines, thinking that the magic of the movies is a far cry from this reality. That's not to say that it isn't beautiful here. It's just before the start of their dry season and everything is drying out, which drives the animals to the few water holes that are left. Deception Valley actually pumps water for the animals so they have enough to live on. The dry season here is very long – about now through November. I remember hearing that on one of the BBC specials I saw about this area of Botswana.

Soon enough our altitude decreases and the pilot points out Deception Valley lodge in the distance. I look ahead and off to the left of the plane and spy two different run ways, several miles apart. They run different directions – perhaps for wind variances. I find out later that the other one is an airstrip for another lodge. Although the flight was a bit bumpy because of the heat, it was nothing out of the ordinary and only one or two of the bumps made my eyes open a little wider than normal for a second or two.

A large Jeep is waiting for us. Well, it's waiting for me, specifically. A guy who looks suspiciously like Steve Irwin - The Crocodile Hunter, the crazy-amazing Australian wildlife guy who got killed a few years ago by the stinger of a ray, is there to greet me and help me out of the plane by taking some of my gear. His name is Adrian.

I get into the jeep via a little ladder hanging down on the driver's side. It seems like a long way up. Adrian offers me a cold bottle of water that I eagerly accept and finish off before our first stop. On our way to the lodge we see all sorts of wildlife. We spy the heaviest flying bird in the world, the Kori Bustard. We see some Greater Kudu, which are like little antelope, and one Steenbok which is a very small little antelope. It has huge ears, and will freeze when it feels threatened. It's funny; they freeze until the moment we stop. Then they must figure they've been spotted, and their "flight" mode kicks in, and they run off. They have straight black little horns that stick straight up in the air and come to a fine point. They're very cute.

When we get to the lodge Wanda, Adrian's wife, greets me. They've been at this lodge for more than five years, which is a long time for this line of work. Most people who run lodges tend to move around a bit from camp to camp.

After a little introduction to the main lodge, another cold drink, and a little snack consisting of a lovely avocado and tomato salad, I am escorted to my room, which is down a boardwalk, elevated just a little off the ground. But not before I get the safety and ground rules. No leaving your cabin at night. No walking to your cabin by yourself in the evening. You can sit on the verandah at night, but if you feel uncomfortable, go inside. It's ok to walk to the lodge in the morning by yourself once it starts getting light. Once we get back from the evening safari, if you want to go back to your room to get something, you always get an escort. These rules are designed to keep everyone safe from the wildlife.

While a friend of our family's was on safari in Botswana several years ago, he heard the story of a woman staying at a camp in northern Botswana who decided to change her shoes before dinner. She didn't tell the guides she was going to walk back to her tent, and she left the group, and walked alone in the dark to her tent. On the way she was attacked by lions, but no one heard because of the noise of pre-dinner conversation going on. As dinner started, her husband started to wonder where she was, and went to look for her. He was attacked as well, but this time the whole camp heard his screams, and the guides came running and chased the lions away before they could kill him. Unfortunately, it was too late for his wife.

It's easy to be lulled into feeling safe out here in the wild. We drive through the bush on open sided jeeps and the animals look at us, as if wondering what kind of animal we are, never seeming to associate us with a food source. Remaining on guard, and aware of your surroundings can be difficult. The story of the wife and the lions has stuck in my head, and I make sure to abide by all the rules, even if I feel I'm being overly cautious.

My place is a little cabin, all by itself, at the end of a long, elevated wooden boardwalk. Other cabins are scattered along the boardwalk, each one separated by enough space for privacy. There's a living room, bedroom and bathroom. The bathroom has a claw foot tub and an outdoor shower, which is enclosed by a wooden fence, made of poles, and elevated a few feet off the ground by a wooden plank floor. As soon as I see it I just know I'm going to enjoy my showers! There are lots of windows on the three sides and two sliding doors that open out on to a verandah that faces the bush. Well, of course it faces the bush, we're surrounded by it on all sides! However, it doesn't face any other cabins or the main lodge.

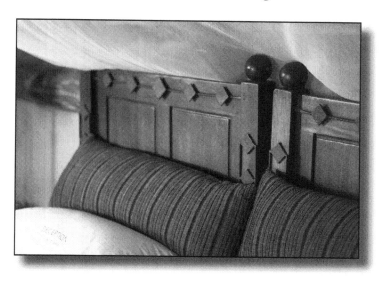

The lodge has a huge patio/verandah, with leather couches and large chairs. There is a wooden railing on which birds like to come and sit, and it looks over the little waterhole that the lodge has created. Inside are a living room with a small library, and a long dining room table with beautiful chandeliers made of wrought iron and ostrich eggs as bulb covers that have holes in them to make a nice pattern with the light.

The next few hours are mine to do with as I please. I meet Adrian back at the lodge at 4:30 p.m. for some tea and a little snack, before heading out on safari. This afternoon it's just Adrian, our tracker, Duma, and me, as I'm the only guest tonight at the lodge. Tomorrow another woman arrives, but I'll have a private safari tonight!

It's hot. Whew, wee! No air conditioning here, but there are ceiling fans. They help. I take off my shoes and socks and all extraneous layers and lay down on the bed. Oh, bad idea. It's hot; not refreshing or comfortable at all. The sheets feel as if they were just taken out of a hot dryer. I get up and walk onto the verandah, which is mostly in the shade. It's hot. Hot breezes hit me in the face. I go back inside and drink another bottle of water. Thinking to myself that I have time, and that although it's hot, it's not going to make me any hotter, I get out my laptop to do a little writing. My laptop thinks it's hot too. One side benefit is that my laptop thinks its battery life is really long. Not sure how that works, but the battery lasts for a really long time. I open all the windows and doors and let as much of the breeze inside as possible.

Teatime, as we know from New Zealand and other previous trips, is a lovely thing. Here iced tea is served – local Rooibos mixed with apple juice. Delicious! And banana bread and little steak and salad wraps. Then we're off. We have more animals to see! Safari time!

We head out on some of the dirt and sand roads surrounding the camp. Our bushman guide, Duma (when I was introduced to him I thought, "of course that's your name."), sits at the front of the jeep in a little chair built out in front of the Jeep. Sometimes he sits on the back of the chair so he can get a little higher perspective. He looks for tracks and animals within sight. When he sees one he puts out his hand in the direction of what he sees. Adrian and Duma talk together to clarify what has been seen, in Duma's native language Naru. He's part of the San group.

We see lion tracks. But it's hard to tell how recent they are because of the wind. There is a pair of lions around but they haven't had any luck finding them. Tracks have been seen fairly close to the lodge, about a kilometer away, so the lions are close. This afternoon the guinea fowl were making warning calls, and Adrian thought perhaps the lions were around. He says if you see guinea fowl in the trees you know there is a lion or some other large mammal predator in the area. If you see them all clustered together under a tree you know there is a hawk in the area. If you know what to look and listen for, there are signs all around you. I'm fascinated to learn just what some of those signs are.

The guinea fowl here are large and, I think, very cute. Perhaps it is just their blue and red heads that I like. It's just after their breeding season so their color is more vivid than normal. The tops of their heads are red, and under their beak and the wattle are a bright blue. And of course, their feathers are that cool black and white pattern – white spots on a black background. Never have I seen so many guinea fowl together at once. There must have been 35 under one tree. I just love them. They like the short grass on the Jeep track and so when we find them, they prefer to run along in front of the Jeep instead of veer off into the bush. It's safer for them on the road. I am reminded of roadrunner cartoons. Although they don't look like the roadrunner, their legs and how they run with a slight wobble from one side to the other, remind me of the Roadrunner.

What they were hiding from was a very large eagle. A Tawny Eagle. If I were a guinea fowl I'd be hiding too. The eagle isn't big enough to carry one off, so they tackle it on the ground and kill it with their strong, sharp claws.

Turning off the "main road" onto a grass track we see a warthog. He's old and very large, and has two youngsters with him. Adrian says they're usually fairly shy and will run off. It's odd that the male has youngsters with him; male warthogs don't usually have anything to do with rearing the young. We get as close as Adrian thinks we can without scaring them off and he turns the engine off. We watch for a while and the second little one comes into view. They're cute. Yes, even baby warthogs can be cute. He says this is my first of the "ugly 5." The ugle five are: warthog, wildebeest, vulture, hyena and malibu stork. When warthogs run they hold their tails up in the air. This helps them find each other in the tall grass.

We move on and see Blue Wildebeest. Then instead of one there are three, crossing the road to get to the water - one male and two female. The male has an all black face, and the females have dark brown faces. All have horns, so it's important to be able to distinguish them by color. When they're grazing you can see, what look like, stripes coming down their flanks from the nape of their neck where there is a bristly short mane.

Birds were making warning calls on the side of the road and so we slow down to investigate. One of the guys spies the cause of the ruckus - a Black Mamba up in the tree to our right. The birds were trying to keep the Mamba away from their chicks in the nests close to the snake. The Mamba is considered the most deadly of snakes.

Some say you'll die within 15 minutes of a bite, however it really depends on what kind of shape you're in, what size you are and how much venom is pumped into your body. We stayed far enough away to not test that theory. These guys are very fast. Within a few seconds it had moved from one side of the tree to the other, through the branches. When taking photos of it, Adrian helped me to find an angle that showed the snakes head and "smile of death" which is the grin that nature decided to bestow upon this menacing creature. Kind of ironic.

Evening is coming on so we stop for a "sundowner" (drinks and hors–devours) along the side of the runway strip. I've asked for sparkling water. A lovely African print table runner is placed on the tailgate at the back of the jeep and a fabulous plate of Kudu meatballs is uncovered. Yum! Exotic meatballs, I never imagined such a thing existed. They're very tasty. Standing alongside the Jeep, flowing ribbons of Quelea glide above the shrubs and trees. These birds are small like sparrows, with a red color. Their carefully orchestrated in-sync group flying puts pairs ice skating to shame with their sheer numbers. Ribbons several hundred feet long rise and fall, undulating to some unheard signal, a rhythm that only the birds know. Duma and I watch in silence for minutes on end, the light in the sky fading to a dark charcoal grey as a storm sidles in ever closer.

Our sundowner is shortened by the approaching storm. We had been watching the wonderful dark blue–grey sky and the amazing display of lightning in the distance when the wind picked up and a dust storm headed towards us. I took my drink and climbed up into the Jeep to ensure my camera equipment was covered. Then we headed off down the track for an evening/nighttime safari, with a large powerful flashlight.

We saw just a few things – one of which was a small bird that looks a lot like an owl. It sits on the ground and is able to sense the movement of flying insects through the whiskers just behind its beak.

Just after we'd driven past the owner's house, which is fairly close to the lodge, the skies opened up and unleashed all the buckets of water that have been held in the sky for over two weeks. For the most part, my equipment was put away. However, I was having issues getting the camera with the large lens to fit back into the camera holster - it just didn't want to go. At this point my hat was on my head and was very handy too for keeping the rain off of me, with its big brim and flap of cloth extending past the base of my neck. I huddled over my equipment protecting it like a small child, from the wet. The right side of my pants was soaked and I could feel the wet material pasted limply on my leg. Luckily that was the one pant leg I'd managed to put back on. The other one was protecting my binoculars. My right arm and shoulder were sopping wet as well.

Just a few minutes after the rain started we arrived at the lodge and pulled in under a covering sheltered, for the most part, from the rain. Yeah, a garage! How convenient! Wendy met us and helped me with my equipment so I could navigate the wet, slippery ladder down from the Jeep.

One large dry towel was handed to me and I started to dry off, the camera equipment first, and then myself. After everything was marginally dry I sat down to a hot cup of herbal tea, and relaxed. What a rewarding day in the bush. Lovely to be the only guest in the Jeep! That way I could sit in the front row and move from side to side as the wildlife dictated. The extra room also allowed me to move to the middle seat when passing close to thorny trees, in order to avoid getting skewered, and to sit in the driest spot (although I don't think anywhere was actually dry!) during the rain.

Dinner was fantastic – a tasty fish mixture in phyllo dough for an appetizer, and then steak (what sort of meat though??) with green beans and carrots and crispy little fingers of potato. Dessert was an orange crepe with a crisp orange glaze around the edges. Adrian and Wendy ate with me and we had a nice conversation. We talked about what work we've done, where we grew up and what our parents did. Adrian's father was a guide in the Krueger national park and a headmaster of a school.

Adrian gave me an escort back to my room. I'd asked what I should do if I needed them in the middle of the night. They kind of just looked at each other and one said, "Well, usually this is it. We drop you off and you just stay there until it's light. But we can give you a two way radio if you would like one." I declined, knowing that I'd be fine. Adrian told a story earlier in the day about one camp he'd stayed at where each guest had the cell number of one of the guides. In the winter it would get cold and the guide would tell the guests that there would be a hot water bottle in their beds when they returned to their rooms, and not to think that it was an animal hiding under the covers. Inevitably one or two folks from each new group of guests would call, scared that an animal was in their bed. Adrian would kindly remind them of the talk about the water bottle, and the guests would insist that that wasn't it, and that the thing was moving. So – no radio or cell phone number for me!

A few times nature called tonight. A call that always must be answered. Pitch black. Black like a cave. Black like the inside of a black can of paint in a cave. Unable to see my hand in front of my face, I feel around in my bed for my iPhone. Finding it I press the "wake up" button and the screen flashes to life, illuminating all that I need to see. Making my way through the mosquito netting and towards the bathroom I repeat the process to light up my cell phone once and scurry along so I don't need to do it a third time. I sit there on the potty and wonder what fauna is living in the bathroom this night, and then I hurry up and pitter patter back to bed, once again employing my iphone as a flashlight, ensuring the mosquito netting is back in place, keeping all the little flying, biting nasties out of my little sanctuary, and lie back down to sleep.

LAURA VAE GATZ

DECEPTION VALLEY LODGE
MONDAY MARCH 15, 2010

This morning I woke up to find a large "flattie" (the nickname they give particular spiders that hug the wall and are very, very flat) on my living room wall. And there's also a beautiful butterfly on the pillow of my couch. The butterfly is keeping me company as I write. Perhaps he's peering over my shoulder to see that I'm writing about him. Oops, now I've disturbed him by trying to get him to crawl onto my finger as I used to do when I was a kid, and he's flown off. Perhaps I'll see him later.

On our morning safari we see a few fairly rare sights. In all his years of guiding Adrian has only seen Aardvark tracks perhaps 8 times. We saw them this morning. Aardvarks can grow up to 140 pounds. They're not the smaller anteaters that we think of in the U.S. These are massive large beasties with powerful forearms and specialized front paws for digging, in order to find those termites!

On my way back to the Jeep from the aardvark tracks, I see these massive ants almost an inch long. I ask what they are and the reply was Matabele ants. Although these ants have large pinchers in front, that's not the part of them that's dangerous for humans, it's their posterior stinger. When they get frightened, as a defensive mechanism, they release an acidic smell. Our tracker picked one up, squeezed it a little, and put it under my nose to smell - definitely not a pleasant smell. Sometimes if the Jeep drives too close to a nest, a good nose can pick up a whiff of that smell. And it is distinctive.

Each day brings with it its particular benefits and downsides. For instance, today, because of the rain and wind last night, we can easily see new tracks. Older tracks have been obscured by the wind and rain, and new tracks press nicely into the damp sand. However, because of the rain, animals had wet grass to eat last night and therefore do not need to use the watering holes immediately. If it had not rained last night we would have probably seen animals at the water holes today. Rain makes the cats hide, but other animals love it and frolic about after it ends. We found some wildebeest tracks today on the road, which left a pattern like he was doing a little dance. Adrian says they aren't themselves after a rain. Maybe it's a happy dance.

It's 1:00 p.m. The heat continues to build, and I seem to playing a solo game of strip poker, perhaps it's "strip safari." First, off came the shirt so that I'm only wearing a cotton camisole, then the pant legs were zipped off and placed in a pile on top of the shirt. Next were the socks, on top again. The heat builds and, with it, a growing sense of lethargy and slight dread. How hot will it get today? Will I be able to take a nap? Will my laptop get so hot that it needs to take a nap too? Will I be the only Botswanan case of a human spontaneously combusting, leaving behind only a heap of ashes? I would probably burn down this nice little casita. That would be a shame. I take a trip into the bathroom, and wetting a washcloth, I wipe it along my arms and legs, leaving the moisture to slowly evaporate. That cools me off. All too soon I'm dry again. Rinse and repeat.

Our new guest arrives. She's from Russia, and just for fun I'm going to call her Svetlana. I'd been looking forward to another guest. The chance to talk, compare notes, get her life story. It's fun to meet fellow travelers. I introduce myself and shake her hand. Weak, stiff, floppy. Can a handshake be stiff and floppy at the same time? Let's just say there was no genuineness to it. That or she's just terribly shy. But I doubt the latter. As she sits down on the verandah to talk with our hosts I am watching and photographing the warthog family who have come to take a drink in the water and later a cooling swim. When I turn around to take part in the conversation my eyes are adjusting from focusing close, on my camera's settings, to focusing far away. Not an easy thing these days. Most people, after they hit forty, start having issues seeing close up. I see close up just fine, it's readjusting to seeing distance that I have trouble with. Oh, I can see distance, it just takes several seconds now, like an old lens with really slow auto focus. I go to smile at Svetlana and think I see a cigarette in her hand. Surely not! I blink a few times and catch a whiff. Horrors! Surely it is. My impartial observer, the voice in my head who always observes objectively, no matter what is going on, is amused at my reaction. Svetlana gets the stink eye from me, and I hold my breath while walking into the lodge, the long way around to be as far away from the smoke and stank as possible. I sigh. Unbelievable. How can you come to a wonderful, wild place, far away from the dirt and pollution of the city and stink it up with a cigarette. Immediately she's on my black list. Gathering my stuff, I walk back to my room, eager to get away from the smell, thinking bad thoughts like "perhaps the lions will suddenly appear tonight and eat her." "That's not nice," my impartial observer says back to me. "I certainly hope she's not in the casita next to mine. That would stink. Literally." Hmmmm. Arriving back at my cabin I lay all my stuff down and start to open windows and doors, with gusto, like you do when you're irritated about something. The handle on one sliding glass door is loose. The door flies open a little too hard, crushing two of my fingers between the handle and the door jam. I exhale in a pained grunt. Oh, "karma!" my impartial observer says a little too gleefully to be impartial. Yeah, karma's a bitch.

In my pained haze I see a beautiful butterfly fluttering against the windowpane, trying to find a way out. In order to distract myself from my fingers, which I'm gingerly exploring to see if they're broken, I grab my camera gently and take some photos of the butterfly on the window, adjusting the exposure to compensate for backlighting.

Being the only guest has been so enjoyable. Svetlana McSmokerson changes all that. It has been such a wonderful opportunity to be able to take photos of what I wanted. To ask that Adrian pull the jeep forward or back a little so I could get a better angle for my shot. To determine what we did next, or how long we tracked an animal before giving up. Ms. Impartial, that little voice in my head, flashes back to the monk Chris (National Geographic Photographer from the Antarctic) met in Tibet who said "Everything will appear as it must." That applies to now (as always) I suppose. Breathe. Relax. Enjoy. And then steal the smoker's cigarettes and lighter later tonight...

Dinner was fantastic. When Svetlana found out it was going to be Babooti her face lit up and she was so excited. She grabbed by arm and said, "You're really going to love this. It's my favorite dish!" Maybe she's not so bad after all. How can someone who loves food like I do be all bad? Well, it was spectacular. A wonderful mix of flavors. I was not able to procure the exact recipe, but if I had, I highly doubt I could easily find kudu meat here in the U.S. Here's the closest I have been able to get to the dish we were served that night.

Botswanan Babooti – Americanized

1 ½ lb. Ground Beef, Lamb, Bison or Turkey
2 Thick Slices Stale bread soaked in milk
1 Egg
2 T Apricot Preserves
1 T Mild Curry Powder
2 T Lemon Juice
Dash Turmeric
1 Large Onion - finely sliced

½ C Raisins
2 Bay Leaves
Coconut
Topping
2 Eggs
½ C Milk

Brown the onion in a large skillet until transparent. Add curry powder, preserves, beaten egg, raisins, bread and about 1/2 C. of milk. Add to meat and mix thoroughly. Split into individual sized corning ware ramekins, place ½ bay leaf on the top of each, and bake for about an hour at 350 degrees. Towards the end, remove the bay leaves, and pour the egg and milk mixture on top, allowing it to cook before removing from the oven. Sprinkle with coconut and brown it a bit. Serve with rice and chutney.

LAURA VAE GATZ

BUSHMAN WALK
TUESDAY MARCH 16, 2010

I was able to take some photos of Oryx today. They're called "the ghost of the bush" because they're very shy and don't usually stick around for photos. We came across three young males and they seemed content to let us up close and personal. Probably about 30 feet away.

Last night's bushman walk was very interesting. Our guide Duma and his brother led us on a walk in the bush, where they had several sites set up to show us how bushman used to live in the Kalahari. Until about 30 years ago when the government came in and relocated the bushmen to towns, Duma's father lived the traditional bushman life.

Duma and his brother, Nxumse (Num—see) took their gear that had been stashed under one of the Jeep's seats and disappeared into the bush for about 15 minutes. When they came back they were dressed in traditional garb, which isn't much. A very modest tied loincloth made out of kudu leather and animal leather sandals with thin lace ties tied up their legs. Over their shoulders they had a kudu-skin bag full of all their traditional tools they needed in everyday life.

The first thing we were shown was a plant whose root helps digestion, if it is chewed, but not swallowed - the Dye plant, which is part of the indigo family.

Next we stopped next to one of the thorn trees we've been dodging as we drive around in the jeep – the Umbrella Thorn bush. The thorns are long, about 2", and very hard and sharp. When we drive too close to one everyone leans in towards the middle of the jeep so we don't get thwacked. The bushmen use these thorns as needles. They use a knife to take off the outer layer of white, then use another thorn to poke a hole in the non-sharp end. Sinew from antelope (oryx or kudu) is used as thread. This sinew often comes from the tendons in the leg of an animal they've killed.

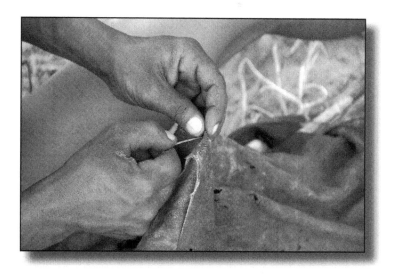

Duma gave me the needle to keep. It's threaded with a little sinew. They use this tool to sew up their animal-hide bags. They first make holes all along the edge of the hide, and then go back with the sinew-threaded needle and sew the ends together. By rolling the ends of the sinew together on their legs they can make a very long strand. Sinew is also used in their bows.

One of their tools is a holder for arrows. It's a root that has been dug out of the ground and put into the fire. The size is about 18" long and 3" in diameter. This makes the outside tough. Then the root is taken out of the fire and, while it's hot is whacked all over. This loosens up the inside of the root so the innards can be removed. Then it is stuffed full of leaves to help the outside shell keep it's shape, and put in a tree to dry for several days. Once it's dry, special animal skin is used to make end caps for it. The knee skin of the different antelopes is very thin and pliable. This is cut into a circle and molded over each end, like cellophane. One end is kept on throughout the drying process, and that is the end that will stay on permanently and not come off. This will be the bottom. The other end is taken off and put back on repeatedly during the drying process. This ensures it fits, but also ensures that it will come off – this is the "lid." Ingenious!

The San often hunt with poison arrows. The tip of the arrow is never poisoned because if you were to scrape yourself you're a goner. Only the short shaft of the arrow is poisoned, the part that is next to the tip. If your arrow hits its target, it will enter into the animal's side deep enough that the poison will begin to enter the animal's bloodstream. The wound is not deep enough to kill it – but that's their plan. The animal runs off. This gets its heart beating fast and the blood pumping, which helps distribute the poison through-out the victim. Once the hunter has hit his target, he and his buddies go off and relax and hang out for a few days. Then they get back up, and start to track the animal. The size of the animal determines how long it takes for the poison to work, and kill the animal. Larger animals of course take longer. These guys are all excellent trackers and this is where they put their skills to good use.

Once they start tracking, it's good luck if they find the long shaft of the arrow because that means the tip must still be buried in the animal. They make the arrows with a detachable tip so they can reuse the long shafts and store them separately from the poisoned parts. The long shaft will come off, and that will keep the tip from being pulled out as the animal crashes through the brush.

In their tradition, it's not the man who makes the kill that gets the meat, it's the man who made the arrow who gets to decide who gets the meat. The arrow making is left to the old men. Old men have the skill to make the arrows and they typically aren't doing hard labor any more so their hands will be less apt to have cuts on them. Cuts would be dangerous when working with the poison.

The poison is collected from beneath the Corkwood bush. A specific kind of worm likes to use this bush to reproduce. The flea beetle works its way into the root and it's the worm-like larvae that are poisonous. So the men will dig with their digging stick in the ground right by the root and will dig up these little nodules. This is where the poison is. Since the arrows are made from metal and metal won't absorb poison, they wrap the very top part of the arrow shaft with sinew, and this is where the poison goes. These little animals only have larvae in the ground for about 6 months of the year. So the poison has to be collected during that part of the year and stored for later use, as is the case with so much in this part of Botswana. 8–10 of the grubs need to be put on each arrow shaft to make it poisonous enough. The poison can remain active on the arrow for up to 50 years – possibly 100 years. So if you find one lying around, don't pick it up!

Fire. As the contestants on Survivor have shown us over and over, fire is hard to make without special tools. Duma and his brother showed us how they make fire. They make fire sticks that they use over and over again. Most of it is the same as you've always seen — two sticks, one stick is flat on the ground, the other stick is twirled quickly and repeatedly on the other, to create enough friction to create a spark. The San have a few variations that make their way of making fire just a little easier and more successful.

The Corkwood bush is the bush the fire sticks are made from. They are cut from branches about a centimeter in diameter. The sticks are put into the fire for a short amount of time. When it's still hot they can straighten the stick, and once it's straight they will pull off the bark and leave it in the sun for a few days to ensure it's nice and dry. One of these sticks will be the bottom stick, and it will get grooves carved into it. One groove is made each time a fire is started. Three cuts are made for each groove, one on top and one on each side. The side cuts allow the hot spark or ash to fall off the side of the stick onto the tinder. The other stick must be very straight because it is used as the vertical stick that is rubbed quickly between the hands. Two people usually work on starting the fire, like a tag team, because it is important to keep at it until the fire is started. I think the Survivor contestants usually give up too quickly. Hard pressure must be used against the bottom stick in order to create enough friction to start the fire. One secret little thing is added to help create additional friction — sand. That's one trick to tell new Survivor contestants!

Storing water is a necessity in the bush because the dry season is about nine months long. The only thing in nature the Bushmen could find, which could hold water for long periods of time, was an ostrich egg. A small hole would be opened at the top with an arrowhead, then with a small stick the egg would be scrambled inside the egg and put on hot ash to cook. This food was then given to the old people in the village who maybe didn't have a lot of teeth and needed soft food to eat, and was also given to young children.

The egg would be washed out with water and scrubbed. Then water would be put in, and it would be sealed with Kalahari Currant leaves, which contain an antibacterial substance, which would keep any bacteria from growing in the water. The egg was then buried in the ground a few feet, to keep it safe, and little twigs were placed sticking out of the ground above it in order to keep predators from digging it up or walking over it.

Water can be gotten from a root called Be Balp Root– or milk root. It looks like a really huge turnip. The one Duma dug up for us was about 10 inches in diameter and 8 inches tall. A knife is used to take the outside off of one side, then the inside meat is carved off in little shavings onto a bed of grass. Once a fair bit has accumulated, it can be picked up, mashed into a wad, and squeezed to produce water. To drink it, place a wad in your fist, point your thumb towards the ground, open your mouth and place your thumb just above it. The "water" will run down your thumb and drip into your mouth. I tried it. Not bad, but really bitter. And it leaves a bitter dry place way in the back of your mouth. However, if it's that or die, I'd choose the Be Balp.

If you're worried about having dirty hands you can use leaves from the Brandy bush. Just pick a few and then rub them together in between your hands. This leaf has an antibacterial property and has enough moisture in it to clean your hands. It's like nature's anti-bacterial gel. One downside – it's just slightly sticky.

On safari in the morning we went looking for animals again (of course!). Our first spot (my spot!) was an Oryx. Well, officially it's not an Oryx, it is a closely related animal called a Gemsbok, but because my guide has been calling them Oryx, I'll do the same. They're beautiful antelope-like creatures, large and stocky with straight horns that reach for the sky. The females have horns that aren't quite straight. Their coloring is the same as the male, so the difference in the horns is one way you can tell they're female. On their face is wonderful black and white pattern, which makes them look like a superhero with a large white mask that has long points on the bottom. Their rump has a black stripe that runs through the tail that is all black. Another black stripe runs along the bottom of each flank. It makes them look like they're outlined in black. Their ears are very large, with big black spots in the middle surrounded by white. Most of the rest of the body is a grayish tan.

The Oryx has the ability to control their body temperature through their face. I can't say I really understand how it works, but the black and white pattern helps with this. Oryx have the ability to control the blood flow to their face and nose. This allows more blood to pump through their head to avoid perspiration, and this can cool them off and save water in their bodies.

I'm amazed at how perfectly content I am to sit in the back of a

Jeep all day looking for wildlife. The landscape here is pretty. Subtly so. Tan grasses, acacia trees, scrubby brush, and the possibility that something amazing is around the next corner. It's certainly a page out of the book on anticipation. Sometimes it's frustrating when you see fresh giraffe tracks but can't turn up a giraffe. Or when the lion tracks are all around you but there's no lion to be found. Sometimes I feel like I want to get out of the Jeep and look underneath it to see if it's hiding there, just playing a little joke on us. The airstrip was filled with tracks, new since we were there last night - three female lions and two babies. The baby tracks were so cute. Perfectly formed, four claws and little tiny pinpricks of claw marks in front.

Adrian told us of a story of a family that came to visit the lodge. Their two children were probably both under ten years of age. They went out on a safari one day. The children had been warned that this was a serious place and they needed to listen to the guide and to their parents and to never go off by themselves. Well, they were tracking a panther and it was in sight when one of the boys hollered out loudly because the other one had taken something that was his. The panther heard this sound and charged the Jeep. Adrian banged with his hand on the Jeep door which managed to frighten the panther away, but not before it got within a meter and a half of the vehicle, with it's eyes locked on the kid that had been making the loud noise. Adrian turned around from the driver's seat and told the parents it was simply too dangerous to take the kids out on safari, and drove back to the lodge.

Adrian said to observe the behavior of large animals, especially big cats, when at wildlife parks or the zoo. They will tend to follow or watch the very old and the very young. Although they might be a little tame because of their circumstances, they're still wild animals and will focus in on the weaker ones, the ones they know they could eat for dinner.

Four-thirty in the afternoon is our time to meet at the lodge for a little "tea" (i.e. tea, coffee, and a little snack to tide us over until dinner at eight), then we head out. Duma sits in the chair on the front of the Jeep and both he and Adrian look for tracks and animals off the road. I look for animals too. What I'm finding is that I have to be actively looking around, as if I'm looking for a shooting star, in order to see some of the animals we find. If I'm spacing out or have my eyes closed because I'm tired, I will miss much of what we find because it may run away from us. I tell you, it's hard work being constantly aware. And there's also a fair bit of luck involved. Just like looking for a shooting star. If you're looking in the wrong part of the sky when a star shoots across the heavens, it's gone in a flash and you're going to miss it. It was the same with the Honey Badger we saw. He was on the side of the road, and by the time I'd located where they were looking, all I saw was his posterior disappearing into the grass on the side of the road. Boy did he make tracks through the grass. We took off after him in the Jeep, following him off-road into the grass, at high speed but he was faster, and then we lost him. If I hadn't been looking around and slightly behind the Jeep this morning we wouldn't have seen the Oryx. Looking for animals here is quite a lot like looking for a needle in a haystack, except this is a 15,000 hectare hay stack, and the needles keep moving, and sometimes blend into the hay.

Keeping this lodge and the little cottages relatively wildlife free must be a full time job. Right now there are ants on the hardwood floors looking for food, a walking stick closer to the bar, a katydid on the French doors, wasp nests on the ceiling fan, bats in the bathrooms, butterflies in my living room, spiders on the walls and large geckos and lizards on the walls hiding around the edges of the picture frames. Ooh yeah, and cute little reverse ladybugs (black with red spots) crawling on the books on the coffee table. It's a veritable cornucopia of wildlife inside the buildings! And I thought all the wildlife would be outside!

LAURA VAE GATZ

LEOPARDS & LIONS OH MY!
MARCH 16, 2010

Tonight was the night. Wow! We saw a leopard. Duma had seen its tracks on the road, going into a grassy area. Then we drove around this area looking for exit tracks, which we didn't find, so it must still be in the bushes. Then I spied it coming out of the bushes onto the road and quickly indicated to Adrian I'd seen it. He stopped the Jeep and backed up a few feet. The leopard saw us and started walking towards us. And it kept coming. And coming. I softly asked Adrian how far he thought it was going to come. He said that these leopards are ones that know the Jeep and are familiar with it. If it got to close he'd bang on the Jeep to scare it away. It got about 10 feet away and stopped. It sat down and looked at us. Then it lay down. The leopard just watched each of us for a while and then yawned.

I had my camera out and was taking photographs. It was almost too close to focus on for my 100-400mm lens. Mentally I was trying to will my camera shutter to be quieter. Admittedly I was a little nervous, but with the assurance from Adrian I knew he'd be watching the leopard carefully and would keep us safe. What an amazing experience to be so close to a leopard, and during the day, and to have it laying down just feet from me. I could hear it breath, see the individual hairs on its body, and see the color of his eyes. My heart was beating a little fast and I had to make an effort to control my breathing in order to not shake the camera. When he looked directly at me I could feel tingling in my fingers and all up and down my arms. I didn't want to look away but I also didn't want to appear to be threatening or challenging. I was desperately trying to remember what I'd heard about making eye contact – was it good or bad?

After about 10 minutes it heard a noise, stood up and walked across another road and into the bush. Adrian thought he was probably going to check out what his sister was doing. Maybe she'd made a kill.

We took the Jeep into the bush, found the male off to our left, and Adrian proceeded on to the large tree ahead of us and to the right. There was the sister. In the tree was a freshly killed Wild African Cat. This is the cat that (most) domestic cats descended from. There aren't many left because a lot of them have bred with domestic cats.

The sister is smaller than her brother. Both are about a year old. We pulled the Jeep in fairly close and she was very relaxed and comfortable. She jumped up into the tree and lay down. After a while she went over to the cat kill to play with it. She's learning how to handle her kills. After playing with it a while, almost dropping and just barely catching it, the cat fell to the ground. She jumped down to retrieve it and take it back up the tree. This happened several times. I'm amazed at how quickly she could move from branch to branch. We had an amazing time watching. Not only is it rare to see a leopard in Botswana in a tree, it's exceptionally rare to see one with a kill, and even rarer still to see one with a kill of its own related species.

When the leopard took its dinner out of the tree and started walking through the grass with it, we decided it was time to leave her in peace. So we drove back out to the road and continued on our way. The sun was approaching the horizon, so it was a good time for the Sundowner, which we had by one of the watering holes. Again there weren't any animals there except for a few ducks. And we were told to stay close because it was still a mystery as to where the Momma leopard was. The girls went to the right for a potty stop, taking care to stop behind the first bush or tree. No room for a lot of modesty here – safety is more important. Everyone knows what you're doing anyway, and people just avert their eyes. I had my sparkling water again, and there were kudu kebabs. We soon cleaned up and were on our way again, this time for the "night safari" with the great big light. It's about the size and shape of a five-pound can of beans, with a handle on the bottom, and one incredibly bright beam of light. The technique is to shine the flashlight into the trees, and along the ground in areas where animals might be. If there are any animals, their eyes will light up like stars. The light doesn't bother animals that are nocturnal; animals that are up and about in the daylight don't like to have the light shining in their eyes. If it's a daytime animal we make sure we get the light off it as quickly as possible.

While driving down the road, Duma and Adrian saw something in the distance and took off down the road like we had rocket fuel in the tanks. I braced my feet on the ledge in front of me, and put one hand on the railing in order to not be tossed about. With the other hand I clutched my extra camera to make sure it stayed inside the Jeep. When I asked what they thought it was Adrian said over his shoulder, "hyena." When we stopped to look at tracks they were lion tracks, and fresh! And then we saw her. A pale tan mass of muscles, off to our left side. A lioness. With each stride she seemed to move yards. I took a sharp intake of breath and exhaled in a whisper, "Ohhhhhh! Wow!" as softly as I could. Camera poised, Duma shone the bright light in her direction as she walked towards the lodge. We turned around and got in front of her so the Jeep could be stopped for photo taking. She stopped at a small water hole just across from the new lodge. The water here is the grey water from showers and such. With her face towards us this was the perfect opportunity for face shots. She was close enough that I could see her tongue lapping up the water. Oh, the muscles in the chest and forearms! Unbelievable. She looked like a great tan hulk crouching there. I put my camera down for several seconds in order to experience this event so that I'd have more memories than simply through the back of my camera. Amazing! What power must be wrapped up in those muscles - even more muscular than the kangaroo we saw in Australia that is built for climbing up mountains.

Then she walked on and we got ahead again, anticipating that she'd come across the road. But she didn't. All of a sudden a loud, deep, very close roar erupts from the bush. The first roar was the loudest. The it repeated, over and over again. Out of my mouth I hear the words, "What's she doing?" Svetlana said, "Are you scared?" I said, "Well, to tell the truth, just a little." Adrian explained that female lions use that call to locate other lions or to let them know where she is - the bush equivalent of a Tweet. And it also means that she's not hunting, because everything within a several kilometer area knows exactly where she is. Then I said, "So it has nothing to do with us." Correct. Ahhh. Cool. The last few roars petered out. As we started to turn around to drive off, she started again and we sat to listen. My heart rate returned to almost normal and I didn't feel as if this might be my last night on earth. When she roared the first time it sounded so close I felt like her hot lioness breath was right in my ear. I think I literally jumped out of my seat. Eyes wide in fear. That'll get your heart a-pumping.

Once we'd gotten back to the lodge the sounds of her roars could still be heard on and off for about twenty minutes. I can still hear the sound of her roar. Roar isn't exactly the correct word; growl isn't either. I think "call" is a good descriptor. Deep, throaty, resonant, gravelly, and almost amplified, as if the lioness was throwing her voice. Amazing how it sounded as if she was sitting in the seat next to me. I think that's the most wild sound I've ever heard, out in the bush. Real, with more than a tinge of danger associated with it. Enough to make me jump and set my heart to beating hard enough to feel as if it might jump out of my chest.

DELTA CAMP
MARCH 17, 2010

Never leave an apple in your open sided tent or you'll come back to find it half eaten with ants swarming all over the leftovers, and a special poop present letting you know someone was here.

Wheeww wheee, it's humid and hot and buggy here. Saw a baboon at lunch, although he didn't stay and eat. But I heard he came for breakfast and almost helped himself to some fruit on the table. The three British couples were talking about it when I arrived. Apparently the baboon jumped up on the long table they were eating at and started walking towards them when one of them had the presence of mind to make a big noise and scare it off. Baboons are fearless, and therefore dangerous.

The birds here are noisy all throughout the afternoon. Caws, chirps, buzzes, pip pips, operatic song at an odd pitch, twirtles, cheeps, chabeeps. Clicks and rasps. Whoo heee wehooo, wehoooo. And in the background a constant hum of frogs and katydids. This place is alive, all around, only feet from me. And there's nothing between me and this vibrant life except air. I'm hoping to keep at least a little space between the mosquitoes and me. I'm feeling a bit exposed. It feels very, very wild here. More alive and wild than at Deception Valley, and you remember how many forms of wildlife had found their way into the buildings there. Those buildings at least had walls. My casita is built around an ancient tree. There are walls, but most of them don't connect with the ceiling; they go most the way up to the tree branches and then stop, leaving a gap. The wall facing the swamp is only two feet high. Above that it's a large open portico to the outdoors, which kind of makes my entire room more like a veranda or a porch, not an enclosure so much.

My first mocorro ride was today. Found out I don't exactly have the right clothes. Almost the right clothes. They're the right color, however the pants are too thin. The thinness is great for coolness, but not good for grasses that tear at and attach themselves to whatever walks by. There is a mess of little stickers all over my pants. The activities at this camp are lot more physical and messy than the last camp. Here there's no riding around in a Jeep. There is gliding through the marshes at eye level with the grasses, lily pads and spider webs, and walking in head-high tall grasses, getting thwacked in the face with sharp edges. There is no dry ground to walk along, well, there is some, but mostly there's a lot of wet, marshy land, dark, squishy and muddy. And holes. Lots of holes and uneven ground.

Once we got to the island across the hippo infested waters from the lodge, we walked for a few minutes and once we were in an open area I got the safety talk. It was a little bit like scared straight. "If I say freeze you freeze. If I say run, you run like hell and climb a tree. If I say back up slowly, back up slowly. No screaming. I'm here to keep you safe. I'm here because of you and you are here because of me." Fair enough. I half expected him to say next, "If I say drop, you drop and give me 50. If I say jump you ask 'how high?'"

Before we took off in the mocorro for the first time I got a slightly different version of the safety talk. This one was specifically about hippos. "If we come across one, don't move, don't talk and don't take photos. Listen for my instructions. If he charges I'll say jump. Then jump and run." In order to clarify I said, "So, you mean, jump over the edge of the boat, and then run for the nearest land?" Yup. Got it. Silently I was mulling over in my head if the instructions included leaving my equipment behind like you're supposed on an airplane in the event of a crash. If it happens, I think I'll take my stuff with me, and hold it over my head. I'm not letting any hippo sink my cameras!

And there were more instructions as I was walking to my hut with the camp manager. I always need to be looking around as I walk to and from my hut. Be aware. If I run into an elephant, turn around and walk back to where I'd come from. Slowly. The elephants and hippos come through camp in the evenings and overnight to get to the other side of the island. I guess that means no typing on my iPhone while walking, eh?

Lying in bed, it's morning and the forest has come alive once again. There's the slightest lightness in the cloudy sky outside my hut. Large animals are moving around close to me. I can hear their movements. And I smell elephant. Did you know elephants have a smell? On the way back to my hut last night we dropped off another couple, and I smelled a thick smell – Rose, one of the British ladies, said that an elephant had been outside their place last night and took a mighty pee right outside their door. She said she couldn't get the smell out of her nose all night. Sleepily listening to the sounds around me now, sometimes it's hard to distinguish the larger animals from the growling in my stomach. I do believe I ate too much at dinner last night.

My tongue is pasted to the roof of my mouth and my lips feel dry and cracked. Time to rehydrate. It's another walk this morning, through the wet dewy grass. Although my clothing will get wet, my insides will be drying out as sweat pours from every available pore, drenching me thoroughly. It's a full time job to keep the sweat from dripping into my eyes, which is highly irritating and stings rather a lot.

I wonder if I should bring both cameras again today. I did use them both yesterday. And Papui, my guide, said he'd carry them for me. Delta camp is almost a little too wild for me. At the end of a two-month trip I can just about say that two nights will be enough, as fascinating as this place is. The little voice in my head occasionally says, "Ok, where's the AC?" or "It would be nice to just sit on the couch with a cold drink and a cat in my lap." Funny how the small conveniences of life suddenly sound so appealing when I'm hot, buggy and uncomfortable. But I tell myself "Be in the moment, realize there's nothing you can do about the heat or the bugs, and hey, you're getting some really good exercise tramping through all this long grass and across uneven ground."

As I sit on the toilet for my morning nature call, I spy my little hut bat again, doing his job, eating the mosquitoes. I squeeze my eyes shut. I know he needs to be here and that he's helping out, but it creeps me out just a little bit because he flies so close to me. I feel a breeze on my hands, then the side of my face. It's a good thing my eyes are closed, because, if they weren't, I'd be flinching. If I hold still he won't fly into me. I know this, and yet....my sister Lisa would be freaking out right about now. She didn't like bats, at all, after having them live in her walls and attic where she lived for several years.

Only a few minutes before my 6:30 wake up call. I suppose wake-up is a little later here in order to give the animals time to get back to where ever they're going to be for the day. Don't want to cut a hippo off from his goal - that would be bad. I'm thinking I don't really want to get up. Maybe staying here and just looking for wildlife outside my open wall would be good enough. Why make an effort? But no, I must get dressed and go out. But I can tell you that I will be very happy to get back for the midday relaxation period.

One of the most exciting things we saw today was a herd of impala. We spied them from a ways away and were able to sneak up on them from downwind, behind a rather large anthill. I had my camera ready to take photographs. I climbed up on the anthill platform, which raised me up several feet above the surrounding landscape, giving me a wonderful vantage point from which to take photographs of the herd. We had snuck up on them so successfully that they weren't running away and I had been looking for some action shots because they run like leaping ballerinas. My guide agreed to flank them and get them running, and told me to be ready because I'd only get one chance. I was ready and took some wonderful action shots, freezing them in flight.

What a wonderful entertainment we had just before dinner, during drinks. Drinks are at seven, because any later and the staff would have to come fetch us from our rooms. As it is, I was minutes away from having an escort from my hut to the lodge because it was getting quite dusky. I left the hut at one minute to seven.

The Lodge has a wonderful veranda that runs the length of the lodge, just two steps down from the main level, and right on the marsh. There sit these wonderful high lounge chairs, strategically placed the correct distance from the wooden railing so that it's a perfect rest for your feet. From this vantage point, the five of us watched the night's entertainment – a wonderful light show put on by nature, in two acts. First the lightning in the distance, both lightning bolts and what my friend Denis calls "heat lightning" which lit up the clouds wonderfully. Some of the tall thunderheads were lit from behind. For an encore, the lightning bugs came out to play and find mates. What an astonishing display. I've never seen so many of them at once. I felt as if the world had been turned upside down and the stars were below the sky, twinkling up a storm. Lovely. When a particularly good flash of lightning occurred, a communal "ahhh" or "good show" was heard from our ranks. My British compadres have been most fun and clever with their comments. Although they might not have said it, their uttering, "Jolly good show!" would not have been out of character.

This morning at first breakfast one of the items of banter between the couples went as follows. It's simple but makes me chuckle. "Did anyone polish your shoes last night? No? Pity you didn't bring your man." I simply must capture a few other choice comments before we all leave tomorrow, they're too precious to forget. Just makes me want to say "Lovely visit, 'ol chap. Pip pip and all that. Cheerio!"

Another story that was told was of a friend of one of the British guys, driving in Germany. A cop pulls the couple over. The officer comes up to the window, which the man rolls down. "You've been drinking," the officer states. The man answers, "Yes, I have been, but my wife is driving." They were driving a car from Britain, which has the steering wheel on the right, not the left.

Last night's dinner was an exercise in avoidance. Avoiding eating extra, unplanned protein, both powdery and not. The candlelight, although it did provide a lovely glow, also provided a focal point for all the bugs within the area, bringing in a myriad of moths, small little bugs including the lightning bugs, which were the only bugs we didn't mind, and several praying mantises. It was quite a feat to keep the bugs out of the drink, and off of the plate. We had rice, and it was necessary to check each fork full in order to ensure none of it was moving, as some of the bugs did a darn good impression of a grain of rice. Then there was what Wanda (Adrian's wife from Deception Valley) calls the peppercorn bugs. They look like a peppercorn, but don't taste as good. The praying mantises were keen on necks and investigating the scenery down the front of people's shirts. We'd all be having a lovely conversation when someone would twitch wildly, flailing hands and arms around their head, ears and neck. Occasionally a quiet little shriek would erupt involuntarily from the victim. It made me feel better that I wasn't the only one prone to such involuntary spasms. It was quite funny, especially in light of the civilized British conversation at the dinner table. Quite out of character normally, but with the local flying distractions, quite understandable.

In the mid afternoon, after the morning walk, after second breakfast, and after a refreshing shower, I find myself laying in bed, scantily clothed due to the heat, and trying to imitate the bird song around me me. E–o–e–o whoo whoo, like a fresh construction worker hooting at a pretty lady. A trilling woo–woo–hoo, whoo–woo–hooo. A throaty caw. I do wonder if any of my neighbors can hear me. Do they think it's just an odd sort of bird, odder than all the rest, or do they think the heat has affected the young American lady? In the bush I was mumbling to the elephant to just take one more step forward and one of the Brits said, What's that?" I just said I was mumbling to elephant. He said "Oh probably just some American endearment, 'Hey, baby, c'mere.'"

LAURA VAE GATZ

IMPALA, IT'S NOT JUST A CAR
MARCH 18, 2010

T his morning was a long hot walk, after a lovely light break-fast of sparkling water, a banana and some of what they call "crunchies." I'm getting the recipe. Sesame seeds and things that look like flax seed. It's quite a nice little bar for breakfast.

Delta Camp Crunchies

Original Recipe	*Roughly Translated*
125ml Flour	*1C Flour*
125ml Sugar	*1C Sugar*
125ml Coconut	*1C Coconut*
125ml Linseed	*1C Flaxseed*
125ml Jungle Oats	*1C Dry Oats*
2 Tbs Honey	*4T Honey*
2tsp Bicarbonate of Soda	*4t Baking Soda*
30ml Hot Water	*4T Hot Water*
200g Melted Butter	*14 oz melted butter (1 ¾ C)*

Mix all dry ingredients together. Mix water, soda, honey and butter together in a separate bowl. Then mix in with the dry ingredients. Place in a flat tray (like a jellyroll pan). Spread nice and flat. Put in the oven at 230'c (about 445'F) until nice and brown.

(I've made these once since I got home and need to adjust the recipe a little so that the ingredients stick together better when baked. One tip — make sure they're well done so they are crunchy, otherwise they're kind of soft and not as good.)

My hut seems to have become quite the little haven for bees and wasps. The wasps are busy building a home just to the left of the headboard on my bed. I will have to tell Leonard, the camp manager, and he can have one of the staff vamoose it. After my afternoon walk I return to my room and the nest is still there. At dinner I ask Leonard if they sprayed it. He says, no, but we did remove the larvae. Looking at him blankly I ask politely, "What?" He said that the wasps are making their next round of larvae. If the larvae are removed, they won't have any reason to continue building the nest. If the nest is removed they'll just build it again. And if they spray it, it's not environmentally friendly.

So, then I ask, didn't they spray the rooms to keep the bugs out? Nope, they don't use any spray, which is why I can't find any in my room. Deception Valley Lodge had spray, but not here. It is interesting to observe the differences between camps.

At lunchtime there was an almighty rainstorm. The thunder was getting closer and closer and cool breezes were sweeping into my room so I quickly gathered my things and headed off towards the lodge before the rain started so I wouldn't have to walk to lunch in the rain. I made it with several minutes to spare. Before the rain hit, the staff were busy unfurling the canvas windbreaks around the edge of the lodge – and then attaching the loops at the bottom of the "curtains" into the little pegs at the bottom of the posts they attach to. This keeps them from banging around or blowing in the wind. A bit like setting up a tent.

Towards the end of lunch, I say to Papeo that I'm not keen on walking through the wet this afternoon - maybe we can just go to the village. The village is several kilometers away from here, and accessible only by walking and mocorro. It's actually a bit more effort than I was after, but not really all that strenuous. However, the afternoon does tend to be hotter than the morning. Here at Delta camp they have to start their afternoon activity before it starts to cool off because of the early hour that the hippos start to move around.

Because it's rained, the going is a little wetter and more difficult than normal on the way to the village. We follow the truck tracks back to the airstrip, which is about 2 kilometers from the camp, and then veer off into the grass. About 1/3 of the track is under water. We walk in the middle of the road when we come to the parts that are underwater, up on the higher ground that is actually covered in thick grass. It's tougher going, but definitely dryer. The grass in the field is still slightly wet and my pants start to get damp. It's another kilometer to the mocorro. This one is made out of fiberglass so it doesn't have any cracks in it, but it does have water because of the rain. Papeo dries it out with a sponge, turns the plastic seat over for me to sit in, and we're off. The plastic seat is the kind of plastic bucket seat you might find in an old school cafeteria – hard, plastic, and "buckety" - kind of molded to the body. Take the metal legs off a hard plastic chair and you've got what I'm sitting on. It's quite nice because it gets me off the floor of the mocorro just an inch or two, far enough to be above any water that remains in the bottom. Once we get to the other side of the water it's another little walk to the village.

The village has maybe 150 or so people. It's called "!Nxoyogh." The "!" is a tongue click that I can't seem to combine with the "N" sound immediately after, and am shy to try. Its population has been declining, as more and more residents become guides for camps. This is good for the people who are guides, but not necessarily good for the village because its population declines.

Just before we arrive in the town I ask Papeo what the appropriate greeting for hello is. He tells me "Dumella" and says it translates to "good morning." I comment that it's no longer morning and he gives me a different word, "Letotzi," followed by "Mma" if it's a woman I'm addressing and "Banna" if it's a little kid. The add-on for a man I wasn't going to attempt to pronounce, so I don't have it recorded. Let's just say it has a tongue click – consonant combination baffling to my mouth. I try my new word out on a few people. I receive a greeting back. Cool. I say hello to one man, "Letotzi," I receive, "Letotzi, Mma," back, and an interesting look from the man. I wonder if he was contemplating my greeting in his native language, Setswana, coming from a white girl. Way far back in the recesses of my brain, "Dumella" sounds familiar. I think it's because it's used in the book series The Ladies Number One Detective Agency, which is set in Botswana.

The homes are round. The walls are made of grass and mud, and sometimes the material from termite mounds. It's very long lasting and hard. That's why you see so many termite mounds around long after the termites have moved out. There's something in the termite's saliva used to make their mounds that make them very hard and resistant to water erosion. Many people use soda cans in the middle of the wall to give it a little structure, and I suppose it also makes the wall less heavy. The roof is pointed and thatched. It is supported on a wooden structure of branches or poles. These poles are several inches outside of the wall and don't touch it. The poles form a frame, which is also a frame for the roof. The grasses I've been walking through are the ones used to thatch the roof. They're very strong, shed water easily and are very plentiful.

Many homes have little areas that are fenced off for a little privacy. I see laundry hanging to dry. One home, and only one home has a small satellite dish. I laugh and pause to take a photo. Papeo says, "That's my home." I say "Really?" ensuring that he's not just giving me a hard time. But it is his home. Good for him, I tell him, asking if he has a generator, which he does. What he needs now though are solar panels to charge the batteries that he has.

This village is very remote. Although there used to be a road from it to Maun (the closest town), it's fallen into disrepair and is not navigable any more. If you were to try to drive from here to Maun it would be a very circuitous route and would take at least 5 hours. It's a trip that should take maybe an hour or two. The only other way to Maun is by mocorro, which is a trip of 3 days each way. They get their supplies flown in to the airstrip Delta Camp uses (another camp called Oddballs uses the airstrip as well, and is just next to Delta Camp) and then they're transported by foot to a mocorro or by speedboat, one of which we saw yesterday.

The only meat they eat must be purchased and flown in. Because of government laws, they're not allowed to hunt on their own lands, but must hunt in a designated hunting area, which does not include that land on which they live. Because of this they have several resident warthogs that have found it a nice safe place to live because they can't be hunted.

There are a few "stores" in town. Simple, square shacks with a large window ledge opening to the front. The doors have padlocks on them, and the window has a sideways door that props open when they're open for business, and locks shut when they're not. Only the basic necessities are on the shelves inside. Flour, sugar, oil. Soda. Everyone in this world is addicted to soda. It's so odd. Inside a disused hut I see a pile of soda cans, waiting, I assume, to be used in the construction of a new hut.

On the edge of town I notice a partially completed structure of cement block, and next to it a pile of light grey bricks. I ask what's going on. Pepeo says that the village is building a structure for the traveling clinic that comes through once a month. For most people here that must be the only health care they ever receive since the closest town is at least 5 hours away one way.

Our last stop is "the supermarket." I would call it the craft market. The ladies have been told that I'm coming. They have all their crafts and goods laid out in a flat, grassless area, on strips of cloth. The one craft of Botswana is shallow baskets and flat tablemats made of the grasses found in this area, dyed with natural dyes, and woven together in beautiful patterns. I select a few and ask whose they are. One lady steps forward. She gives me the price when asked, and I decide not to bargain. Whatever I give them will be a more than fair price for me and may help them out quite a bit. There are also little mocorros about 8 inches long, a few necklaces with beads made from grass, and bracelets as well.

With my purchases in Papeo's capable hands, we set off back towards the mocorro. The sun is starting to get low in the sky and it's time to head back. The path doesn't seem quite so long this time. As we head out into the water I notice the amazing clouds on the horizon, a combination of dark grey storm clouds and towering puffy white thunderheads. The contrast of the sky with the late afternoon light on the green grasses is stunning. I ask Papeo to turn the mocorro a little so I can get a nice shot. The sky is reflecting in the still water, making a wonderful scene. Rich and vibrant. Full of life. The sun goes behind a cloud and it's instantly cooler. I sit back and relax, soaking up the colors and enjoying the quiet watery sounds of the pole coming out of the water to be repositioned for the next push.

As I was getting ready for bed last night I took off my wet hiking boots and socks. Whew wheee. Finky Steet! (stinky feet). There's just something magical that happens when you walk around all day in the damp and wet, walking through the bush, and in and out of swamp water. The aroma is just breathtaking. Literally. I didn't want to leave my socks out because they would have a fine layer of dew on them in the morning, so I put them in the trunk provided to keep your things from disappearing at the little crafty hands of monkeys. This morning, they were no less fragrant. As soon as the sun came out this morning I lay them on the bed to air out, and put my hikers (slang I've picked up along the way for my hiking boots – probably in New Zealand) on the ledge of my hut, taking care to tie the laces around a branch in order to keep them from falling over the edge. Although the hikers don't look much dryer, the socks are considerably less finky. I don the socks again and make plans to take advantage of the next lodge's laundry service.

LAURA VAE GATZ

MENO AKWENA
MARCH 19, 2010

Wow. I feel like I'm in Out of Africa. I am the only guest here at Meno Akwena. I'd been booked at Mapula Lodge. Part of that camp is underwater because of high water and this is the alternate camp they've booked me into. It is a tent camp. It's a permanent camp, but the rooms are tents. Now, it's not like sleeping on the floor, oh no! There are sleeping beds out on the verandah, and water in brass containers and a washbasin for washing your hands and face. Bucket showers, but a real flushing toilet – all outside. When I say "bucket shower" it's not a literal bucket made out of wood or plastic, it is a huge brass urn, suspended from a high tree branch, with a shower head attached to the spigot on the bottom. It's very chi chi for a bucket shower. A raised wooden platform has been built over a drain as the shower floor, so you're not standing in water. Wooden towel racks are on one side, far enough out of the way as to keep the towels dry. On the other side there is a wooden shelf in a convenient spot to put soap, shampoo and razors. And along the far wall are two sinks built into a cement cabinet. The sources of water are two copper urns. The view from the shower is spectacular. It looks over the edge of the cliff, down at least 50 feet to the bank of the river. Although there is a fence around the shower area, the side by the river is a little lower, which allows me to peer over the top and down onto the riverbed, where elephants and hippos like to cool off and play.

There is a fence all the way around my campsite except on the riverside because it's a very steep slope. During my shower I could hear and see the elephants playing in the water as the sun set. Man, you can't get better than that. AND the water was still warm. This place is so cool.

Max is my driver. He picked me up at the Maun airport. From Delta Camp it was a ten-minute flight to pick up a couple at another camp, and then 20 minutes on to Maun. Then about 30 minutes of waiting before Max showed up – although Svetlana's plane flew in just minutes after we landed. We had a happy reunion, strangely happy to see each other. She said they saw about ten giraffe and more female lions the day after I left. Then it was at least a two-hour drive to the Camp. What a long trip it seemed today. We stopped about an hour into our drive for a snack and drink by a lake. Then we went "over the border" meaning we went through a checkpoint and across the fence line. This fence line has a little bit of a story that has to do with a demarcation line between cattle that are free from foot and mouth disease and those that aren't. We had to sanitize our shoes in a small plastic container, much like we did in Antarctica, when coming back to the ship from land. The whole shoe sanitizing procedure was rather informal, given the other lengths they go to in order to stop vehicles.

The roads here are good but full of possible obstacles. The cattle, goats and donkeys are all free range and like to hang out close to the edge of the road. Any one of them could decide to cross the road at any time. I'd compare this to Michigan where deer like to dart across the road, especially around dusk. The same thing happens here, except with domesticated animals.

People, close to the edge of the road, are using a pair of donkeys to pull a cart, others are riding on the horses, with only thick blankets to sit on. I have not seen any bicycles here. Odd. Perhaps it's just too sandy on the unpaved roads here for bikes to be of much use.

There are signs on the side of the road marking small cattle stations or people's homes, but they don't have writing or an address on them. You have to look for them, or you might take them as random bits of rubbish. One family marks their cattle post with a bit of metal, some are painted, others not. Could be an old car door or a broken milk crate or part of a chair. Or even a car bumper. I can imagine the directions to their place the first time someone visits. "Yeah, we're about 55 minutes outside of Maun, on the main road. We'll be on your left, just look for the old car bumper about 5 kilometers after the chair with three legs. You can't miss it."

Occasionally I'll see a small group of people on the side of the road. Eventually I figured out they were all waiting for a bus. The bus stops on the side of the road seem to be pretty informal and I can't find any sign indicating it's a bus stop. Perhaps the buses just stop wherever they see people waiting. There are a lot of people waiting on the sides of the road – in the shade wherever they can find it.

The elephants were spectacular today. In this area it's mostly older male elephants around because the females and babies are in the places where they know there's been water for a long time. The river here just started flowing year-round the last few years. Before that it was only seasonal. Looks like weather patterns are changing all over the world.

So, back to the elephants. I must have watched the ones playing in the river for almost an hour. First I ran to get my camera. Then I ran back for my monopod. I wasn't running very far as my tent compound is right above the banks of the river. Prime real estate for viewing the playing elephants. At first there were three. Then two more joined them. It looked like there was a rite of passage the new ones had to go through in order to access the water. They were thoroughly checked out by the first three, then when they passed muster, they were allowed to get wet. Very funny. The first three had been playing in the water for at least twenty minutes before the others joined them. They were all splashing about, draping their trunks over each other's backs, facing-off in mock fights in the water, wrapping their trunks together and around each other's tusks. Out of the water they would charge each other. I even saw one of them fart in the water. I said to no one in particular – "I saw that!"

Out of the water, elephant farts are even better. They're...melodius, like a little primal music. Juicy. Reverberating. They sound like a little elephant tune. Interesting. I have to say I've never, in my life, ever thought about elephant farts. Now I'll be able to hear them in my sleep. Literally. At least there is a fence around my tent so I know if the elephants do pass through camp while I'm here they'll be able to pee only so close to my tent!

Tomorrow is a full day safari. Whew, it's going to be hot. I will make sure I have batteries and memory cards with me for the trip. Maybe I'll just bring my whole backpack with me. That's not a bad idea.

The plan for the morning is to wake up at first light, slowly, very slowly, unzip the tent, and creep out of it, as if I'm hunting game, and maybe I'll be able to see some of the night predators taking their last sip of water before heading back inland before the sunrise.

Then breakfast is at seven, and we're off as soon as I'm done. It takes about forty-five minutes to get in to the park – the Central Kalahari Game Reserve.

With bubbling noises coming from the river with elephants blowing bubbles in the water, to the katydids in the background, to the sound of my tiki torch that shows me the way to the bathroom, I am ready to drift off to sleep, knowing that tomorrow will be a fascinating adventure. Good night world!

A lovely group of people came in while I was out on safari.

They're doing a mobile safari but stopped here for a night. One of the ladies, Pam, is traveling with her niece and nephew, showing them a little of Africa. She lives out of her car when she is here, and it's a very cool car. A Range Rover all decked out to live in. We hit it off and are going to keep in touch. She'll pop in to see me in Dallas when she's back in the states. What she does in Botswana, when she's here, is build libraries for schools. The government is working on it, but has a very long list. So some schools are down the list quite a ways. They've said to Pam, that if she can get the building built, they'll supply the books and other organizational things.

Botswana is a very new country, and has made great progress in the last 40 years since their independence. They used to be a British protectorate, but were never a colony. When they got their independence there was basically no infrastructure. A year after independence was declared, diamonds were found here. That, of course, was amazing timing, and gave Botswana a nice income with which to create infrastructure. The road we took to Meno Akwena is only ten years old. Before that, the main road was a wide sand road. I've never seen so much sand in one country before. I know Botswana is mostly a desert, but not all deserts have this much sand. In the winter the grasses die off and the areas that are grassy now become mostly sand. Hard to imagine how different the landscape must look in June, July and August.

When asked, David, the owner of the camp, says he's happy to have guests of any age. He tells parents, when they inquire about bringing kids on safari, that he loves having children as guests, because when out on safari and the children make noise, any sort of noise, it attracts the predators. He says he's never seen such well-behaved children. His comment communicates to the parents very clearly that their children need to behave, and puts the burden of making that happen on them as well.

Noticing the position of the sun in the sky I decide it's time for a shower. If I take it before the sun sets I have a much better chance of avoiding the mosquitoes, which is a good thing when you're standing around outside naked! Sometimes it's too easy to forget that avoiding mosquito bites is about more than avoid itchy bites, it's about possibly avoiding malaria. Once again, the elephants are playing in the water as I shower. The sun gets lower and lower in the sky, creating a lovely sky, which morphs from blue to orange.

Afterwards, I change back into my clothes, being careful to put my shoes on immediately after the shower, before walking anywhere, in order to avoid any possibility of a scorpion sting. One of the ladies that works here told us at dinner about her scorpion sting she got several months ago. From what I understand the scorpion stings here are on a whole different plane of pain than ones from the southwestern desert in the U.S. Even within Botswana there are several different kinds of scorpions, some more venomous than others. Most scorpion bites here happen at night. The scorpion has a passive hunting strategy – they hang out just under the sand and sting as a barefooted person walks over the top of them. The sting she got incapacitated her for at least three days. She said that no painkillers even put a dent in the pain. All she could do was lie on the bed and wait for time to pass; she couldn't even talk to anyone. Or eat. It felt like there was a white hot poker in her heel, but that the pain affected her entire body making it difficult to breathe and making her muscles cramp.

The elephants are still at it, playing in the water. And I hear another sound. It sounds like hippos. It is! There are three hippos in the same area as the elephants, and the hippos are fighting in the water. Although I'm quickly losing the light, this is too good an opportunity to pass up. I unzip my tent quickly, duck into it, grab my camera, long lens and monopod and walk to the edge of the cliff, maneuvering myself on the high bank in order to see the hippos' heads and jaws. Not being familiar with hippo behavior I'm unsure if they're really fighting or just messing around. Hippo's jaws remind me of the commercial for the "Reach" toothbrush where the add talks about the concept of a "flip top head" which would make it easier to reach the back teeth effectively when brushing. I think hippos have a flip top head. And what a shape! I believe God had quite a sense of humor when making hippos. They have a massive head, eyes that stick up above the water, and a huge, enormous nose area. Right under the eyes, hippo heads get very narrow, then their upper jaw blooms into a massive nose/snout. When looking at a hippo with it's huge open maw, from above, the head looks like a child's drawing. What animal would have such a massive head, then get really narrow only to have such a wide snout? Almost looks like a factory flaw.

As I am photographing the hippos and elephants in the fading light, the staff comes through to light the lamps in my compound - two on the porch, one inside the tent, one each in bathroom and shower, and one tiki torch. The lamps look like small hurricane lamps, but the base is made from plastic, not glass. And the fuel isn't propane it's bio fuel. It doesn't get hot, and does not produce any smoke. Bio fuel is made from plants. When asked, that's the most specific answer I could get. I wonder if it's like saffron oil or canola oil? After doing a little research once I returned home, I found that it could be what some refer to as the magic bean. Also known as Physic nut, Jatropha curcas, or Pourghere. The plant requires very little water to grow, and each plant can live for more than forty years. And as it drops old dead leaves, it nourishes the soil and helps with soil erosion.

Before bed, one last pee. I duck into the bathroom and am greeted by my friend the large flatty (spider). Although I don't know for sure it's probably a Selenopidae Anyphops. Also known as a wall crab spider. I say "Hello," like we're old friends and I expected him to be sitting just across from the toilet. I don't even flinch anymore. They're just part of the furniture. Like a decorative spider. Just there for ambience. Hardly ever see them move. Although when they do move I know they move very fast. However, I also wouldn't be surprised if I pried one off the wall to find little plastic suction cups underneath and a label proclaiming "made in China."

The walk back to my tent is a little too dark as I remember the Jurassic size millipede tracks from this morning and the one I just saw on the way to my tent earlier.

My tent is in an enclosure. A fence about 6–7 feet high, made mostly of good size branches and brush. The way into my enclosure is through an opening with removable poles. David's suggestion was to keep the poles in place when I'm in or out. Having the opening sealed off keeps the large animals and predators from coming around to check things out. So each time I leave I lift 3–4 poles out of their track, move them to the side, and reverse the process once on the other side. The more I go in and out the fewer poles I remove, trying to see just how few poles I can get away with removing. Two is the minimum, and that's only if I don't have a backpack on.

Max, my guide, and I go out for an all day safari. Although we did not find the rhinos we were looking for, we did see many, many elephants and were able to watch them at close quarters for long periods of time. All the "ele's" we found were males, some old ones and some young ones who are old enough to get kicked out of the breeding herd. The breeding herd is what it sounds like, a herd of females and young elephants. When the males reach puberty, around age twelve, they'll get kicked out of the breeding herd and will have to go hang out with the males. When this happens they meet up with the old men, to learn a bit about life and learn all their tips and tricks. Education time. As we would get close the elephants were immediately aware of us, each one investigating us in his own way. One might lift its trunk up to smell us on the wind. Another might just look at us, and still another might prefer a mock charge.

A mock charge is interesting. Each one is different. First the elephant starts walking towards the vehicle, then it might bring its ears forward and come forward quickly, making himself look as large as possible. When we don't flinch they lose interest in us.

Elephants are fascinating to watch. They're so large, and, most of the time, so quiet. They have a heavy, elegant gracefulness about them.

So, this camp, Meno Akwena, has been here for 7 years. David used to do mobile safaris, but then in order to be considered as part of the park area, they needed to make a permanent camp. This persuaded the government to have wildlife access to the river in this area. A camp provides income for the country, employment for locals, and also encourages land and animal conservation. So the fence that divides cattle from wild life is open in the area where Meno Akwena is.

Once David decided to have a permanent camp, they started off kind of basic, without decorating it all at once. He's been adding things as he goes along, which I think helps add to the ambience. He had the beautiful wooden boxes that are used in mobile safaris, designed especially for him. They are now all over the camp, used for many different things, and are beautiful and project nostalgia. In the main area they are used as both room dividers and storage. One faces forward, and two backwards, making for a place to store dishes and glasses, a place to put the breakfast buffet and tea service, and in the back there are places for other storage. These boxes are beautiful and so cleverly made. Each one is like a small trunk. The lid opens on hinges and stays open with supports on each side. The insides are removable and hold plates, cups, a tray for silverware, and places for covered pots full of food. One of these boxes came with us on our all day safari and held lunch.

Other decorations are brought in from India, through a friend of David's, such as the brass hand-hammered urns that hold water. They're both beautiful and useful. I find them in my bathroom, shower, communal bathroom and the lodge area. Being a "tent camp" these are these urns are the main areas for washing hands around camp. Underneath each urn is a brass bowl to catch the water.

David's brother made many of the furniture pieces around the main area of camp. By the fire pit are a few iron love seats. The great thing about iron in this part of the world is that you don't have to worry about the bugs eating it. They're beautiful and fit right into the old-world feel. Some of the staff made the other wooden chairs that encircle the fire pit.

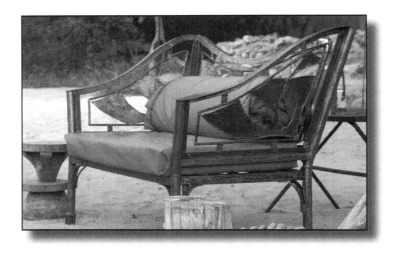

The main eating/hang out area has 4 or 5 old parachutes hung as a canopy overhead. It's quite a nice effect. A mix between circus, Bedouin camp and posh British Indian tent-camping. But the furnishings decorating the room cancel out any tendency towards thinking the place looks like a circus, it's, in my mind, Hemingwayesque.

One night the appetizer was Tomato Soup. I'm not a tomato soup fan really, but I like it a little better than lentil soup, so I almost passed. But I decided to give it a Girl Scout taste. It was fantastic!

Everyone at the table seemed to have the same opinion. When I mentioned I was interested in getting the recipe the woman across the table from me mentioned she'd like it as well. So we asked for it and here it is. The cook didn't exactly have a recipe but she came out from the kitchen and told us what is in it. I transcribed it into my sketch pad, in which I'd been making notes once the battery on my laptop gave out.

Meno Akwena Tomato Soup

1 T Butter
1 Onion – fry in butter
4 Tomatoes – skin, chop, mix with onions
Partial cube of chicken stock - add
Simonzola cheese (Italian style mild blue cheese)
Fresh cream – a little, at the end
Salt
Pepper
Pinch of Sugar
Boil onions and tomatoes till cooked, along with partial cube of chicken stock. Then mash. Add cheese and cream. Then add sugar, salt and pepper. Voila! That's it.

It is so peaceful sitting on the edge of the river, high up on this steep bank, steep enough to discourage animals from climbing up it. The water bubbling in the splash pool to my left, the sounds of breakfast being cleared, the clank of dishes, and the sneezes of someone with hay fever. The birds seem to be the only animals close to the water this morning. The elephants and hippos must have gotten their fill of the water last night because they're absent. Hornbills and Frankolins caw and tweet. No traffic, no cell phones, no TV or radio. No airplanes. Ahh, delightful.

SANTAWANI:
THREE WISHES GRANTED
MARCH 21, 2010

I've left Mena Akweno and have flown to Santawani. I had quite an awesome afternoon. As we were heading out of camp, the camp manager (and my guide), Doctor, and I were getting to know each other. Two of the typical topics of conversation in this situation are what animals I've seen and which ones I would like to see. Knowing that guides cannot produce animals on command, I said that I hadn't seen giraffes yet, and that it would be cool if we ran into some, or could look in some of the places they like to hang out, but that I would be thrilled with whatever we saw. Less than a minute after I'd stated this we drove around a large curve, and bam, there were the giraffes! It was as if my desire had summoned them out of thin air. There were several of them, all sizes and colors. I never knew that giraffes came in so many different colors and patterns. You can definitely tell them apart from each other. They're so graceful, which I wouldn't have expected, being so tall. After we were done watching the giraffes about twenty minutes later, I tapped Doctor on the shoulder and said "Well, that was cool. I'd like to see some zebras now." And I laughed. We drove on off down the road, and not more than a few minutes later, there were the zebras, just off the side of the road, grazing." I laughed, quietly of course, and thought this was a pretty excellent way to start the day. Hmmm, what did I want to see next?? Apparently it was mine for the asking.

After the zebras wandered off, we did too, and we stumbled fortuitously into a huge herd of elephants. There were so many that both Doctor and I started to count them. 65–70 elephants! When we came upon them they were grazing on the move and heading towards water. Doctor could tell they would cross right in front of us, so we parked the Jeep and just watched them come. Mothers and youngsters, babies just weeks old, and then more elephants of all sizes. Amazing. Such large masses all moving through the grass and trees virtually silently. I could almost feel the masses disturb the flow of air. If I'd been blind I'm sure I would have been able to sense the presence of large bodies moving.

Part of the herd has come across a large watering hole and is slowly moving across it, like an approaching line of soldiers storming a beach. They walk into the water, drinking as they go, trunks stretched out in front of them, sucking in the cool water, and then transferring it from their trunks to their mouths. It is such a peaceful scene. And then, all of a sudden there is a commotion and elephants are moving out of the water. Something seems to have disturbed their slow advance across the pond. I look more closely and see that what I thought was a short young elephant, is actually a hippopotamus. The elephants have invaded his quiet pond. And he's not happy about it! He scares the elephants away by charging them in different directions until they leave. Before they leave the elephants merely back up, trumpeting loudly and looking decidedly anxious. I'm sure the mothers are worried about their young. No doubt the hippo could do a little damage to one of the young. Doctor and I are quietly laughing. How funny that this short animal can scare off elephants. It makes me think of the troll that lives under the bridge in fairy tales who demands payment for passage over his bridge.

We eventually drive on, still amazed at the sheer numbers of elephants herding together. Doctor says he's never seen so many in one herd. Our tracker picks up some lion tracks that are very fresh. We follow them, on and off the road. We meet up with another safari vehicle, one from another camp. It's chock full of people. I think almost every seat is full which means they have at least 9 people. I silently chuckle to myself. Tee hee, I've got my own private safari! We head off in one direction and they head off in a slightly different direction. We're both tracking the same lions. We can tell they've lost the trail, because we're still on it, and their Jeep isn't anywhere near ours.

We see the lions; they're on the other side of a line of trees. Now we just have to figure out how to get over there. As we're driving around the trees we hear the other Jeep driving back and forth, apparently lost. Not only have they lost the trail; they don't seem to be able to follow our trail either. Unbelievable. Perhaps their tracker is sick today, or the guide left his glasses at home.

There are two lions, a male and a female. The male is about seven, the female about ten. They are sitting fairly close to each other, about two yards sits between them. I watch the female yawn and stretch and rolled over onto her back. The male is watching her as if she is something yummy to eat. The male is clearly interested in the female, and she doesn't seem all that into him. It's as if she'll tolerate his presence, but she doesn't really want to carry on a conversation with him. He's sitting there, apparently contemplating the best way to get her interested in him. Then he makes his move. He stands up and slowly walks over to her. She is sitting now, all four paws and belly on the ground, and her head is up. He approaches her from behind, slowly walking on either side of her body, so as to not step on her. He softly bites the back of her neck as if asking a question. She already knew what her answer would be, and that was a resounding "No!" in the form of a quick growl thrown over her left shoulder in rebuke. "No! You're too young for me and it's too hot." I can just imagine her conveying in that growl. She gets up and trots off into the scrubby bushes.

Doctor knows we'll never be able to navigate in those bushes and we drive off, content to have seen what we did. The other Jeep finally showed up just a few minutes before the female lion took off into the bushes. I never could figure out what took them so long.

Amazing. Simply amazing! To see this interaction in the wild is just a dream come true. It's like sticking my head into the television while watching a BBC or National Geographic documentary on Africa, except this is better, it's live. It's real! These lions aren't in a fenced park or in a zoo. They're out here in the wild; free to roam where they want to without restrictions. Living in the city most of my life, growing up watching Marlin Perkins on Mutual of Omaha's Wild Kingdom on Sundays, and later in life, the Discovery channel and the Animal Channel, being here in person is almost surreal. I feel alive. I'm happy and content. And excited! I could ride around on safari for the next month and be perfectly content to watch whatever we come across. It's simply fascinating to see what is around the next bend, to watch each species' behavior, and to not have any timelines to do it in.

What an amazing three hours. I can't believe that's all it was. We saw giraffes, elephants and lions all within that time period, and we didn't even drive that far. Oh, the giraffes - six of them! As we flew into camp I'd seen one – that was my first – but we were 1000 feet up in the air and I only saw it for a few seconds before we'd flown past it. So, to see 6 of them right around the corner from camp was breathtaking. Wowza!

After the midday relaxation period we went back out on safari. We ran into another Jeep, and Doctor and their driver conferred. The driver told Doctor that they'd seen wild dogs just down the road. Wild dogs are endangered and, if we could find them, would be a rare viewing opportunity. So Doctor yelled over his shoulder, "Get ready, we're going to go really fast. So hang on!" And he gave us several seconds to get ready before he took off, and then he really took off, fast! That's the fastest I think I've gone in one of those Jeeps. We must have been going at least 50 miles an hour, down a grooved, bumpy, potholed dirt road. Just before we got to the "T" in the road we slowed way down. This apparently was where the wild dog sighting was. And there they were, lying in twos and threes, along the side of the road, in the shade, and just off the road in the grass. How exciting! When Doctor said "wild dogs" I had no idea what to expect. I expected domesticated dogs that had gone feral. But African Wild Dogs are their own species. They are also known as the Painted Wolf, or Painted Dog. It is the only species in the genus Lycaon.

They're an endangered species. There might not be more than 3000-5000 in the world. They are very strong and fast and have incredible endurance. They work together as a pack and kill their prey while it's still running, literally tearing it apart with their teeth. Studies have shown that their kill success rate is around 80%, whereas lions' average kill rate is 30%. Lions and hyenas will often follow the pack, knowing their great success in making kills in order to steal their dinner from them.

I think there are several problems that plague their population. First they need to have large areas where animals are protected so that there is a good population of prey to eat. Second, only one female breeds within a pack – the alpha female. Although there may be several females of breeding age, only the alpha reproduces. Once the alpha dies another female takes over as alpha and will start to breed. Although the female may have up to 10 in a litter, the little ones have to keep up with the pack as they hunt, almost from the time they're born. That can be a hard thing for a newborn to do. So, as a result, there is a high mortality rate amongst young ones. Predators that are following the pack can pick off any slow youngsters lagging behind the pack.

We sit to watch the dogs for a good twenty minutes. They're very social animals, licking and grooming each other, and playing, pretending to fight. Two of the dogs are curious about our vehicle and cautiously wander up to take a closer look. They must have come within ten feet. My camera shutter kept clicking away. Occasionally I would take the camera away from my face for a few minutes to watch without several layers of glass being between the action and me. I know it's important to sporadically stop shooting and enjoy the moment, without the camera. But it's still a hard thing for me to do.

I've never seen dogs like these. They are definitely their own species; much different from any domesticated dog I've ever seen. They're all leg (all the better to run with, my sweetie!). Their ears are huge, and round, and stick up away from their heads, as if permanently on alert (all the better to hear you with, my sweetie!). And their teeth are huge (yes...all the better to eat you with....). African Wild Dog has a Bite Force Quotient (BFQ) of 142 – the highest of any currently living carnivorous mammal. The BFQ is essentially the strength of bite as measured against the animal's mass. In comparison, the BFQ for lions is 112, and 98 for the leopard. And Fluffy, your house cat has a BFQ of 58. Doctor said that these animals can rip their prey apart while it is still running. And, as other predators follow these animals, eating their prey quickly is an important habit.

I captured an image of one of these dogs yawning. Man, those teeth look sharp! The dark face of the dog I caught yawning combined with his sharp teeth reminds me of Cujo, the crazy rabid dog from the 1983 movie. Yeah, I know Cujo was a St. Bernard, and these dogs don't look a thing like him, but nonetheless, something in the back of my head says "Cujo" when they yawn and show all their teeth. It's quite a menacing sight if you lose track of the fact that they're only yawning.

Ok, It's after dinner now and I've got to get to sleep. Our morning starts at 5:30 a.m. with a wake up call, first breakfast at six and then we head out around 6:30 a.m. I'm back on the schedule I had at Deception Valley. I like it here. I was a little concerned about the rooms because although they're nice, they're not exciting and different like the other places I've stayed. However, I can't say as I care now that I know the wildlife is fantastic. I'd sleep anywhere if it meant we'd keep seeing the kind of wildlife we saw today!

MY WHAT BIG TEETH YOU HAVE!
MARCH 23, 2010

Yeah, he looks ferocious, but he's just yawning. It's early evening and time for big cats to wake up and go to work... hunting. This is the time to wrap up the naps, stretch, sharpen the claws on trees, say hi to everyone, and get on the road. Our road. As the lions start to move around a little I ask Doctor what would happen if I got out of the Jeep this close to the lions. I prefaced my question with "I'm not actually thinking of doing this, but I'm wondering...." Doctor said that at close range, once I separated myself from the Jeep, I would be within the cats' comfort zone and they would charge me. If I came up on them from farther away, they'd probably just run away. It's all about fight or flight and how close you are when they see you. Good to know.

Another stray thought wanders through my brain, and this one I do not put into words out loud. This one is simply for my pleasure. I wonder if lions have "elevator butt" like my cats do. You know, the phenomenon that makes cats raise their posteriors up in the air when they're scratched on their back, just north of their tails. I wonder if anyone knows. I don't suppose that's a test that has been performed in the wild, or if it has, that no one has lived to tell about it.

Both the dogs and lions take long naps in the afternoon, conserving their energy in the heat of the day so they can hunt later on. We can see the full and extended bellies of the dogs and know they've eaten a good meal recently. In fact, we know it was an impala, as we saw one of the puppies carrying the impala head across the road in order to chew on it. The lions on the other hand look hungry. Not that they're malnourished – they're not, they look nice and healthy. But their tummies are flat and their breathing is slow. After a meal their tummies will look round and full and their breathing will be hard as their bodies work to digest what they've just eaten.

As the sun dips closer towards the horizon, the lions begin to stir. They yawn and stretch, one female does a yoga move – downward facing dog. I knew that was a good stretch. It's the same stretch my cats do after a nap. They walk around and lick each other, greeting one another, and getting ready to go out hunting.

A few of the lions wander off, and we later figure out that they were after the wild dogs we'd just visited. They scattered that group; we can hear the dogs trying to communicate with each other to regroup. It will probably take all night for them to find each other, which will put a damper on their hunting activities tonight. And it might put some of the younger pups in danger if a predator spots them. I wonder if the lions killed any of the dogs. I find it hard to reconcile that both sets of animals I've watched today could be killed by other animals. Granted, the lions are pretty much at the top of the food chain, but all the other animals have predators.

The balance of the lions that didn't take off after the African Wild Dogs start to head out towards the road. We back our Jeep up and place it in the road so the lions will walk right past us. The pride moves from the shade of the trees into the tall grass just off the side of the road in front of us. I'm amazed to see just how camouflaged the lions are in the grass. They almost disappear. Occasionally I'd see a tail swishing through the grass, apparently without a body.

Several young lions are sitting in the grass, in a row, one behind the other. The front lion yawns, and shows me all of his teeth, all the way back to his molars. What a mouthful of sharp choppers. I capture the entire sequence with my camera, taking eight frames a second.

Now the lions are on the move again, and coming straight towards us. They're so beautiful in the grass, almost the same color.

They move with such quiet grace, slicing through the blades without making a sound. They're so close now I can count their whiskers. One lion looks off to his left, towards the Jeep and I swear he's sizing me up. He slows down. Then stops. He decides to take a breather, and sits less than one leap away from the side of the Jeep, just even with me. I'm feeling two different emotions. I'm thrilled to be able to watch this lion so closely. And on the other hand I feel just a little scared. I watch my movements, make sure none of them are fast, and I once again find that he's almost too close to photograph with my 100-400mm lens. What must he be thinking? What's going on in that lion's head? Eventually he wanders off with the other lions, starting to get down to the business of hunting.

It is so interesting to find these large groups of animals and then to sit and watch their behavior as they get used to the vehicle being there. The giraffes are a bit too on guard to get back to what they were doing before we got there, but the dogs and lions either ignore us or get back to business fairly quickly.

I wonder which animals will die tonight. Kind of sad, really, but each species has to find its own way to live. As we drive past herds of impala and giraffe, we told them who was on the hunt tonight and to be careful. Maybe they should start running now.

STUCK IN THE MUD
MARCH 24, 2010

This morning was interesting, and slightly amusing. Knowing that I have all day to get somewhere is nice. It means that any issues I run into don't really matter. In the wee hours of the morning thunder awoke me. I thought to myself "Gee, that's probably not good." A little while later it started to rain, and it rained hard and then softer on and off for the next 7–8 hours. Not having flown in the rain I wasn't sure what to expect. Doctor thought the runway should be fine.

After breakfast we headed out to the runway. I remembered the waterproof cover for my camera bag and put it around the bag. The staff put my suitcase in a lovely lime green plastic bag to keep it dry. Perfect. Now I just needed something to keep me dry. After waiting in the rain for about 10 minutes watching the jackals hanging out on the runway, Doctor remembered there were raincoats in the Jeep and offered me one. I put one on and used another to cover my camera bag, just for good measure. Then the call came in on the radio that the plane was going to be 15 minutes late; more time to watch the jackals, and time for me to "mark my territory" one last time. The raincoat came in very handy for that; just like a little personal tent.

The plane eventually landed, but I wasn't watching. I was watching Doctor watching, and he wasn't listening to me ask if the plane had landed, he was watching something very intently. The plane had done a low fly by without the landing gear down, to take a look at the airstrip, and I hadn't heard it come back. But all of a sudden, when I turned around to see what Doctor was looking at, there was the plane, about 50 feet behind us, off the runway in the grass.

That's odd. Hmmmm. I wonder if he did that on purpose?

The pilot got out. It was Stephen – I've flown with him before. He says to Doctor "I thought you said the runway was fine." He was stuck in the mud. Well, it's not exactly mud, it's more like really soft wet sand, which apparently has the same effect on plane wheels as mud. Doctor walked up and down the runway. The middle was nice and firm. It's made on a slope so that the water drains off. The middle is the highest and hardest, and then as you progress to the edge it gets muddy and soft. I think the pilot got worried about the runway and pulled off to the side thinking the grass would be firmer, but it wasn't. So there was a bit of hemming and hawing and finally Doctor came back looking for a rope.

The one in the truck was too short so he radioed the lodge for longer rope. A truck with rope came out a few minutes later. Then they needed more manpower. I asked if I could help but was turned down (which is fine, I would have gotten really dirty). Another radio call was placed to the lodge, this time for manpower. Another Jeep comes with the other two guys from camp. They came with long wooden planks to roll the plane wheels up onto. Then began the process of digging the wheels out of the muck, getting the planks under the plane wheels, and hooking the plane up to the truck so it could be slowly towed. Good thing the plane was small. All it took was a few guys to lift the front of the plane up so a board could be slid under the front wheel. The side wheels were a little more tricky, and involved pushing up on each wing, one at a time.

By the time the plane was back on the runway they'd been at it for about an hour. I watched the conversation between the pilot and Doctor. Stephen was pointing and shaking his head quite a bit. It looked to me as if he might want to take off without me, afraid of getting stuck in the mud again. However, he thanked the guys for their help, I said goodbye to everyone all over again, and my stuff was transferred to the plane. I walked across the runway, trying to find the least muddy spots, and got on the plane. Stephen said, "Don't worry about the mud," as I gingerly set my muck-covered boots on the nice clean carpet inside. I hated to get it dirty but there was no way around it.

As we taxied down the runway to turn around at the end I was fervently sending up one short prayer, "Don't let us get stuck in the mud, don't let us get stuck in the mud, don't let us get stuck in the mud." As He always does, God came through and we didn't get stuck. We turned around and took off, through the mud puddles, through the muck, and past the guys in the truck who were waiting to make sure we actually got airborne before heading back to the lodge. I waved goodbye, and then waved goodbye to the three giraffes that had come to see us off. I think the jackals had already run off, or I would have waved goodbye to them too.

It was a lovely flight into Kasane. On this Cessna 206, the fastest plane in Maun, it takes just over an hour to fly to Kasane. We flew at a very low altitude, lower than the other planes I've taken. I'm sure it was to avoid flying in the clouds. The landscape here fascinates me. Ever changing: the plants, shrubs, grasses and trees change every few minutes with the change in soil, moistness of the area and other factors I'm not aware of. Simply amazing how one moment we're flying above an acacia tree forest and the next we're on wide open plains filled with water grasses. The next we are on a dry plain with very few trees. Ohh, there goes one lonely baobab tree. So cool! Their nickname is "the upside down tree," because, the way they're built it looks like the branches are roots. The trunks are very fat and round, and so are the branches. I think it looks like a drawing a kid would make of a tree. They're ancient trees, living several hundred years, some possibly even longer, and they can get massive. Around the Makgadikgadi salt pans east of where I stayed at Meno Akwena those trees are abundant. This pan is a large salt pan in the middle of the dry savanna in north-eastern Botswana, and it is one of the largest salt pans in the world. Salt pans are a result of dry lake beds, when the dry surface is primarily salt.

Flying along, running into showers here and there, I watch the landscape fly by, changing, keeping my eyes open for wildlife. Although I don't see any giraffes this time, I do spot several wildebeest, elephants, and a few unidentifiable mammals along the way.

Although very curious how the day was going to turn out, I wasn't concerned. Every other connection and transfer had worked out just fine. This one was a bit more of a mystery than the others, and a little more complicated. Most of the others had been a light airplane flight from one lodge's runway to another. This transfer didn't seem to have all the pieces, or at least I wasn't aware of all of them. I had figured out that I was flying from Sankuyu to Kasane, and then it seemed that I was going to have a transfer to the Livingstone airport where someone from Chundukwa would pick me up. What I hadn't realized is that Zambia is across the river from Botswana. And there isn't a bridge. And close to Kasane, the Zambezi River is the border between Namibia, Zambia, Zimbabwe and Botswana.

All my transfers went smoothly, even though there was quite a wait at the airport for my first pickup. There had been a little confusion when the plane was late (because of getting stuck in the mud). I love to look back on times when I put something in God's hands, because I can always see in hindsight how He takes care of me. This is one more of those examples.

So, my transfer from the Kasane airport picked me up and took me across the Botswana-Zambia border, which is right at the Zambezi River. I filled out the departure forms for Botswana and had my passport stamped. Then we drove about 100 yards further and I was transferred to a small boat along with my luggage. I waved goodbye to my driver, but he was already headed back to his van. We traversed the swift moving Zambezi River, where I was met with another driver. We drove a few feet and I went through immigration on the Zambia side, which took just a minute, and 50USD. Glad I was prepared for that. That was the only thing that hadn't been included in my "all inclusive" safari. Then we were on our way.

On both sides of the river, trucks are lined up waiting to cross. The ferry that takes them across is a one–truck–at–a–time ferry, and because the water is so high, it takes 3–4 times the normal time to cross because the ferry must fight the pull of the quick flow of the water. There must have been 75–100 trucks waiting to cross on the Botswana side, and almost that many on the Zambia side. When the river isn't high it can take 3–4 days to cross the river because of the truck traffic backup and paperwork issues. Now it's up to two weeks.

Zambia's main industries are copper mining and tourism. The tourism industry started about 18–20 years ago as Zimbabwe's political troubles started. Tourism shifted from there to Zambia, and Livingstone became the tourism capital of Zambia. About 250,000 people live in Livingstone, which is right on the Zambezi and very close to Victoria falls.

The turnoff for Chundukwa lodge is off the main road at the ferry crossing going into Livingstone. It's a very small sign and easy to miss. They're about 5 minutes down a dirt road, and right on the river, just past the practice polo fields for the local polo cross team. Polo Cross is big here in Zambia, and it's different than Polo, it's more like a cross between Polo and Lacrosse. There are six riders on each team and each team is split into two groups. Each group plays three sessions of 6 minutes each. The goal of the game is to score goals by throwing the ball between your goal posts using a cane stick that has a racket head with a loose thread net. This is used to scoop and carry the ball, which is sponge rubber and about four inches in diameter. Too bad I'm not here on Sunday or I could watch them practice.

After the camp manager, Charmaine, introduces herself and her Boston Terrier, Thug, she tells me they're on "flood alert." When I see my accommodations I understand why. They're little huts right over the water. So when you're inside it appears as if you're on a little houseboat. The "verandah" of this little place is actually inside my bedroom and not outside – it's the fourth "wall" which looks out over the water, similar to the fourth wall at Delta camp – it's a half wall with a good view. The river here totally reminds me of the Niagara River in Buffalo, New York, as it approaches Niagara Falls. It's wide, flat and swift moving.

Chundukwa is a series of eight small huts or chalets overhanging the river. One wall, as I've mentioned, is open to the river. The bathroom is back across the small walkway to the chalet, on dry ground; in its own little enclosure. It's open air too, with a peaked roof like the sleeping area. The bathroom is around the corner from the entrance so no one can see you, and the tub/shower is sunken into the floor. For privacy a reed curtain can be lowered in the entranceway, but there's an open window facing my lodge.

The bedroom is simple, rustic and perfect. The mosquito netting extends a foot or two beyond the bed so there is room to move around. The top is a solid fabric, and the netting starts on the sides. I'm amazed at how much comfort a mosquito net can give me. It's like my own little fortress against all the creepy crawlies. Well, at least against 99.9% of them.

Both things people have told me to do while I'm here are closed due to the high water. I believe I will just have to come back in the winter to go out to Livingstone Island and to do the white water rafting.

After dinner by candlelight and a talk later around the fire pit, I am escorted back to my room with my head filled with all the little nasties that could plague my night. Charmaine told great stories about blister beetles and spiders with sacks on their backs, snakes and monitor lizards, hazardous hippos and creepy crawlies. Blister beetles secrete a blistering agent, Cantharidin, which is used in the medical world to remove warts. Isn't that nice? A blister beetle can land on you and as you go to brush it off you'll aggravate it and it will leave a trail of secretion on your body as well as your hand. And the blisters it leaves behind contain Cantharidin as well, so if one oozes or pops, and you unconsciously open it at night, you can spread your blisters across your body while you're sleeping. Mmmm, such a soothing bedtime story.

I slide underneath my mosquito netting just as quickly as possible, wondering if I can make it until after sunrise to use the bathroom again. And the colony of spiders in the trees along the bank of the river is calling to mind the great spider movie, "Arachnophobia." It's really creepy, especially because my room doesn't really "close." Oh sure, there's a door, but that's not going to keep out the spiders. Charmaine says that they have to take a broom to the insides and outsides of the rooms twice a day in order to keep the spider webs at bay. Everywhere I walk I hold my arms out in front of me so they catch any spider webs in my path, instead of my face. I keep my head up, looking to see if any spiders are hanging down from the trees, and I actually walk slightly bent over like I'm rushing out to greet a helicopter, as if afraid I'll run into the spinning blades.

Before dinner I was treated to a sunset cruise on the Zambezi. Lovely. I do have to say that I was a little nervous each time the driver cut the engine to let us drift for a while. He must know the boat and engine very well because he'd wait until the last second to start the engine back up before we hit a clump of trees in the middle of the river, or almost drifted into a bush on the Zimbabwe side.

It's peaceful on the river. The water currents are not, though. We drifted over upwelling and strangely silent areas of water, and through small whirlpools where the water flowed around submerged rocks. Being on the water, I think even more now, this river reminds me of the Niagara River in New York state. Knowing that it eventually flows over falls makes me nervous. In the back of my head, thoughts are forming as to what I would do if the engine wouldn't start and my driver suddenly had a heart attack and died. Swim? Probably not – with hippos and crocs in the water there's no guarantee I'd make it. Jump off onto one of the trees in the middle of the river? Maybe. I wonder how long it would take for someone to find me. And with the river still rising, I'd have to find a really large tree so I could climb up past where the water could possibly rise. And it would have to be a tree I was sure could hold my weight. It would be a bad thing to find one only to have it start to bend over, bringing me slowly closer and closer to the water.

The beautiful clouds distract me from these slightly disturbing thoughts and I gaze up at the moon that has been getting fuller every night. I'll probably be back home in the U.S. before it's full again. Ignoring that thought I try to decide what I think IS in the moon. It's certainly not a man in the moon. I've always thought it looks like Bugs Bunny or at least a rabbit. Taking a photo of it so I can enlarge it on my camera, I look at the image and agree. It looks like a rabbit. Craters are barely visible as well, just at the edge where the moon gets dark. Fascinating.

The driver brings out drinks and snacks. Oohhhh, popcorn and chips and peanuts! The peanuts I find out later are grown locally. They're in red skins and are very tasty. The chips are some strange flavor like steak sauce, but still enjoyable. But the best surprise is the popcorn. It's fresh, salty and tastes like it was made the old fashioned way, over a stove with oil. Yum. I eat one kernel at a time, watching the sun slowly slip towards the horizon, the hippos making their deep rumbling grunts and crocodiles somewhere slipping silently into the water looking for dinner. It's a lovely ending to a long, but fulfilling day.

Morning now and I'm sitting at the edge of my room, on my "verandah," watching the golden light on the river. Branches and flotsam float by as well as some unidentifiable white pieces. After getting Mom's binoculars out to investigate, I discover they are suds. Is someone doing laundry upstream?

A knock comes at the door. It must be 7:30, time for tea. How lovely. Hot tea, sugar, milk and a banana muffin. Perfect. The water-weeds just outside my room move around. It's an odd thing. They don't just move a little, the numerous clumps actually rearrange themselves from minute to minute. Sometimes they won't move for several minutes, but then all of a sudden they're on the move again, leaves rubbing against each other as if bracing themselves against the movement. What is this unseen force causing them to move? Is it simply the underwater currents? Is it a large animal? I love that these are the kinds of things I have time to contemplate. As I do, I hear the rumblings of hippos in the background, barking good mornings to their fellow rotund water beasts. Baboons (or perhaps monkeys) on the island across the river don't want to be left out of this morning's cacophony and add their growling hoots. Life is good here on the Zambezi.

Thug is the resident domesticated dog here at Chundukwa. He

belongs to Charmaine. When she was looking after a friend's dog, it gave birth on her patio, to Thug and his brothers and sisters, and Thug chose her from the moment he saw her, following her around and chasing off any other dog who tried to come near her. Although Charmaine hadn't wanted a dog at that point, she realized that this was the dog she'd had a dream about in the past and decided that she should keep him. They've been best friends ever since.

Thug is such a happy dog, a Jack Russell Terrier, with the cutest face, and a lovely black and white pattern. He chases the butterflies, changing stride almost in mid leap. The skinks are in danger from him too. One lives by the plunge pool and during lunch yesterday Thug would take off when he spotted it. There is something else he chases that is on the edge of the boardwalk over the water. Charmaine is worried that one day he's not going to be able to stop fast enough and end in up in the water, which is a problem because of the crocs. Thug doesn't like the deep water. And the reason is because of a beaver.

One of Charmaine's friends has a beaver and for some strange reason he and Thug are friends. The beaver, of course, likes to be in the water and wants Thug to be in the water and swim like he does. Thug wants to pull the beaver out of the water so the beaver can play on land like Thug does. And so a little tug of war ensues. When the beaver wins, Thug ends up in the water with the beaver trying to pull Thug under the water so he, too, can swim underwater like a beaver. So, Charmaine can never leave the two to play by themselves.

UP IN THE AIR
MARCH 25, 2010

Today I rode in a helicopter, one of those experiences that had been eluding me. Mom and I were supposed to have done it at Franz Josef Glacier in New Zealand, but the weather was a bit too wet. What an experience! Charmaine called yesterday to book time. She was to find out for sure if they allowed cameras in the microlights or not, and if not, to book the helicopter. She booked the helicopter. The microlights sure looked cool. That might be what I do next time, but I know I'd have been itching to take photographs. They have a camera mounted on the bottom of the microlight, and you can purchase the pictures later....what a crock!

When she booked, the helicopter people said they only had a 15-minute time slot available; no half hour flights were available. Two Germans were ahead of me paying, and the helicopter guy asked if they wanted 15 minute or 30 minute. When they found out the 30 minute was double the price of the 15, they decided to stick with the 15. I tried to convince them otherwise. When I told the man behind the front counter that I really wanted the 30 minute, he said "Well, I've booked you with these two gentlemen." That seemed a little too convenient for him and a little fishy because I think "these two gentlemen" had just walked in off the street. So I said, "Well, I really would like 30 minutes," and walked slowly out the door without paying. I went to find the rest room and to give him some time to contemplate losing a sale. By the time I had come back he'd miraculously found time for me one hour later at 11:00 a.m. It pays to be persistent. The thirty minute flight included a flight through the narrow gorge, past Victoria falls.

So my driver and I got back in the car and went in search of Chitenge (pronounced stenge), the cloth Zambian women wrap around themselves for skirts. Once you reach the age of 16, you must wear Chitenge at home. If you are leaving the house you can choose to wear whatever you want, but at home, according to my guide, you must wear the Chitenge.

The cloth is 2 meters long and almost as wide as from my waist to the floor. They're made from cotton and printed with very bright colors. Of course the two that I found that appealed to me were blue, because blues and aquas are my favorite colors. I tried to find some other nice patterns, but the only ones I liked were blue.

Then we got the call that two other people had shown up for a 30-minute helicopter ride and could we come back now? Too funny! Ten minutes later we were back, and I paid the man my money. I introduced myself to the couple and found out that they had booked this a long time ago. Interesting...

Apparently Benny was the man to talk to in order to get to ride next to the pilot. I introduced myself to him and shook his hand before I knew this. My driver for the day told him that I needed to sit in the front seat. How nice of him!

When it was time to get on the helicopter, I followed Benny, who held the doors open for the departing guests who had just taken their flight. He indicated for me to get in the front seat, which I did. Very cool. The helicopter had windows underneath, where you place your feet, like a glass-bottomed boat. On the side there were small sliding windows so I could shoot directly out without having to shoot through the window pane, and there was also a window in the ceiling, I suspect in order for the pilot to be able to see the rotors turning. The pilot greets us, and gives us a short run down of the itinerary, hands us headphones to put on because of the extremely loud sound the helicopter makes, and so that we can hear him talking – there is a microphone installed in the headphones. As I clutch my camera, he suggests I take the lens hood off. He said if I stuck it out the window with the lens hood on, that lens hood would be gone for good. I thank him for the suggestion and promptly take the lens hood off. Later when I do stick part of the lens out the window I can feel the force of the winds against the camera and am very happy he said something before I got that far.

Taking off in a helicopter was exactly as I had envisioned it. You just take off. All of a sudden you're air born, nose down, and sailing over the ground, then you rise up and it's so smooth. Upon closer inspection it's not completely smooth, which is something I noticed as soon as I started to take photos. There is a distinct vibration. It's not violent, in fact it's easy to ignore, except when the camera comes in contact with the side of the window. I'm shooting at 1/1250th of a second to counteract any movement.

We fly over the falls, from different angles. Because the water is so high right now it's really hard to see much of the falls. It is easy to see the water just before it goes over the falls, but the gorge it falls into is only 18 meters (52 feet) wide, and twice as far down as Niagara Falls. So, the best time to visit, strangely enough, is during the winter season when there is less water.

The updrafts are so strong from the force of the water pouring over the falls, that it rains straight up, and the falls form vapor clouds twice as high as the falls are, so you can see the falls, or really, where the falls are, from miles away.

After we fly around the falls it's time to fly through the gorge, past the falls and the bridge they bungee jump from. Wow. This is the highlight of the helicopter ride. I feel like I'm in an iMax movie for the first time, flying through a gorge. How strange is it that the best real moments remind me of moments in the movies? Isn't that a bit backwards?? I take a movie so I can play back these moments later and bring back some of the memories. We fly low over the water, past some of the larger rapids. At one point I remember murmuring "holy crap" at the size of one rapid. A crazy person could surf that! Naturally this is not the season in which they raft down the rapids. For that you have to wait until winter. Just one more reason to come back.

After the ride, I walk around feeling like I'm walking on air. The couple that flew with me agrees that the flight through the gorge was the highlight.

Next we drove through some of the back streets of Livingstone, which look like a run down old western town, with boardwalks, and wooden posts holding up shed roofs, which keep the boardwalks in the shade. As we get out of the car I feel strange, and very conspicuously white. We pop into a shop so I can look at other Chitenge. Indians run many of the shops in this part of town. I bargain with one of the shop owners and I walk away with one Chitenge for $3. Such a deal!

Then it's on to the craft market, where I have about thirty minutes to make it down the long row of shops, each selling roughly the same items. Each shop is a bit different and I find myself migrating to the shops with the women. I notice as I walk down the line that more and more shops have women running them. I think I am being watched. And I think they notice I like buying from women, so they have the woman greet me. I am not stupid...but their ploy does work.

"Come into my shop. Looking is free. Let me show you something I made." Uhh huh. Once in the shop they'll often stand between you and the exit. However they aren't really pressuring me and they won't stand in my way if I want to leave, they all just want a sale, and I understand. It is hard to leave one shop with a purchase and not walk into the next one. Lutheran guilt catches me off guard and makes me self-conscious.

Then we're on to the falls. I've heard it's very wet. So I am prepared, or so I think. Mom, thank you very much. Your advice to keep an extra pair of shoes came in extremely handy today. I wore my extra pair to the falls and brought my boots so I would have something to change into.

Before we get to the wet part, we stop for lunch, which has been packed for us. Charmaine has been very careful to not pack anything I am allergic to, and I am thankful. No bread! Before very long we have a visitor, a baboon. He's interested in our lunch. In order to keep him busy long enough for us to eat lunch, my guide throws him a bit of his sandwich, which the baboon dissects, leaving the meat parts on the ground. Did you know that baboons are vegetarians? This baboon remains a respectful distance, but doesn't respond to my efforts to shoo him off further. Next I notice a second, smaller, baboon casing the joint. He stays his distance and hides behind part of the fencing, off to our right. I can see only his tail.

It is not very appetizing having baboons around. Although it was a good photo opportunity, and I did take some photographs, they scratch a lot, and they also have really red butts. I know that's just how they're made, but I don't want to be looking at that while I'm eating. Go away baboons!

Wet does not even begin to describe the falls, walking around them when the water is high is more like snorkeling. I should have forgotten the raincoat and either gone naked or in my swimsuit. And bringing a camera is useless unless it's an underwater camera. Hey, that would have been perfect! However, I still wouldn't have been able to see much. If you wait long enough, and look towards the falls, eventually the wind shifts for a few moments, and then there are the falls, through the mist, and then they close in again, hiding the falls like Brigadoon.

The raincoat I'm in is a jobber that snaps up the side, leaving openings where water can, and does, get in. By the end of our walk there isn't a dry centimeter left on me. My camera gear and other pack stay relatively dry, each inside it's own waterproof container.

The path we follow is made of rocks, like small cobblestones, in order to give the path a bit of traction. Because of where it is, it's wet during most of the wet season, and therefore tends to grow something akin to green slime, surely some sort of seaweed! I'm sure it's actually a kind of moss. We walk from a bright blue sunny sky into a wet, raining, rainforest within the space of 10 feet. Fascinating! The rain is hard but feels good. I can feel the cold drops through my raincoat. The rain comes in bursts, like waves. Sometimes it's straight in my face, other times it blows from below and billows my raincoat out around me as if I'm some sort of aquatic Marilyn Monroe.

I'm reminded of the time I was in Myanmar with my friend Judy. It was April, the hottest month, and also in the height of the New Year and Water Festival. During this festival, pretty much anyone outside is fair game to be doused with water. Kids stand on the side of the street with big buckets full of water and toss it at anyone who passes by. Older kids ride around in trucks with 50 gallon drums filled with water, dumping smaller buckets-full on those poor folks riding motor scooters or motorcycles that they pass.

Judy and I were each in a tuk tuk, a little cart with a seat, pulled behind a bike, where we sit, and get pedaled around town. Boy, those kids saw us coming a mile away, two "Farengi" (foreigners) riding down the street. They would run up with their buckets and say (pronunciation, not spelling) "Sawadee beep mai!" (Happy New Year) We would reply in kind and then they would empty the contents of their buckets on us at point blank range. One kid with a 5-gallon bucket did so with enough force to wash my glasses right off my face. After a few moments of panic, and trying to get my tuk-tuk driver to stop, I found them on the 8"x8" platform at my feet. Whew, close call!

Anyway, the force of the water here at Victoria Falls feels a lot like those kids throwing water on me. Except about 100 kids all throwing water at once. We're buffeted by water. Actually buffeted, blown around, beat upon, moved by. The water is a force to be reckoned with. I think it's actually alive, like a sea sprite, except this one would be a water fall sprite, I suppose. I'm standing on the edge of the gorge, waiting for the winds to shift so that I can see the falls for a moment. I watch the spray, and it looks exactly like it's raining upside down. The spray is in little droplets like rain, and it's heading straight for the sky. What an amazing sight. Then the wind shifts, blows the amazing sight right in my face and I decide that's enough of the amazing sight. Time to move on.

Our path turns into a river. We're walking in several inches of swiftly running water. As we descend stairs, they too have become a waterfall. Along the way are viewing areas, positioned a little closer to the falls than most of the walkway. If we stand still long enough we catch a brief glimpse of the falls before the mist closes in around them again. At one point there is a decision to make – the inside or outside path. I say the outside path, as I know I am already as wet as

I can possibly get. We walk down a sloping path, green with algae in between the rocks that stick up for traction. I walk slowly and carefully, as if on ice, slowly shifting my weight to each front foot before trusting its grip. My shoes are squishy inside, full of water, but I can't hear any sound they make because of the roar of the falls. Ever since white people first saw the falls back in the mid 1800's the local name for the falls has been "The water that thunders," and it is a very fitting name.

Exploring the falls has been a little like an amusement park ride, the kind you reluctantly agree to go on, knowing you'll get wet, but not fully understanding just how wet you'll get. It's like Splash Mountain, the Log Ride, and A Wet'N Wild Water park, all rolled into one, with a side of category two hurricane.

The town here is named after one of the early white missionaries and adventurers, David Livingstone, who is said to be the first white man to have seen the falls, and roamed around this area, exploring, and driven to find a water way into the interior. The phrase "Dr. Livingstone, I presume?" comes from this time and man. At one point he "disappeared" and was not heard from for several years. A journalist from the U.S., Henry Stanley, suggested an expedition be mounted to go find Livingston in Africa, which he did. When he found him, he proclaimed, "Dr. Livingston, I presume?" There is much written about these two, which I plan to investigate and read a bit of after I return home. Since I don't know the details yet, I won't include them here, but from the stories I've heard, they were both quite the characters.

The "Golden Hour" here is followed by the "Malarial Hour." It sounds like a television show, "And here's the Malarial Hour, with your guests Mozzie and Quito!" And the lead-in music surges and the hosts walk on the stage......fade out to commercial with the announcer "The Malarial Hour, brought to you by Tabard and Doom.

Why get bit when you don't have to?"

Commercial, "Hi, and welcome to Africa. Our mosquitoes don't know what Deet is. So don't try to use it here because they'll just eat you up anyway. Oh sure, use it if you like the smell as an aftershave, but I have a suggestion for you while you enjoy your stay on our little continent. Use Tabard or Doom. Mosquitoes won't go near it. Find it at your local grocer or pharmacy. In spray, lotion, coil or patch for your heater. All the forms you like the best. Stay safe! You're in malaria country. And now back to the Malarial Hour."

Seriously, it's 6:00 p.m. here in Zimbabwe, and it's time to put back on whatever clothes I'd taken off. Zipped off pant legs get zipped back on. Long sleeve shirt gets donned. Tabard gets reapplied, and I check my memory banks to ensure that, yes, I did take my Malarone today.

BACK IN JO'BURG
MARCH 26, 2010

I t's almost time to leave for the airport. I am completely looking forward to four real walls, an indoor shower without bugs, and seeing Walter's five lovable Rhodesian Ridgebacks again. Wonder if they'll remember me? Then a little laundry action, syncing my blog, and Skyping with Beth's school kids to fill them in on my last two weeks of safari, a home cooked dinner, then off to bed. Quite a full day all packed into just a few hours.

One last weekend of fun is all I have left of my two month sabbatical. Saturday I fly to Cape Town, pick up a car, and drive to my B&B on the coast. I'll have the rest of Saturday and Sunday, and most of Monday before I fly out to London, that is, unless British Airways has decided to strike. Not being by any news portal, I haven't heard where all that stands.

Goodbye hippos and monitor lizards. Goodbye billions and billions of creepy spiders. Goodbye creepy crawlies in my tub and sink. Goodbye ants on the floor and giant flying wasps in my room. Goodbye damp wet smelly socks. Goodbye spider webs in my path. Goodbye mysterious scary sounds in the night that make me sit up and listen silently for more before lying back down.

Goodbye beautiful sunrises and sunsets. Goodbye spectacular cloud formations and soft evening light. Goodbye outdoors, I will miss you. I'll visit whenever I can. Goodbye amazing animals, you are so cool and wild, be well, and try not to get eaten. Goodbye all the wonderful people I met; some of you I will see again, others not. Be well, travel safely and enjoy what you do. Goodbye strange bird cries that wake me up in the morning. Goodbye yogurt and eggs for breakfast. I think I'm going to take a break from you for a while. Don't take it personally. It's me, not you. Goodbye little tiny planes, I'm taking a break from you too. You were great and I enjoyed the low flights over the bush, but I'm going back to my big planes with air conditioning, hot towels and bathrooms; again, nothing personal.

Hello clean cool sheets, windows with screens on them. Hello kitties, don't hate me too much. Hello ice cubes and fresh vegetables. Hello car and garage and couch. Hello work and coworkers. What's changed since I've been gone? What's my next project to work on? Hello friends, I've missed you all! Can't wait to catch up. Hello Internet, wi–fi, and Skype whenever I want it. Hello free texting!

I arrived in Johannesburg on time, and Walter was there to pick me up. Once I got back to his house, greeted his pack of Rhodesian Ridgebacks, and took a long and luxurious shower, I got ready to Skype Beth's 4th grade class, for the second time. The time difference between Johannesburg, South Africa, and Fort Collins, Colorado, is 8 hours - Johannesburg being 8 hours ahead of Colorado. This time, we're on the same day - Friday.

The kids are very excited, both to talk to me, and because today is the last day before their Spring Break, so they're a bit more restless than the first time we Skyped, but they're just as interested.

Their questions ranged from "What kind of houses do people live in in Africa?" to "What was your favorite animal?" to "What kind of food did you eat in Botswana?" Beth had shared photographs from my blog with her kids, and she mentioned how large their eyes got when they saw the close-ups of the elephants and leopards.

This time I think everyone got to ask a question. I shared stories about the danger of hippos, talked about how my lodging was sometimes open to the outside so that the only thing between me and the wildlife was a mosquito net, and that my room was visited by a monkey when I left an apple sitting on my bed. I explained the safety factor of staying in the Jeep while on safari, and how the animals don't associate you with food as long as you're "part of the Jeep." They were quite impressed that we were just yards away from a large pride of lions, and that one of the herds of elephants I saw, numbered more than seventy. When asked what my favorite part of the trip was, I was silent for a moment, as I tried to figure out the answer. My answer was that each part of the trip was so different that it's hard to identify a clear winner, so I mentioned several of my favorite parts, and mentioned a few things I'd learned, which I've listed at the end of my entry for March 28th.

What fun to talk to the kids again! Exciting to know that an entire class has been tracking my trip around the world. I wonder if this experience will encourage any of them to become avid travelers, or maybe to become a photographer or an oceanographer. You never know the impact you have on people!

LOTS AND LOTS OF LUGGAGE
MARCH 27, 2010

D id I really leave this much stuff behind? Wowza! My gracious host has purchased me a small duffle bag for my extra things. It's just perfect. After a trip to the store for money and more Tabard bug lotion, I return to pack my stuff. At first I packed all my African purchases in my new duffle, but it was really heavy, so I unpacked everything and switched the stuff around. Now my purchases are in my older green duffle and all my other stuff is in the new duffle, which will be checked. I've marked it with red duct tape so that I can easily recognize it when it comes out at the baggage carousel. Nothing like new luggage to confuse you when you're traveling! I snap a quick photo of it with my iPhone, just in case. I'm all packed up again, my clothes have been washed, dried and ironed!

Yeah, I'm ready to be home. Never thought I'd say that, but hey, it's the end of my trip, I have to go home anyway, I might as well be excited about it. Time to give some luvin' to my kitties, settle back into every day life, and make some good improvements. There's nothing like a little trip around the world to give you a greater perspective on life.

I've learned a few things. No, I'm not going to share them all, but I may share a few here. One thing I've learned is that when traveling, there's really not a whole lot you need to take with you. In the future I will travel even lighter than I have been: fewer socks and undies, fewer clothes, a few less "what ifs," and fewer miscellaneous things. However, you still never know what you're going to need. If I had sprained an ankle, or gotten sick or broken something I would have needed some of the "what ifs" I brought with me but didn't use. I'll pack two external hard drives, fewer memory cards, no USB drives, fewer lenses, more lens cleaning cloths, leave the sunglasses at home, and double check the power plug requirements for each country.

DRIVING ON THE LEFT, AGAIN
MARCH 28, 2010

This scene is neither Cape Town nor the Cape of Good Hope, just a scene along the way between the two...

I picked up my car at the Cape Town airport. It was a long walk to get there, and I wonder if anything will change between now and June when the World Cup starts? Can't imagine everyone walking all that way. My name was not on the "Gold Club" list for some reason so I had to stand in line. My seatmate from the airplane was in the same boat, and was being helped when I walked up. We briefly chatted about how nice it is to simply walk out to your car and not have to go through all the rigamarole at the counter. Why does it take so long? What are they doing behind the counter? What could possibly take that long??

I have a white Yaris. Good. I've driven this car before — with Beth in Ireland. I'm feeling completely at home as I drive out of the parking lot, directions to Antrim Villa in my hands. Easily I find the N2 towards Cape Town, and after reminding myself to "stay to the left," I ease out onto the highway. Because it's Saturday, it's also construction day and there's a backup as the highway is taken down to one lane in either direction. Everyone is busy fixing roads in South Africa because of the upcoming World Cup. The slow down gives me time to locate myself on my iPhone GPS, and review the directions I have, so I know ahead of time what my next turn is going to be.

I find the B&B without any problem. Along the way, in the brief moments I'm not watching out for pedestrians or bikes in the road, opening car doors from parked cars, or red lights, I try to look around for landmarks I might need later. I manage to locate a few, but the road I'm on, High, is like Colfax in Denver, an endless sea of city businesses, in endless city blocks.

Antrim Villa is one block off the main street, and close to the water, up on a little hill. It's in a residential area, like Impangele in Jo'burg, it's behind a gate and has buckets of security. In order to enter the house I have to make it through the front gate to park the car, another door with a code box to get into the area where the house is, one more code on the side door to the house, and then use my key to get into my room. This reminds me of getting into my place when I worked in downtown Chicago. I think I needed 4 keys to make it from the front door to my room there: the front door, the inner door, a code to make the elevator go, the key to the floor, the key to the suite and a key to my room. Wait, that's 5!

The place is cute, it's decorated contemporary Ikea with a Caribbean–African theme. The building must be vintage because it has exceptionally high 14 foot painted patterned ceilings with patterns that extend down into moulding. All rooms have two single beds pushed together, a large window that opens without a screen, en suite bathroom, a wardrobe to put your things in, a complimentary safe to use, and nice lighting. No television, clock or radio. There are fans for the hot days, reading lights by the bed, and a tub and a shower in the bathroom. A two and a half foot diameter white paper lantern hovers above my bed, straight out of Ikea, tan sisal rug on the floor over light hardwood floors, beautiful delicate rattan chair in the corner, and bamboo attached to the wall as a headboard. Three silver hooks hang behind the vintage Victorian door with low brass door knob and lovely carved wood facade. There are three South African woven (what I call) hot plate mats, adorning the wall to lend some African flavor.

It's around noon and my room is almost ready. I bring in my luggage and select a few items to bring with me on my day trip, including my wallet, camera and hat. Then with a few directions I head out, driving south along the southeastern side of the Cape peninsula, taking the M6 to the M65, past Camps Bay, Hout Bay, and over Chapman's Peak. Chapman's Peak is a toll road – or at least you have to pay a toll to go over it. And then you have to keep your receipt to show a man a little ways on.

Although the driving was along fairly narrow, curvy roads in misty conditions, it wasn't too bad. If someone impatient got behind me I simply found a convenient space to pull over to let them pass. No way was I going to let someone pressure me into driving faster than was comfortable or let them ruin my leisurely drive. It's funny how I'm so relaxed as a driver when I am on vacation. Of course, it's all perspective. There's no business meeting I have to be at by 9:00 a.m., there's no doctor's appointment I have to get to on time, and there are no cats to feed or food to buy at the grocer.

By the time I'd reached the entrance point to the Cape of Good Hope Park, I'd been driving for about 2 hours and had stopped a few places for scenic photos and a little food. My first stop was the visitor's center, which has a few baboon visitors of its own. There are signs along the way warning patrons to be careful of baboons, not to feed them, interact with them, drive too fast around them or try to get your things back from them if they take something.

The first turnoff after the information center (which had lovely bathrooms and very old cypress trees) was the Cape of Good Hope, which is, I just discovered, not the most southern point in Africa. Hmmmpf. It is the most southern point of the peninsula. And it is an old famous landmark because of the tall ships that sailed around the bottom of Africa, many of them meeting their doom on the rocks around this area. The other stop I made was the Cape Point, where the lighthouse is. There is a funicular that takes you up the mountain so you don't have to walk up the slope and all the stairs, but it is being "upgraded" (perhaps that should be read as "repaired" and "prepared for the World Cup" as so many other things seem to be), and wasn't available. A ticket could be purchased to have a minivan drive you up the hill. I passed on that option and decided to walk. It's a goodly little hike and I was breathing hard when I got to the top. The pathway is a combination of slopes and stairs. The altitude gain is probably only 500 feet, possibly 750. The weather was nice, cool and breezy, which kept me at a nice temperature even though carrying my camera gear. People I passed spoke many different languages. One I hear around the world, in every port I pass, is German. Those Germans love to travel.

With some of the last 20% of my iPhone battery, I looked up the sunset time for Cape Town so I could estimate when I needed to head for home to avoid being on the road at dark. Finding your way home the first time in a new town can be challenging enough, without adding the extra dimension of darkness. I took different roads home and saw some beautiful landscape, some wine country and lovely rich neighborhoods full of fenced, guarded estates with nicely manicured lawns built amongst old-growth trees.

The Antrim Villa gates closed behind me before it got dark. After dropping my things off in my room I took the car back out to find some dinner. Dinner ended up being determined by where a parking spot could be found. I got take-away; chicken skewers and what was supposed to be mashed sweet potatoes, but ended up being just potatoes. It was good and I ate it back at the B&B while watching part of the movie "Australia," with Hugh Jackman and Nicole Kidman. Then it was time for bed. It had been a long day, starting in Johannesburg, and I'd done quite a bit of driving.

Breakfast was very good; it was as they advertised, a Scandinavian buffet consisting of cereals, plain yogurt, meats and cheeses, fresh bread and croissants, juices, cut up vegetables, and fresh fruits. And there were muffins and something they serve here that is like a biscotti, but not as crunchy. I took a muffin, some butter, a yogurt and some baby tomatoes for lunch, and had a flashback to traveling with Mom and Dad in Copenhagen last summer and the lunches we'd make from our breakfast buffet.

After breakfast I consulted the map and discovered that conveniently I am staying just a block and a half away from the craft market that Walter suggested I visit. I couldn't be staying much closer. I walked across a street and a soccer field, and wandered around the market as most vendors were getting set up. It is a great time to arrive because many of the sellers are busy getting their wares out and don't pay quite as much attention to a visitor as they normally would. I enjoy wandering without being the center of attention.

The booths they're putting together catch my eye and I stop to chat with one guy. The booths are very simple but would suit my purpose if I were to sell my photographs at a market. Iron bars form a frame – vertical and horizontal sides, to make a 3-sided box. Then to reinforce it, some have a horizontal bar half way up, others don't. Those that don't will take rope to tie tightly between the vertical supports creating a line to hang things. Ingenious, fairly inexpensive but heavy, and heavy enough to not blow away in a wind. Not fancy like those little tents with the pointy white roofs, but those are really light (and fast to put up). I wonder if I have any friends who weld??

Something catches my eye, as I'm walking slowly, talking to myself, telling myself to be careful what I buy or I'll have to buy yet another suitcase to put it in. Then I wonder how much luggage gets purchased in the name of excessive purchases while traveling? How many people have a basement or an attic with extra luggage they bought while traveling just so they could get their stuff home? Once I get home I'll have at least three bags; two purchased on this trip, and one purchased in Thailand.

I start talking to a guy, Derack. He's the artist of these fascinating metal animals. He cuts shapes out of old oil barrels, shapes them, and welds them together. His work is really nice. He turns a piece over to show me all the welds. Another piece he picks up and shows me how all the different pieces form together to create an animal shape. He names a price. I pull out my iPhone to see how much that is in U.S. I counter offer just above 1/2 his offer. And then the haggling begins. He tells me how much time they take to make and how it's all done by hand. I show him how much money I have, which is not enough, but he's willing to take British Pounds, which is great because I really don't need any and I'd like to use them up. After settling on a price I pay partly in South African Rand and partly in Pounds. He tells me I'm getting a special price because I'm his first customer of the day. Uh huh. Riiiight. Somehow, at markets, I'm always special. How do I get so lucky??

I take my purchase and wander away to sit on some steps to see what kind of cash I still have. USD. Ok, I stash different amounts in different pockets, hoping I'll be able to remember which pocket has which amount in it. I remember that I'd really like some carved animals in graduated sizes, because at home I have a set of camels from Egypt, ranging from 1/2" to 2" tall, and elephants from 1/2" to 5" tall, from Vietnam. The first place doesn't have animals that are small enough and I remember seeing another place. As I walk away, the guy I was talking to at the first booth, Romeo, hollers after me to come back, and I keep walking, conspicuous as one of the first shoppers of the day. He appears at my side as I'm about to walk up to the other booth I'd remembered seeing with little figurines. What he's doing is showing this new guy that he brought me to his place, but I mention that I'd seen this place before and was heading here. Romeo hangs around during my whole transaction.

Of course I change my mind from my original intention, seeing that what I want really isn't available. However, these carvings are nicer and more intricate than what Romeo had at his booth. I decide on 5 figurines: a large and small elephant, a leopard, lion, and a cape buffalo. I've seen all those animals. The guy had been encouraging me to get "the big 5," but I haven't seen the big 5, I'm missing the rhinoceros. These will be nice. Ok, time to go.

As I head out of the market I hear singing, through the windows of the building I'm next to. I walk slowly around the corner, wondering if it is a church, not wanting to interfere with the service if the front doors are open. Sure enough, it's a church, and there's a small group of folks inside. I perch on the step right by the temporary banner with the name of the church and service times on it. After sitting there for just a few minutes a woman comes out and asks me to come in. So I thank her and come in, sitting in the row just behind the last row of people. A minority once again, I feel just a little uncomfortable, but there is a woman singing with heart and soul and a microphone at the front of the room. She's got the soul goin' on. She walks back and forth, raising the microphone with her head and her hands. The crowd is swaying and dancing. Booties are shaking and hands are above everyone's shoulders. Being a Lutheran, I didn't grow up moving much in church. We certainly never raised our hands above our shoulders.

The swaying reminds me of choir class in 7th grade junior high, Mr. Summerville's class. Although we had a few African Americans in our class, most of us were poor uncoordinated white folk. Getting a bunch of gangly 7th graders to sway in rhythm to the music must have been a bit like herding cats. Mr. Summerville would let us sway, and once we had gotten that down pat, we were allowed to shuffle our feet from side to side. That was graduation to the next level. However, if the rhythm fell apart, it was back to swaying without any foot movement. I think most of the time we were a disappointment to him. He must have wondered how we all could have been born with so little ability to keep a beat.

Church started at 9 and I showed up just as they were getting started. After the rowdy beginning songs, they settled down to some that were slower and more spiritual. Ones with easy words repeated several times, so that even I could join in. Then the preacher got up and talked, for a long time. For at least an hour at least, maybe longer. But his sermon was good. Sometimes his story was a little disjointed, but it was still good. He talked about the harvest, and how each of our harvest times is different. We've all planted different seeds, and each of us has different times to harvest them. He talked about how man was not meant to be lazy. That humans have very few holidays. Then he related that to the harvest and how those that sleep during the harvest will be hungry. One of the things I remember is that "we should not love sleep." This is in the Bible – in Proverbs. That's too bad, because I dearly love sleep. Then he went on to say that those that work can enjoy their sleep as a reward. I didn't 100% agree with all that he said, but he knew his scripture and even managed to get the gospel in there at some point. For a while I was a little worried he wouldn't get to it. We ended with the collection of offerings and tithes. Those with tithes were to come up and receive a special prayer. Those with offerings were to hold their offering up and the preacher asked God to bless both the offering and the one giving it. It was a very nice touch, and I think, made each person think about what they were offering to God. After the offering I slipped out as it was going on 11:30.

The sun was still shining and I decided to figure out my way to Table Mountain, so I could go up in the cable car and see the view. It's not very far from here, just down Kloof road, and then up the hill. I found a parking spot amongst the myriad of cars already parked along the road. Everyone else seems to have had the same idea. "Hey, the sun is out and we can see the mountain! Hurry before it closes in again." I walked to the end of the line, and somewhere in the back of my mind I remember reading on the web before leaving this morning that I could purchase a ticket over the Internet and skip the line to purchase a ticket. The sign about 20 feet in front of me in line said "45 minutes from here to purchase your ticket. Save time next time and purchase your ticket online." So I pulled out my iPhone and tried to do just that. The Internet connection was very slow, and ultimately it would not take me to the last screen I needed to get to. And the final straw was that the ticket had to be printed out. Well, that's no good. The British guys behind me finally quit the line right around the time I was thinking the same thing. It was going to be around 200R to go up and back, and the clouds were starting to close in around the peak. How much did I really want to do this? Yes, it's what people do when they come to Cape Town, but that doesn't mean I have to do it. It's just a big tall pointy hill with a great view. I got really great views yesterday on my drive to the Cape and back. Convinced I could do something better with my money, and not convinced that the views would be good by the time I got to the top, I popped out of line and went to find my car which was farther away than I had remembered it being. After managing to turn around, I drove back down the hill and stopped in Camp Bay to hang out and enjoy the sun and the sand. There's a lovely seaside village that reminds me of Palm Beach, Florida. It's all very white and posh and full of white people in bathing suits, barefoot, and tanned. Just off the beach I found a lovely stump under a tree and pulled out my yogurt – butter – muffin – tomato lunch to eat. After a quick look through my bag, I settled on the handle end of my long nail file to eat my yogurt with. It worked quite well even if it was a bit slow. Then I spread butter on my muffin and ate that as well.

That's when I saw an older couple picking their way gently across the grass in front of me. The lady went to sit on the low wooden railing so her husband could take a photo of her on the beach. I stashed my food away and walked up to him to ask if they would like their photo together. It must be my honest face that allows people to trust that I won't run off with their camera. They thought a photograph together would be a lovely idea. So he joined his bride and they asked where I was from. They'd just been traveling on the QEII (Queen Elizabeth II) that had been in Sydney just around the time Mom and I were there. They'd sailed for 17 days from Sydney and got off the ship yesterday. That got me thinking about cruise ships and how different it is to travel on a ship, surrounded by other people on the same trip, than to travel on your own. Both are good, but very different ways of traveling.

The Pick–And–Save was calling my name, whispering "Come to me for dinner," and so I crossed the street and went inside looking for something appetizing. A banana or two, goat cheese, rice crackers and a red pepper will be my dinner tonight. And for a beverage, lovely sparkling water. Ahhh, wonderful; simple, fresh and healthy.

Done with sightseeing, I think for the whole trip, I headed back down the coast road looking for a gas station so I can fill the tank before returning the car to the airport tomorrow. All gas stations here are full service, just like in Oregon, and they take debit cards, but my debit card doesn't work like that here so I needed to have cash. This was one little tip I picked up in the literature in the room from Antrim Villa - very convenient to know that.

There are new guests at the Villa. They've just called, and then quickly arrived. It's a couple of film crews that just wrapped up, one from shooting a commercial, another from filming a movie. They've brought champagne and share a glass with me. They're all perfectly lovely, but there goes my peace and quiet. I tip toe over to the manager's office and nicely ask if there's a room that's maybe a little bit away from everyone else because I've just been informed (in a humorous way) that they don't plan on being quiet tonight. She shows me room #1; I'm currently in room #2. It's not really any farther away from the action. She tells me they have another villa just down the road that I could move to, and after I make sure that it's not too much trouble she gives me directions, takes my gate remote and keys and sends me off with a new gate code and the manager's name, Brenda.

I'm off. Up to the High Road, a road several blocks south–ish, then a right and a left. I'm there. I park in a no parking zone because I don't see any alternative, and put on my hazards. I enter my secret number to the gate and it opens to a lovely whitewashed building with a semicircular staircase opening out onto a paved pool area surrounded by gemstone colored pillows. It looks like a Caribbean paradise. I walk down the pavers, which are perfectly spaced for my stride, and up a few short flights of stairs, through a gate covered in bougainvillea, and around the corner through the main door. "Hello?" I call. I take a few steps farther inside and walk part way into the kitchen. "Hello?" I call again. I hear a faint hello from around the corner. I follow the sound of the voice and ask, "Brenda?" Yes. I tell her who I am and why I'm here. We go through a little paperwork and I get my new gate opener and keys and can pick from the three rooms available. They're all lovely. The ceilings here are even higher than at Antrim.

This villa is called Bickley House, and the building is even older than Antrim. The inner courtyards make the place. The first courtyard is up the stairs from the small parking area around the pool. The next is through the next gate by the front door. There are several small tables and wrought iron chairs for eating breakfast. There is another courtyard behind the kitchen, not for guests, and then there is MY courtyard. French doors open out into a lovely courtyard with high white washed stucco walls. There is a wide area to sit, by the wall, lined with thick olive cushions. The floor is paved with round rocks in a pattern, and two trees grow close to the high walls, providing shade from different corners. Ivy grows along the wall and I feel like I'm in a secluded Italian villa far, far away. Well, I am far, far away, from home, but I don't feel like I'm in Cape Town, South Africa.

Cape Town is a bit of a surprise. I'd heard it had a bit more of a European feel to it than most other parts of Africa. It's more cosmopolitan and first world than anywhere else I've been in Africa. It's also a "cape" town – you know, it's on the water. I imagine it must be much like parts of the Italian coast; areas I haven't been to, but have seen in the movies. Here, whitewashed buildings perch on the sides of hills that slope down to the aqua ocean. Beautiful.

After I talked with my friend Beth's 4th grade class (in the US), she emailed me to ask if there were any "Big Truths" that I'd learned from my experiences. I said, "How about a few smaller truths?" Here's what I wrote back: Big truths...umm...how about a few smaller truths?

- Most places aren't as scary as they seem.

- Most things will NOT eat you.

- I am sensitive to wheat, no doubt about it!

- I really don't need a shower every day or even every other day.

- I should not be afraid to dream bigger than I have been.

- I really don't need to eat all that much.

- I don't like to talk much, I prefer to listen.

- I'm really not shy, I just don't like to inconvenience people or be intrusive.

- Someone is always willing to help if I need it.

- I miss my friends and family.

- I would like to have a dog some day.

- I love animals - wild ones, other people's pets...

- There's usually a way to get what you want. Just be patient, keep smiling and don't take no for an answer.

- Siestas are good.

- Other things I've learned:

- I prefer Beefy Bovril to Marmite or Vegemite, but why people would spread this on their toast is beyond me.

- When using a power plug adapter, it's helpful to have the third prong - it helps the adapter stay in the socket so that it's making a connection.

- Carry a cigarette lighter adapter with you on safari and you can recharge things in the safari vehicle during the day.

- Buy the local mosquito repellant.

- Spray your clothes with Permithrin if you're going to a malarial area. It will last up to 6 weeks.

- Trip Advisor has not led me wrong. If you toss out the best and the worst comments about a place, you'll come out right on target.

- I've learned how to do the "handshake with a tip" movement fairly smoothly. Never thought I'd figure it out. Along with that, keep the money you're going to give for a tip in a place you can get to right away, like a pocket.

- Having your luggage marked with colored
  duct tape is very helpful when looking
  for it on the luggage carousel.

- When driving in a car made for driving on the
  left side of the road, controls for the wipers and
  turn signals are reversed. Turn signals on the left,
  wipers on the right. The clutch, gas and brake
  are in the same configuration as we're used to.

- If in a country where you're not supposed to drink
  the water, keep your mouth shut in the shower
  and keep the water out of your eyes. Then put
  a bottle of water in the sink the night before to
  remind you not to brush with the tap water. It's
  amazing how automatic it is to turn on the tap.

- People are interested in how the economy is
  in the US, because our economy affects theirs
  (usually), so have some short comment stored
  away in the back of your mind to share.

- Take a photo of where you parked your
  car, find a landmark, then look back
  occasionally as you walk away to see what it
  will look like when you're coming back.

- Supermarkets, or corner markets are a great
  inexpensive place to get lunch and dinner. They have
  fresh fruits and vegetables, cold drinks, yogurt, and
  usually a place with prepared meats and sandwiches.

THE LONG WAY HOME
MARCH 29, 2010

It was sunny when I woke up this morning. Knowing I didn't have anywhere to go all day until my flight at 8:30 tonight, I lazed in bed until about 8:00 a.m. What a lovely, cool morning. Waking up in a new room is great. Everything is new to my senses so it can be appreciated. The ceilings are high, the beds comfortable. The walls over 18 inches thick, and the floor made out of something like painted concrete so it's cool and smooth. The cool white comforter is the perfect weight and not hot. Breakfast is great again, and again I take some things for lunch. Online I make reservations for going up the mountain in the cable car to Table Mountain, and print out my ticket.

Feeling smart, I retrace my route from yesterday back to the mountain. It's busier than yesterday. I have to park even further away and the line to buy tickets is much longer, but today they have umbrellas up along the line to help people stay in the shade. How nice it is to walk right to the gate and not wait in that long line again. The waiting time is only about 20-30 minutes.

The cable car holds about 20-25 people. The floor moves which is ingenious. It gives everyone a chance to have a good view. The folks in front of me, in the direction the floor was moving didn't quite grasp the concept of the moving floor. Before the car headed up the operator announced to "Stand clear of the walls. Do not hang onto the handles. The floor will rotate in a circle." These folks had gotten into the car and moved in front of the only open window. When the floor started to move, they were hanging on to the handrails on the side of the car, trying to stand still, in front of the window. I was moving with the floor and was being shoved up against them. I quickly tried to explain that they should not hang on, and that the floor was moving. Eventually they figured it out after I and a few others told them the same thing. It was like a 5 car pileup on the highway until they figured it out.

The weather was perfect at the top. Cool, slightly breezy, and clouds below us wafting in and out and over lower mountain points. After the crush of the line and the cable car issues it was peaceful and tranquil. I took my time roaming around, enjoying the view, having lunch from my bag, watching other people, and relaxing.

It's two long flights from here to home. The first, on British Airways, which is still flying long-haul flights despite their cabin crews being on strike, gets me into London, Heathrow. Then I have a three-hour layover and catch the second flight on American that flies straight into Dallas. It's gonna be a long day, however, I am flying business class so I'll be comfortable, and any extra time in the airport I can spend in one of the lounges. I don't have to claim my luggage in London, but I do have to go through security again, because of the extra precautions for planes flying into the U.S.

I made it home without incident; nothing of note happened, which is how you want it when you're traveling for more than twenty-four hours at one time. Smooth is good. My airport pickup was smooth as well. It did feel odd to be back in the U.S., driving on the right side of the road, seeing familiar sights I haven't seen in two months. I saw my house with new eyes too. It's odd, I didn't remember my living room carpet was tan berber. How odd it is to be away from home for any length of time and return. Things look different. All of sudden, things you've seen every day, when you're not traveling, jump out at you as peculiar or odd. I notice the unevenness of the curtains, one wall looks particularly bare, and I remember that I have two cats. Ok, I didn't really forget about them, but seeing them waiting for me at the door was a reality check. "Oh, yeah, I'm responsible for two furry little beings."

I'm back. I am not excited by this. I never am, but it is inevitable, unless I somehow become independently wealthy, which is not a possibility anytime in the near future. I have accepted that I have to come home and work. Adjusting will take a little time.

And then, only a few short minutes after I walk into my house, little responsibilities started creeping up to pull on my pant leg, tugging to remind me that they'd been waiting for me to come home. Oh yeah, right. I have responsibilities. I can't say that I missed them, at all. In fact, many of them I forgot I had. I had not realized how limited my responsibilities were on the road. Now I understand how that is part of the appeal of travel. And it is an advantage when focusing on photography and writing. The lack of responsibilities allows me to center my attention on a limited number of things.

Coming home I first felt like a fairy, feeling all free and footloose, but, once I had touched down on earth, little threads reached out to wrap around my arms and legs, fingers and neck, tying me to the ground, grounding me. No longer a fairy. I forgot, I'm not supposed to be able to fly. Except that I know how to now…

Time to keep my feet on the ground, and keep my head proceeding slowly towards my dreams. Time to make the money. Time to make the donuts. My Sixty Sunsets in the Southern Hemisphere have come to an end. I wonder what my next adventure will be? I suppose, "All things will appear as they must."

ACKNOWLEDGEMENTS

So many people have contributed to this book, some knowingly, some unwittingly. Many folks I met during my travels took the time to repeat information or help me with dates or spelling to ensure that my facts were correct.

I am grateful to the staff and crew of the National Geographic Explorer. Thanks to Michael Nolan, staff photographer, for your friendship and photography tips; Chris Rainier, National Geographic photographer, for sharing your brother, great photography tips, and fascinating stories; Captain Oliver Kreuse, for taking us over to those great icebergs, braking for whales, finding and sneaking up on that one, lone Emperor penguin, and for getting us fifteen feet off the shore of Deception island on the day of a summer blizzard; Tom Ritchie and Stefan Lundgren for your vast knowledge, Peter Puleston, for your laughter and making sure I didn't get lost in Ushuaia; fellow passenger Sheila Lummis, you are a ray of sunshine; and Bev Honchorek, the best roommate ever.

On Easter Island, to Sharon Diotte, for your warm hospitality and orienteering; Edmundo Edwards, primary resident archeologist, for the food, friendship, romps around the island, and for your bountiful and gripping stories.

In New Zealand, to Graham Highet, our fearless leader, for your good humor, luggage wrangling skills, surprise side trips, and for the stuffed sheep - baahhhh! Ben, our bus driver to Milford Sound, thanks for repeating parts of your stories, and for helping me keep my facts straight; and to our entire gang - you know who you are! You really made New Zealand and Australia a wonderful experience. I miss you all! And to Mom, you're a wonderful travel buddy. What wonderful, unforgettable experiences we had. You always had your thinking cap on, making great suggestions for the book, and for all your superior editing skills. Never forget, "I'm an Austraaaaalian!"

In South Africa, to Walter Guyer, at the Impangele Bed & Breakfast in Johannesburg. Thank you for keeping your cell phone with you so you could pick me up a day early from the airport! Thank you for your excellent local knowledge, for the personalized tours, shopping trips to local gems, fabulous dinners and conversation, and your sweet family of Rhodesian Ridgebacks.

In Botswana, to Adrian and Wanda, the managers of Deception Valley Lodge, and tracker Duma. What a wonderful welcome to Botswana. Thank you for sharing your local knowledge and for tirelessly tracking elusive animals; you're very gifted. And many thanks for introducing me to boboti, that typical African dish. The wonderful quartet of British safari guests at Delta Camp - Rose and Simon, Janet and Gerald, your turns of phrase are fantastic, as are your stories. Thank you for the delightful company and unexpected entertainment. Papeo, my macorro driver and guide, thank you for keeping me safe, for showing me your village, and for all the interesting animal facts. Doctor at Santawani, you're just delightful. What fun we had on safari. Your humor and laugh are unforgettable. I'll always be able to hear your voice in my head exclaiming "Is it?"

Many, many thanks to my editors: Joanne E. Gatz (my mom) and Donald F. Gatz (my dad), and my old friend, Elizabeth Grimm. Mom and Dad, thank you for all your suggestions, for your faithful editing, and for sticking with me through multiple revisions. I'm always amazed at the ways in which you support me, through my many adventures.

RESOURCES
APPENDIX A

Airline/Plane Ticket

One World Pass – Around the World Ticket - 5 continents – Business Class

Web: http://www.oneworld.com/ow/air-travel-options/round-the-world-fares/oneworld-explorer#travel-the-globe-with-round-the-world-fares

Santiago, Chile

Lodging: *Rick's B&B*

Carlos Antunez con Pedro de Valdivia, Providencia, Santiago Chile

ricks_bedandbreakfast@hotmail.com

I stayed in the "YARI-2 room for 31,500 CLP.

Airport pickup is 18,000 CLP each way, by their own taxi.

Lodging: Grand Hyatt Santiago

Antarctica

Lindblad Expeditions

1.800.EXPEDITION

web: www.expeditions.com

Expedition: Antarctica – The Great White Continent – 14 days

Easter Island

Lodging: *Te'Ora*
Web: http://easterislandteora.bizland.com/english/
email: info@rapanuiteora.com
Proprietress: Sharon Diotte
Payment: only takes cash, in Chilean Pesos, no credit cards.
I stayed in the "Nui" suite for $55,000 Chilean Pesos/night.
Very helpful, provides lots of information. Picks up and
drops off at the airport.

New Zealand/Australia

Auckland Lodging: *Duxton Hotel*
Web: http://www.duxton-hotel-auckland.com/?gclid=C
Oqgm6KklKICFRCfnAodcUxYIg
http://www.duxtonhotels.com/
Email: Res@auckland.duxton.co.nz
$159/night
Airport pickup $60, each way.

Lodging: *Mercure Auckland Windsor*
Web: http://www.mercure.com/gb/hotel-4976-mercu-
re-auckland-windsor/index.shtml

Overseas Adventure Travel (OAT)
Phone: 800-493-6824
http://www.oattravel.com/
Trip: Pure New Zealand – 16 days
Post Trip: Australia's Great Barrier Reef and Sydney – 7
days

Africa

Expert Botswana
Web: http://www.expertbotswana.com/
Email: info@expertbotswana.com
Phone: +27 21 418 725

Johannesburg Lodging
8 The Drive, Westdene/Benoni, 1501, South Africa
Web: http://www.impangele.com
Proprietor: Walter Guyer
R625 (during my trip, about $86/night)
Accepts Visa, Mastercard, and Cash (Rand, USD, Euro, GBP).

Safari Camps:
Deception Valley Lodge
Web: http://www.dvl.co.za/

Delta Camp
Web: http://www.expertbotswana.com/safari/okavango-delta/delta-camp.aspx

Meno Akwena
Web: http://www.kalaharikavango.com/

Sankuyu/Santawani
(I was supposed to stay at Sankuyu Bush camp, which is a tented camp, but it was closed for renovations. I stayed at Santawani instead, which is simple and comfortable.)
http://lodgesofbotswana.com/camps_lodges/santawani

Chundukwa River Lodge, Zambia
http://www.chundukwariverlodge.com/

Cape Town Lodging: *Antrim Villa and Bickley House*
12 Antrim Rd, Three Anchor Bay, Cape Town, Western
Cape 8005, South Africa
High percentage of guests are European, which is
appealing to me.
Phone: +27 21 762 154

PACKING LIST
APPENDIX B

To Do (pre–departure)
- buy travel insurance within 15 days of 1st deposit
- buy air ticket
- prepare bank accounts
- reserve hotel rooms
- photocopy documents & email to self
- prep medical prescriptions
- recharge camera batteries
- unplug appliances at home
- lock up valuables at home
- take out garbage at home
- give itinerary to family/friends
- arrange for sabbatical from job
- turn email "out of office" message and VM
- reformat all media for cameras x 20

Essentials
- passport
- folder of important travel info
- cash
- credit card
- ATM cards
- day pack
- brown suitcase
- green rolling duffle
- photo backpack

- monopod
- butt pack
- travel wallet
- ipod
- bite guards
- computer
- hiking boots

Clothes

- jeans
- fleece kayak pants
- fleece kayak top
- travel pants w/ zip off legs
- waterproof pants
- pajama bottoms
- sleeping top
- blue Nautica sweater
- underwear
- bamboo long johns
- swimming suit
- camisole, blk, ivory
- safari shirt
- short sleeve Talbots, teal, maroon, pink
- cardigan Talbots
- thin 1st layer socks/kneehigh
- long thermal socks
- hiking socks
- socks for walking shoes
- light blue jacket shell
- Eddie Bauer wind–breaker in a pocket
- thin blue fleece

Accessories

- umbrella
- binoculars
- safari hat
- fleece hat
- Antarctic mucklucks
- hiking boots
- shower shoes
- Merrell shoes– brown
- over–mitten
- snorkel mask & snorkel
- eye mask
- extra glasses
- chain for glasses
- baseball cap
- handkerchief
- orthotics
- necklace/Taiwan/mosq repellant
- Eddie Bauer backpack in a pocket

Toiletries

- shampoo
- hair mousse
- toothpaste
- toothbrush
- hair brush
- floss picks x 10
- feminine hygiene products
- nail clippers
- razor
- wet wipes

- chap stick x 2
- face moisturizer
- shower cap for cameras x 3

Medical/Health

- cold pills
- Band–Aids
- Q–tips
- sunscreen
- bug spray
- ear plugs
- daily vitamin packs x 70
- Excedrin
- Immodium
- Ibuprofen
- Sudafed
- cough drops
- allergy pills
- anti–malarial prescription
- antibiotic prescription
- Vicodin
- Cipro
- motion sickness

Electronics/Gadgets

- flashlight
- reading light
- plug converter x 2
- USB drive x 8
- headphones
- Compact flash cards (for camera)

- monopod
- Canon 7D Camera x 2
- 28–300 Tamron lens OR 28–200Canon
- 50mm lens
- Denis's 100–400mm lens
- 16–35mm wide angle lens
- iPhone
- iPhone wall charger cable
- iPhone USB cable
- iPhone car charger
- laptop sleeve
- laptop computer
- laptop power
- laptop power wall adapter
- 7D battery charger
- Canon 990 memory
- Canon 990is camera
- Canon 990 charger
- Canon 990 batteries
- ball head for tripod
- laptop DC adapter
- Canon 7d manual
- mini external HD
- airplane charger gadget

Misc.

- laundry detergent
- pens x 3
- pencils
- cable lock
- plastic bags

– ziplock bags
– sewing kit
– tennis balls (for stretching/massaging)
– vials for sand x 8
– divers card: PADI
– dryer sheets x 10 (for mosquito repellant)
- compression bags x3

NEW ZEALAND SLANG
APPENDIX C

Across the Ditch – across the Tasman Sea

All Black – New Zealand national rugby team

Anklebiter – toddler, small child

Anti–clockwise – counter–clockwise

Aotearoa – Maori name for New Zealand meaning land of the long
    white cloud

Bach – holiday home

Banger – sausage, as in bangers and mash

Barbie – barbecue

Beaut – great; good fun; "that'll be beaut mate"

Bloke – man

Blow me down – an expression of surprise

Bugger – damn!

Boohai – awry; out of the way non–existent place. As in "up the
    boohai shooting pukeko's with a long–handled shovel": said
    in response to "Where are you going?", and meaning either
    "Mind your own business" or "I'm just wandering around".
    Or "up the boohai" (out of place; awry)

Box of budgies – cheerful, happy, very good

Bungy – kiwi slang for elastic strap, as in Bungee Jumping

Caravan – mobile home that you tow behind your car

Cheers – thanks

Cheerio – goodbye

Cheerio – name for a cocktail sausage

Chemist – pharmacy, drug store. Also a euphemism for druggist.

Chocka – full, overflowing

Chook – chicken

Chips – deep fried slices of potato but much thicker than a French fry
Chuddy – chewing gum
Chunder – vomit, throw up
Cockie – farmer
Courgette – zuchini
Cuppa – cup of tea, as in cuppa tea
Dear – expensive
Dole – unemployment benefit
Dodgy – bad, unreliable, not good
Down the gurgler – failed plan
Drongo – stupid fool, idiot
Dunny – toilet, bathroom, lavatory
Ear bashing – someone talking incessantly
Entree – appetizer, hors d'oeurve
Fizzy drink – soda pop
Flannel – wash cloth, face cloth
Flat – apartment, name for rental accommodation that is shared
Footie – rugby union or league, as in "going to watch the footie"
G'day – universal kiwi greeting, also spelled gidday
Going bush – take a break, become reclusive
Good on ya, mate! – congratulations, well done, proud of someone
Good as gold – feeling good, not a problem, yes
Gumboots or gummies – rubber boots, wellingtons
Grotty – dirty
Handle – pint of beer
Happy as larry – very happy
Hei matau – traditional Maori pendant, made from bone or green-
    stone carving in the shape of a highly stylized fish hook
Hen fruit – eggs
Hokey Pokey – 'sea foam' candy or special New Zealand ice cream
    flavor

Hongi – traditional Maori greeting, done by pressing one's nose to another person's nose

How's it going mate? – kiwi greeting

Kia Ora – hello (Maori origin)

Kiwi – New Zealander

Knackered – exhausted, tired, lethargic

Kumara – sweet potato

Lift – elevator

Lolly – candy

Loo – bathroom, toilet

Long drop – outdoor toilet, hole in ground

Mad as a meat axe – very angry or crazy

Main – primary dish of a meal

Marmite – popular spread, made from yeast extract

Mate – buddy

Motorway – freeway

Mozzie – mosquito

Naff off – go away, get lost, leave me alone

Nana – grandmother, grandma

Nappy – diaper

OE – Overseas Experience, many students go on their OE after finishing university, see the world

Oldies – parents

On the never never – paying for something using layby, or layaway; not paying straight away

Oz – Australia

Pack a sad – bad mood, morose, ill–humoured, broken, as in "she packed a sad"

Pakeha – non–Maori person

Panel beater – auto repair shop, panel shop

Pav – pavlova, dessert usually topped with kiwifruit and cream

Petrol – gasoline, gas

Pong – bad smell

Quite nice – a term used when you can't really think of anything better to say ; as in "her hat is quite nice", and you often mean the opposite!

Rellies – relatives, family

Ring – to telephone somebody, as in "I'll give you a ring"

Rubbish – garbage, trash

Scarce as hen's teeth – very scarce, rare

Shandy – drink made with lemonade and beer

Sheila – slang for woman/female

Silver fern – native plant, often used as the national symbol

Snarky – mixture of sarcasm and nasty

Sparrow fart – very early in the morning, sunrise

Stubby – small glass bottle of beer

Sunnies – sunglasses

Suss – to figure out

Ta – thanks

Take–aways – food to be taken away and eaten, fast food outlet

Togs – swimsuit, bathing costume

Torch – flashlight

Trots – diarrhea as in "having a dose of the trots"

Tramping – hiking

Vegemite – spread for toast or bread. Indescribable, but missed by many expat Kiwi's. It tastes of yeasty soy sauce.

Waiwai express – walking, "We are taking the Waiwai express across the hill"

Whinge – complain, moan

Wop–wops – situated off the beaten track, out of the way location

Yack – to have a conversation with a friend, to talk

ANIMALS AND BIRDS I SAW AT EACH CAMP IN AFRICA
APPENDIX D

(I visited these camps between the dates of March 13-26, 2010)

Deception Valley Lodge, Central Kalahari
Lion
Leopard
Warthog
Kudu
Oryx
Blue Wildebeest
Bat eared fox
Jackal
Wild African cat
Steenbok
Kauron
Helmeted Guinea fowl
Marricou
Egyptian goose
Batteleur
Steppe Eagle
Tawny Eagle
African Eagle hawk
Red billed frankolin
Common quail
Secretary bird
Kori busterd

Red crested korhaan
Ruckus cheeked nightjar
Lilac breasted Roller
Yellow billed hornbill
Queleas
Shaft tailed whydah
Yellow billed Shrike
Black shouldered kite
Vulture
Cape teal
Pale chanting goshawk
Yellow weaver

Delta Camp, Okavango Delta
Black collared Barbit
Open Billed Stork
Green Spotted Dove
Gymnogene
Woodland Kingfisher
Elephant
Hippopotamus
Bochle Zebra
Red Lechwe antelope
Immature Helmeted Guinea fowl butterfly
African monarch
Impala
Vertet monkeys
Swamp Boubou bird
Heglunds Robin
Grey Lourie
Lesser Strep Swallows

Meno Akwena, on the banks of the Boteti River, Central Kalahari

Grand Scraper Thrush

European Bee Eater

Tawny Eagle

White Backed Vulture

Marshall Eagle

Santawani/Sankuyu

Giraffe

Spur winged goose-largest goose in area

69-70 elephants- females with babies, youngest a few weeks old

Crimson bush shrike

13 African wild dogs- or painted wolves

Long tailed glossy starling

Tsessebe Antelope - male and female

Red backed shrike

Spur winged goose

Egyptian geese

Little bee eaters

White faced ducks

Common sand piper

Black winged Stoat

Red backed shrike

Battaleur Eagle

Yellow Billed Hornbill

Wild Dogs (painted wolves)

Blue Wildebeest

Flap Necked Chameleon

Lesser Bush Baby

Red Billed Buffalo Weaver

Natale Cryer Butterfly

Crimson Bush Shrike
Hyena
Crested Frankolins
Red billed Frankolins
Pride of 12 lions
Second wild dog spotting
Zebra
Blacksmith Plover

HEALTH TIPS
APPENDIX E

Face Masks

I like to pack a few masks. You never know when you're going to be sitting next to someone who is sick, or directly in front of someone with a wicked cough who has the habit of not covering his or her mouth. There are several kinds I use. One type of mask is the kind you'd wear in the hospital when visiting someone with a compromised immune system. The kind that has loops to place over your ears and covers the face from nose to chin, with a little metal strip to pinch by the nose. These are good for several hours.

There are also other masks. If you've ever visited Asia you'll find colorful cotton masks that are used to keep exhaust fumes and dust off of commuters' faces while driving motorcycles and scooters. These are not only useful; they're fashionable and inexpensive! I bought a few for my Mother when I was in Vietnam and that's her mask of choice for when she flies. It's kind of cute – a blue and grey plaid pattern.

And then there are the type of masks you'll find in the hardware store, for contractors, painters and anyone who is trying to avoid breathing dust particles or fumes. Some have a one–way vent that make it easier to exhale. Ultimately you just need to decide what your tastes and comfort factors are.

Germ Avoidance

One more note about germ avoidance. You can't always avoid picking them up, but you can help avoid getting them into your system so they make you sick.

Wash your hands. A lot. Sing the "Happy Birthday" song or "Row, Row, Row, Your Boat" through once, and make sure to soap between your fingers, your fingernails and the front and back of your hands, and then rinse for as long as you soaped up.

Don't touch the door on the way out of the bathroom!

Train yourself to not touch your face. Don't rub your eyes, pick your nose or your teeth, or wipe your nose on your hand. As gross as some of that sounds, you know you do it! Use a tissue.

Immune System Helpers

- Be kind to your immune system. Here's the short list I try to live by. Sometimes I don't do everything, but I try to think "big picture" in the immune system area.

- Get plenty of sleep before traveling.

- Stay hydrated.

- Don't eat salty or sugary snacks on the plane or drink alcohol. Salt and alcohol dehydrate you and that can lead to a lowering of the immune system or DVTs (blood clots). Sugar and alcohol impair your immune system for several hours after ingesting it.

- Take an immune booster before and during your flights for that extra "kick." I use both Airborne and Shaklee's Defend and Resist. I also take vitamins daily. Vitamin C, D, and a good multi vitamin can all boost your immune system.

- When walking into a bathroom stall, get two pieces of toilet paper before touching anything. Use one to pull the door shut and the other to lock it. Use the same method on the way out.

- Being sick while traveling is not fun. Nothing makes you want your Mommy more, at any age, than being sick on the road. Taking a few extra precautions and being practiced at them can make a big difference in your health while traveling.

LAURA VAE GATZ

Laura's Travel Principles
Appendix F

- Pack as little as possible; less than you think you need.

- Look up, look around, be in the moment.

- Take time out to be awed by nature.

- Intentionally "turn off and tune out" media input.

- Notice and appreciate the little things.

- Cultivate curiosity; try new foods and experiences.

- Keep notes of your thoughts and travels.

- Smile and be courteous.

- Instead of getting upset during travel difficulties, step outside of your circumstances and enjoy the experience. Issues while traveling make great stories later.

- Learn these six words/phrases/questions in the local language, and use them: Hello, Thank you, Excuse me, Where is the bathroom, How much is this, Goodbye!

RECOMMENDED BOOKS
APPENDIX G

101 Tips for Women Traveling Alone
by Harriet Lewis
ASIN: B002RCMFMU

Globtrotter Dogma, 100 Canons for Escaping the Rat Race
by Bruce Northam
ISBN-10: 1577312163
ISBN-13: 978-1577312161

A Year in the World, Journeys of a Passionate Travel
by Frances Mayes
ISBN-10: 0767910060
ISBN-13: 978-0767910064

The Crystal Desert, Summers in Antarctica
by David G. Campbell
ISBN-10: 0618219218
ISBN-13: 978-0618219216

Penguins of the World
by Wayne Lynch
ISBN-10: 1554072743
ISBN-13: 978-1554072743

The Practical Nomad, How to Travel Around the World
by Edward Hasbrouck
ISBN-10: 1566918286
ISBN-13: 978-156691828

The Safari Companion, A Guide to Watching African Mammals
by Richard D. Estes
ISBN-10: 1890132446
ISBN-13: 978-1890132446

A Woman's Passion for travel, True Stories of World Wanderlust
ISBN-10: 1932361146
ISBN-13: 978-1932361148

Wild Honey
by Bookey Peek
ISBN-10: 1921037350
ISBN-13: 978-1921037351

AUTHOR BIO

Laura Vae Gatz was given a camera at a young age, and has yet to put it down. An avid adventure traveler, landscape and nature photographer and writer, Laura travels the world capturing word and visual images of culture, creatures, and the inevitable dialogue in one's head while traveling alone. Last year a friend pointed out to her that she'd traveled to all 7 continents in just 13 months. She's published a dozen Coffee Table photography books from her travels, available online, and in 2009, published a limited edition Photo Book of a vintage family camp on the shores of Lake Michigan. Africa via Antarctica: Sixty Sunsets in the Southern Hemisphere is her first published work of her adventures.

Laura Vae Gatz was born in Ann Arbor, Michigan, grew up in central Illinois and received a Bachelor of Arts degree from Valparaiso University. She also attended Brooks Institute of Photography in Santa Barbara, California for post graduate work. When she's not traveling or taking a sabbatical, Laura works full-time in Dallas, Texas as a Senior Project Manager in IT, for a Fortune 100 company.

OTHER BOOKS BY LAURA V GATZ

Africa via Antarctica:
Sixty Sunsets in the Southern Hemisphere
ebook, for Kindle, Nook and iPad
available online at Amazon, Barnes & Noble and the
iBookstore, respectively

Sixty Sunsets in the Southern Hemisphere
Volume I - Antarctica
Hard Cover, 13"x11", Dust Jacket, Full Color Photo Essay,
80 pages, available at blurb.com

Sixty Sunsets in the Southern Hemisphere
Volume II - Easter Island, New Zealand & Australia
Hard Cover, 13"x11", Dust Jacket, Full Color Photo Essay,
110 pages, available at blurb.com

Sixty Sunsets in the Southern Hemisphere
Volume III - Africa
Hard Cover, 13"x11", Dust Jacket, Full Color Photo Essay,
144 pages, available at blurb.com

Baltic Adventures
Hard Cover, 13"x11", Dust Jacket, Full Color Photo Essay,
110 pages, available at blurb.com

A Year in the Saddle: Roping and Riding in Texas
Hard Cover, 7"x7", Dust Jacket, Full Color Photo Essay,
136 pages, available at blurb.com

Made in the USA
Charleston, SC
22 June 2013